Dear You...

May your Journey be filled
with Love, Peace, and Joy!

Let the World receive
EVERYTHING you came
here to give!

All my Best...

Adrian

THE
JOURNEY

THE JOURNEY

A Path of Self-Discovery
and Reinvention

PART I: SETTING THE DESTINATION AND THE ITINERARY

ADRIAN LUZZI

THE JOURNEY
A PATH OF SELF-DISCOVERY AND REINVENTION

iUniverse books may be ordered through booksellers or by contacting:

iUniverse
1663 Liberty Drive
Bloomington, IN 47403
www.iuniverse.com
1-800-Authors (1-800-288-4677)

ISBN: 978-1-4917-7961-3 (sc)
ISBN: 978-1-4917-7962-0 (e)

Library of Congress Control Number: 2015916670

Print information available on the last page.

iUniverse rev. date: 11/23/2015

CONTENTS

CHAPTER TWO
Finding True North

ACKNOWLEDGEMENTS

I dedicate this book to the love of my life, my sweetheart and beloved wife who has been the inspiration of everything significant I have ever done. Her unconditional love, support, encouragement, care and advice illuminated my life in ways I would have never imagined. It is because of her love and the inspiration she engendered in my soul that I was able to transform this recollection of scattered thoughts and turn them into a more compelling story for those in the quest of their true life paths. Dear Lili, my love … you are on every single word of this book and on every chapter of my life!

I will be eternally grateful to our three beautiful children who I love with all my heart and to whom I would give everything life has given me … and more. They have transformed my life in ways they will never imagine, like angels on Earth making the impossible possible. It is because of them, their love and glowing charm that I am who I am, gradually becoming who I was meant to be.

I feel an immense amount of love and thankfulness for my parents, they were the first ones to shape my heart, filling it with a secret recipe of enchanted affection that poured the concrete foundations that allowed everything else to be built. Whoever I will end up being has its roots in the little baby that I once was, a small and helpless creature so much cared and nurtured by a young couple as new to raising a first born as experienced about providing endless love. They lived for us, five children incessantly asking for their support and protection, against all odds. Mom and Dad, I love you dearly!

Life has blessed me with the gift of friendship and I was incredible fortunate to cross the paths of a few loving souls who have illuminated my way showing me a side of life I was not familiar with, serendipitous acts of kindness that redefined what true companionship was all about. They have been a source of inspiration and joy through the many twists and turns of life, enlightening me with their glow like stars on the sky, being always there when you need their light. I am grateful for their ongoing support of my writing efforts and for encouraging me to share my inner work with the world. I feel privileged for their friendship and want all of them to know how deep in my heart they will always be.

If there is a thin line between true friends and family, JoAnn Fisher was able to erase that line completely and become family to all of us, lovingly holding us in her arms ever since the first day we came to the United States of America, full of hope and dreams while empty of everything else. I would confidently say that true friends are mystically joined even before they meet for the first time as if their spirits were heavenly bound in a dimension far and above human comprehension. Thank you JoAnn for everything you always did for us, you were a true blessing in our life. Your charm and endless aim to open your heart to us has been imprinted in love ink throughout the pages of this book!

My passage through the corporate world has unquestionably augmented my wisdom and the understanding of both basic and complex human traits, opening my eyes to a reality secretly hidden from my still naïve conception of behavioral drives. I am grateful for all the experiences I had to go through as they have shaped aspects of the old me in such a way that allowed a more compassionate, a more considerate, a more persistent and a more patient person to emerge. When I think of the business world, there is one person in particular to whom I will be always indebted for his trust, kindness, mentorship and selfless intent to help our family when we needed it the most, somebody who in his own way and without knowing it, immensely contributed to build the foundations of this book. I will be forever thankful to John DeBlase for helping us relocate to the United States of America sparking the start of a new life, both for our family and for our future generations. Thank you John for your principle based leadership examples, for being yourself regardless of the circumstances and for helping me prioritize what matters most. You trusted me beyond reason synchronistically shortening the distance between who I was and who I am. Somewhat you saw in me more than what was visible and in so doing you allowed and fostered the best in me to emerge.

I cannot finish my thanksgiving without expressing an immeasurable and deeply felt gratitude to David Johnson who has so graciously devoted his life to help us change ours. Dave has been my one and only investment coach and someone who so passionately taught me everything I know about the markets, fueling the elaboration of a countless number of metaphors between trading and life. Thank you Dave for having such a big heart and for the many sacrifices you made to give us the best of you. Your legacy to us goes well beyond the field of trading and has enabled many of us to become more loving and caring human beings, a serendipitous gift I have treasured dearly. You made this book possible by helping me advance in the mesmerizing process of finding my true self.

We are who we are not only because of what we did but most importantly because of what others did for us. What we do with our life is nothing but a tribute to them, a sort of unspoken act of appreciation for the unconditional love and care of those that believed in us. The time will come when we will have to do it for others, spreading the love we have received and nurtured throughout the course of our lives, and in so doing create a mystical cycle of eternal lovefulness.

INTRODUCTION

If I would be asked how to succeed in life and honor our Creator, I would answer … *have BIG Dreams and never stop chasing them!*

Either you have dreams or you don't …

If you have dreams, either you chase them or you don't …

If you chase your dreams, either you make them come true or you die trying …

And either way you must be at peace, for your job on Earth would have been well done!

This book is about having BIG dreams, believing in them and always chasing them. It has been written in a rather symbolic, simple, plain, yet unabbreviated language. The concepts presented here are the result of everyday life lessons learned by the author with the utmost altruistic intent to grow, to mature, to become wiser, more caring, more loving and to adopt a more sensitive stand to the human condition. The application of the reflections in this book will vary from person to person and will require the individual's interpretation according to his or her own value system, life stage and personal circumstances. There are no magic formulas, no ten-step plans, no shortcuts to learning, only a collection of personal experiences translated into reflections and thought provoking questions aimed at helping the world become a better place to live. If nothing else, this book is intended to trigger the sort of inner dialog that would eventually lead some courageous beings to know more about themselves and in so doing discover the fascinating yet unexplored terrain of their inner lives.

There is no scientific proof of the statements made in this book nor any structured process of recollection, organization and articulation of the presented themes other than the focus on the easiness of their comprehension. It was on purpose that some topics have been developed in an ample, perhaps rather ambiguous tone, opening the door for the reader to make his or her own assimilation of the topics without constraining or restricting the beauty of the human imagination and confining it to a narrow view of what can be elaborated into something larger, richer, more beautiful and more meaningful to the reader's reality. I hereby offer my apologies if some of the essays contained in this volume are confusing, troubling or puzzling. I have to admit that I sometimes have sought to generate such a state of confusion not only in you but also in myself. Confusion leads to clarity, and clarity opens the gate to wisdom, a rather inevitable sequence of events without which, learning would find a difficult if not an impossible way to be born.

For a reflection to evolve and become a source of clarity, we have to grant it the attribute of confusion first. It is only then when valuable and unknown insights will eventually emerge. I plead guilty of that charge and hope it is well worth the symbolic struggle that accompanies the process of understanding something that seems complex and intriguing first, only to lead us to a more holistic appreciation of the reality both outside and inside of us. As I describe in some of the following passages, there are no complex or simple matters, either we comprehend them or we don't, and in either case, it does not have to be forever, we change, we grow and we evolve. Anything we learn can and may need to be un-learned to allow room for advanced, more profound and elaborated concepts to be assimilated. What was once complex becomes explicable, simple, and what was once simple, may come back to us with new and renewed aspects of it that can turn it perplexing and puzzling. What once was may not necessarily continue to be, the Universe is in constant motion … and so do us.

I want to also acknowledge that many reflections will revolve on the same underlying subject matters, as if trying to uncover all their facets by looking at them from multiple perspectives and angles. Repetition is key to memorization and a base for the foundation of behavioral changes that accompany the learning of something new and conceptually compelling. If learning represents the first step towards mastery by providing us with new knowledge, practice constitutes the second, enabling us to build the skills that applied knowledge would consistently craft.

Those that can tolerate the temporary stage of uncertainty that travels along with us in the expedition to discover who we are meant to be will be the recipients of immense treasures, golden gems trusted to us by Nature and the Universe. We are all we can be and become and whether or not we are courageous enough to go for it will not change anything. The *who* we are expected to be is there, patiently waiting for us, confidently knowing that one day we will show up at its doorstep. For those committed to follow the guidance of their hearts, becoming their true selves is not a matter of "if" but a matter of "when."

Seeking to become who we were meant to be is the most important task every human being can pursue and the simplest yet most complex undertaking we can possibly conceive as it will require the very best in us, both at the surface and at the innermost confines of our souls.

This book is a wholehearted attempt to help those interested in embarking in such a mysterious yet captivating journey, providing them with the strength, the wisdom, the persistence and the patience to never give up in the process of chasing their dreams, their burning wishes, aspirations and most beautiful visions of a future still yet to come. As Thomas Henry Huxley once wrote "Perhaps the most valuable result of all education is the ability to make yourself do the thing you have to do, when it ought to be done, whether you like it or not.", I too believe that educating ourselves in the most profound life aspects is a paramount task to maximize our contribution to the world while leaving an everlasting legacy to the future generations coming after us.

We are all here for a reason, and whether that reason has been disclosed to us or not, it does not matter. If we are open, willing and daring, we will be gently guided towards accomplishing it, whether we know it or not. All we have to do and all we should care about is to give our very best in the pursuit of such a call … everything else is irrelevant, insignificant and should be regarded as a far second priority.

Life is God's gift to us, what we do with it is our gift to God – Amish proverb

CHAPTER ONE

Facing the Unknown

THE BEGINNINGS

Curiosity is a human attribute that creates an inner itch to answer the inquiries posed by the mind in an effort to recognize the source of such conscious or unconscious wondering, namely an unknown companion knocking on the door of the certain. Some individuals have a more developed sense of curiosity and expand it beyond the field of everyday life to reach and embrace more philosophical and spiritual realms like the origins of mankind or the purpose of our existence. In a holistic characterization of the trait, one may rate curiosity as a rather positive aspect of the restless mind and the main reason why some people never stop asking questions that propel their growth and maturity beyond any stretches of imagination. Needless to say, along with curiosity comes the evolution of the world.

I was curious from the day I was born, both in ordinary and extraordinary ways, always wondering about those things I could not easily explain. Posing questions was so natural to me that I got used to live in such state of mind and undergo the subsequent and inevitable process of sleeping on puzzling crosswords for days, months, or even years. It was through the routine of dwelling on difficult-to-understand subjects that I gradually escorted myself into the habit of tolerating ambiguity and accepting that some matters would remain mysterious until the right time would come, a time when I would be ready to comprehend.

Pursuing an engineering degree was in part the result of wondering how a television set worked, an intellectual effort to identify what kind of magic made it possible for a person to become virtually encapsulated in a wooden box and speak live to an audience sitting miles away from him. It was the same curiosity, although in a more profound way, what started to create a sense of unease about the meaning of life and the reason of our existence. Human kind was something so complex and elaborated that could not be just an accident of nature, a misconception of a Higher Power, or a mistake of the Universe in the pursuit of a progression towards a future state of being. There had to be some overarching explanations behind why we were here and what was expected from us. The Darwinist evolution of the species theory, although scientifically sound, was not enough of a justification to my quest for answers. I was looking for something more philosophical and less scientific, more spiritual and less logical, more mystical and less conventional, something I may never be able to proof but strongly believe in.

Philosophers, scholars, and scientists of all times revolved around the same type of puzzling themes and debated for centuries, perhaps millennia, trying to crack the codes scripted inside the meaning of life and the ultimate purpose of the human race. For as much as my inner need of originality was concerned, the path I was trying to embark myself into was not a new wisdom chasing expedition but an old and perplexing paradox still unresolved. It was not going to be that easy for a twentieth century ordinary man to engage in a sound discussion that has sustained the passage of time and challenged multiple generations of great thinkers. My courage and restlessness was bold enough to set me in motion, to be daring enough to pursue acceptable explanations for immensely relevant mysteries, yet I could not avoid the feelings of arrogance for aspiring to belong to a community of selected minds whose knowledge was light years ahead of mine and in a so doing climb to levels of complexity that would blow my paradigms away. Whether I liked it or not, the same question chased me in different ways and shapes, over and over again. *What are we here for?*

I inadvertently became a voracious reader of different schools of thought while immersing myself in a self-discovery process that required the virtual companionship of famous experts on matters of the mind, people like Carl Jung, Viktor Frankl, Abraham Maslow, Erich Fromm,

Carl Rogers, Rollo May, Antonio Damasio, and Scott Peck to name a few. What I learned through those years of self-awareness would have not been accomplished without the invaluable help of those great scholars who in one way or another provoked my thinking and catapulted my curiosity astray. If I had questions before starting, I ended up with many more after my research was somewhat completed. It all seemed as if after becoming slightly more educated, my ignorance on matters of higher complexity was escalating in direct proportion of my efforts to crack the code of universal wisdom. Although I was sensing some progress in the direction I was urged to move, the number of unanswered questions did not seem to confirm my advancement.

Three notable figures in the field of mind research deserve a great deal of the credit for my self-education in the sense that their findings ignited my passion and fueled my engagement to astronomical levels. First and foremost my capacity to think unconventionally was dramatically improved by Carl Jung's elaborations of the unconscious (individual and collective) and the themes gravitating around the idea of *significant* coincidences, the simple yet rock solid foundation of the *synchronicity* construct. Second, I am highly indebted to Viktor Frankl and his logotherapy theory, the search for meaning and the profound notion of the ultimate human freedom, *the ability to choose our own response in any given set of circumstances.* It is by pivoting on the idea of being the owner of our own choices, no matter how adverse the surrounding environment could be, that I was able to go through many stages of my life *free* from the external conditioning and pressures that would expect me to act otherwise than what my inner voice would dictate. Frankl's *Man's search for meaning* book was a crucial turning point in my own quest for purpose and the confirmation that the first overarching wondering I had was not only my own but many others' dilemmas as well ... and quite certainly something worth living and dying for.

Finally, I am incredible grateful to Abraham Maslow for his constructs around the self-actualization theory and the ultimate pursuit ingrained in the individuation process. Maslow's ideas of thrusting us above and beyond the mere need-gratification layers and into the realm of self-actualization, provoked a myriad of thoughts in the endless journey to fulfill my lifelong call and in so doing decode the ultimate realization of my existence: *who I was meant to be and what I came here for.*

Once the philosophical level was more or less in a certain state of equilibrium, an intense passion for the study of human motivation started to take prey of me and I devoured any book I could find on the subject. I became inadvertently captivated by the concept of self-directed behavior which induced me into the study of intrinsic motivation, a field I regarded as extremely intriguing and mesmerizing. It was through the curiosity to learn more about intrinsic drivers that I mystically stumbled with the research of Deci and Ryan, who spent years analyzing the motives and personality traits of self-motivated individuals. Needless to say, I am extremely thankful to both of them for their rigorous work and research which sprung me in ways I would have never imagined while at the same time empowered me to discover many of my own motivational dynamics.

Still inquisitive about the experience that self-motivated individuals would go through, I serendipitously encountered an author whose name I was afraid to mispronounce and for whom I have developed an immense amount of admiration and respect, Mihalyi Csiksentmihalyi. What a pleasure was to learn about Csiksentmihalyi's *flow* theory and the experiences of those individuals reaching such a level of self-motivated behavior. Without a single doubt, I could have not elaborated my reflections about self-driven individuals and polished the notions neighboring extreme focus, consistent commitment and undisputable mastery without Csiksentmihalyi's research and findings.

The unexpected exposure to such a vast amount of mind blowing knowledge made me feel extremely privileged to the point of being unable to avoid the question of *what was expected from me after such a generous access to universal wisdom?* Deep inside I knew there was a plan, it was just too premature for me to imagine what it would look like, as if its shape and form would simply be outside of the reach of what I could conceive at that time. Mysteriously enough, a great deal of patience invaded me and made me company as the journey of my life started to unfold. Along with the peace of mind that graciously took prey of me, I felt the love and the duty for what was about to emerge.

The parallels among Csiksentmihalyi's *flow* state, Maslow's *peak experiences in self-actualized individuals*, and Deci-Ryan's *intrinsic motivation* theory was astonishing and clearly a pattern of something much greater than three independent schools of thought taken individually. I was at the verge of a *significant* coincidence, the intersection of three separate but intimately related fields of research that were guiding my quest in one direction: *finding the optimal way to do what one must do while experiencing joy at doing it.*

I observed myself for years, writing any specifics that would relate to the subject of self-motivation and purpose simultaneously benchmarking my perception of how others would go through the same motivational dilemma. The more I thought about it, the more convinced I was that all of us without exception, were born unique and special in our own ways and that all of us carry a mission in life, something that only us can do wonderfully well, whether we know of it or not, whether we like it or not. Some were born musicians and expected to enlighten the world with their musical creations, others were born parents and entrusted with the noble and generally underestimated task of raising loving, happy and socially responsible children, others were born teachers, engineers, sport men and women, nurses, caregivers, scientists, soldiers and the list goes on and on.

By then, I felt I had bitten the apple of knowledge and the Pandora's box had been open. Why was I given access to such a powerful truth that only a few others would know about? What was I supposed to do with it? There had to be a reason, a compelling and noble reason and I had to find it.

While I could indisputably feel I was in the right path to something meaningful, all I had done was create more questions for which I had no answers and the feeling of having spent all these years to become more puzzled than when I originally started could not be avoided. Deep inside I continued to feel that my quest was advancing and so the magnitude and caliper of my conscious ignorance on the themes I was after.

GETTING DEEPER TO FIND THE ANSWERS

Asking yourself questions, especially the right and most provoking ones, is not a guarantee to get answers, at least not immediately. As a matter of fact, more often than not, the result of asking complex questions is the perfect formula to end up even more confused, regardless if the original intrigue was satisfied or not ... the wisdom ladder is always leaning on the ignorance wall, and if nothing else you will become more aware of your lack of knowledge. This is the way it worked with me and if that happens to you, I would suggest you take it as part of the process of moving yourself to a higher level of complexity. Those related and more complex inquisitions were always there, it was just that your brain did not have access to them because it was operating at a simpler, less complex realm. The process of mobilizing yourself to find answers for difficult matters has to be seen as part of the continuous practice of elevating your thinking to the next level, engaging both the conscious and unconscious sides of your mind to arrive at places you have never been before, not with this intensity or frequency.

Being an engineer by profession, I have spent years resolving problems, both technical and human related, and as far as I can tell it is part of my nature, my DNA construct. After you do something for over fifty years, you learn some of the basics, which in the case of complex problem solving, I can summarize as follows:

- Complex problems are never resolved without creating other problems, normally of higher level of complexity
- The process of trying to resolve difficult problems can be painful, but almost always leaves you with a sweet taste, a learning of some sort, regardless if the problem was resolved or not, as if the process of seeking the solution with everything you have at reach would somewhat ease your eager mind and take you to a calmer state of being.

- When you expose yourself to something significantly more difficult than the most difficult circumstance you have ever been through, you may feel you are not going to make it, you just can't imagine a way out of it. You have to keep trying. The fact that you can't visualize what will come next is responsible for the mental agony of conceiving an unreasonably high number of possibilities, most of which have a realistically low probability of occurrence, but you don't know it, you have never been there before, hence your uncertainty and disdain.

- The solution to complex life circumstances generally lies at a higher level of complexity than the one where those circumstances were created (credits to Albert Einstein). You can't see the light at the end of the tunnel because you are still operating at the same level of complexity where the problem was created. To find the answers, you will have to learn some things you don't know. Persisting at the resolution effort will give you access to the knowledge you need to acquire and putting that domain knowledge into practice will give you the skills you need to overcome the present challenges. Only then you will be able to see the way out. Don't give up!

- Many of the most difficult problems in your life will transform you in one way or another. In other words, there will be a You *before* and another You *after* the problem is finally resolved

- It is not uncommon to find ourselves immersed in adverse contexts without a clear appreciation of the reasons why. Very often and in the midst of the struggle, all we want, wish and desire is that the problem goes away!

- For as adverse the circumstances may have been, it is likely that the growth you have experienced and the new *You* that has emerged out of them will outweigh the suffering. If asked whether or not it was worth it, chances are you may say *yes*. Furthermore, if asked whether or not you would go through it again if given the opportunity and assuming you will get both the pain and the learning, chances are you will also say *yes*.

7

Nobody stumbles with noteworthy life matters they will not be able to *eventually* manage (eventually is the key word here), especially if they try *hard* and *long* enough. There is a reason for you to ask yourself those questions, the same reason that moved you to pick this book from the shelf or the internet store, it was just meant to happen, it was a part of what you must do. Whether or not you believe in God, Nature, the Universe, or any sort of Higher Power, you may find intriguing how some things keep coming at you throughout the course of your life, sometimes in different ways or shapes, perhaps camouflaged to go unnoticed or unperceived but in categorically similar or related ways.

All of us were born with unique talents and powers, attributes of our personality that form a distinct pattern, something that us and nobody but us have, the things that differentiate us from our fellow humans. Whatever those talents are, whether realized or not, developed or still latent, they were given to us for a reason, they are powers of some sort and all noteworthy powers come with responsibility. We are all carriers of distinctive qualifications, skill muscle, certain altruistic attributes, abilities with which we can do better or contribute more in our specific fields than the average person can, something that differentiates us from everybody else.

*We may or may not know what that something is, but it is there,
it was given to us without conditions of any kind, in a loving and
caring way. Only the hope that we will do what we are expected
to do was put in our hands and in our hearts, and it is up to us to
fulfill that hope, it is up to us to honor the life we were given.*

If you imagine the Universe as a giant ecosystem that tends to both preserve itself from extinction and continuously advance to higher forms of existence, you can explain why some species constantly evolve and transform themselves to adapt and adjust to changing environmental circumstances. We are one of those species, the most complex and capable creatures on Earth and it would not be surprising to think that our task is not only to preserve our kind but to enhance it. The powers that were given to us, this uniqueness that makes us who we are, different from the person next to us, is the *key to unlock the best and the greatest hidden in the eggshell of our life.* The Universe expects us to do something with those powers, they were not given to us by accident or chance, we were meant to have them. The matter to discern is not *if* we have special powers, gifts, qualities or attributes but *what* those powers are, which leads to the ultimate question of every human on Earth: *What our mission in life is.*

    Who we are is defined by *what we do*, however a totally different question is: *who we were meant to be*, which is defined by what we *must* do, and even when the resolution of that mystery may reside in the future, it is our responsibility to start inquiring right here, right now, if nothing else, to keep going back at it, over and over again. Note that I have purposely skipped the subject surrounding *who we are going to be*, and the reason being is that I want that question to be answered not now but after you finish this book. The *who* we were expected to be was defined when we were born, maybe prior to that, a timing that indeed does not really matter. The crucial concept to grasp is that we were meant to be *somebody* and not somebody else, to do *something* and not something else, a special way of being and doing, unique in our own way.

    It is the becoming of that somebody and the doing of that something what will make us the who we were meant to be. Only then, we will be able to fully realize ourselves, make us whole, complete and at peace.

    The answers to the most significant life questions lie within us, somewhere deep inside within the confines of our inner self. If we truly want to know, we will have to dig deeper, to go to places we have never been before, at least at conscious level, to find the true and genuine components of the marvelous creation called *self.* After doing it for years, diving deeper and wider into the realms of self-discovery and reinvention, I can tell that finding the meaning of the fundamental aspects of your life is one of the most fascinating and transforming processes you can ever embark into. Although not easy at times, as you will have to face the mysteries of the unknown, it is a quest full of treasures and golden gems, raw diamonds of magnificent proportions, invaluable gifts you will stumble with in a serendipitous and synchronistic manner, gifts that will find you before you find them, and ultimately, gifts you will get to keep for the rest of your life.

Whenever you get ready to start asking the right questions, don't look for answers out there, everything of true value lies within the confines of your own self! It is in the innermost parts of your own persona where everything started and it is right there where everything will end.

HUMAN CHOICE

All living creatures on Earth operate on some sort of *natural* way (derived from the word *nature*), sometimes instinctual and life preserving and in the case of humans also driven by conscious choice. It is ironic that humans, the most advanced creatures on Earth, were given the freedom of *altering* the expected behavioral pattern they were supposed to follow for the ecosystem to function in an orderly manner. We were empowered with decision making abilities, a sort of free will, the type of self-determination that Viktor Frankl referred to, the option *to decide what to do in any given set of circumstances*. Plants don't get to choose, nor do most animals as they operate in ways according to their nature and they behave in a pseudo instinctual manner to preserve their species throughout the years to come. Choice is a tremendously powerful behavioral driver and an attribute granted *only* to the superior species on Earth: *human beings*.

I must stress this view as it is paramount to the understanding of our responsibility in life as a whole. As Viktor Frankl pointed out, choice is the ultimate human freedom, and we must accept that choice is inevitable, *we exercise choice even if we do not choose*. Not choosing is either actively or passively *choosing not to choose*, inaction is a possible response to a life circumstance, and relatively often the right one. We must be conscious that we *always* have the ability, the right, and the duty to *decide* what to think, what do, or not to.

The outside world will sometimes find ways to limit the span of our choice by making it *easier* to pick some things over others, to conform the expected patterns of behavior and to *go with the flow*. I tend to call it crowd behavior, what eight out of ten people would do in a circumstance like that. We all fall in that category many times a day, we all eat, sleep, work (for a living or desire), etc. I do not intent to imply that crowd behavior is something to avoid, with one exception. There are times when something inside tells you this is not what you should be doing, that this is not the *right* thing for you to pursue at that time, at that particular stage in your life. We are elevating the conversation to a higher level of complexity, beyond the daily routine of mundane, life as usual domain and entering into the category of *must-do* things we all have to pursue in our individual and unique life quests.

Parents, care givers, teachers, police officers, doctors, nurses, and everybody else in a position that can meaningfully affect the life of others will find this conception rather appealing, being responsible for another human is such an undeniable call for action that one can hardly miscarry that responsibility and not regard it as one of the most important aspects of our lives. It is in those instances when we need to think carefully and exercise Choice (with capital C).

Defying the crowd is not easy and although it comes out naturally for some people, it is not the preferred response for the masses as it requires uncommonly high amounts of inner confidence along with a somewhat marked disregard for public opinion. If you decide to follow your own way, eventually defying conventional wisdom, you may not be sure that what you are about to do will work, especially if you have not mastered it yet, and it is perfectly reasonable to feel that way, to not know for sure but rather strongly believe in what you will do. If the outer world is expecting you to do something else, there will be plenty of reassurances as to why you should do it, conformity to massive behavioral patterns is always the easiest way out and the fastest path to *together-land*. Life many times teaches us that easy is not better, especially when *easy* will not take us where we must go. Just because most everybody else we know is doing something may not necessarily mean we *have* to do it as well (we are not them and they are not us). We must think by ourselves!

We were all given an inner sensor, a kind of life compass that will always point to the *true North* of life, our *own* true North. We all have it, no exceptions. Where is it? The easiest and most common place to find it is in your heart. Your heart will talk to you, you just need to learn how to listen and also how to ask when you are not listening what you need to know. Some people talk to their hearts all the time, not necessarily knowing that they do it. Some may not even call it a conversation, they may rather say it is a feeling, a hunch, a sort of intuition, an inner voice, their conscience, etc. It is your most inner and truest side talking to you in a loving and caring way, being candid on what you should do, what you must do. Listen to it!

Stephen Covey referred to this type of inner dialog as a three step process:

1. Ask with intent
2. Listen without excuse
3. Act with courage

Simple and beautiful! ... When it is time to ask, ask your heart! Your heart will never fool you, although it may tell you things you may not want to hear or not want to do, either out of difficulty, change to the status quo, crowd defiance, etc. Whatever the reason, never argue with your heart in the significant aspects of your life. Your mind will only see the short term, the here and now, the immediate impact of your actions, but your heart can see beyond, the long run, the whole nine yards, the full spectrum. Your heart can *see* things your mind cannot, especially under pressure or stress, when your reptilian brain (this is a part of your brain responsible for survival) has been commanded to be in charge.

The most primitive part of your brain functions reside in the amygdale and is responsible to make quick decisions with the ultimate intent of preserving your life, generally in the form of fight or flight type of actions. There is a reason for that part of our brain to be active in challenging situations; however its structure and complexity are so archaic that it cannot distinguish between a true life threatening circumstance and a difficult challenge to overcome, something not posing a substantial risk but requiring a thorough, well elaborated answer, something far from a quick fix. From that premise, conventional logic would suggest that life threatening situations may require you to follow your instincts, put the amygdale in control, and do not err on the side of your heart. Well ... I will have to challenge that assumption, even at the price of risking my life. When Viktor Frankl described his stay at death camps in World War II, he narrated the stories of some men, although few in number, that would take their only meal intake, a small dry and hard-to-bite piece of bread and give it to others that seemed more desperate, weaker, or about to die out of starvation. The ones giving away their daily meal intake, if nothing else something helping them to live one more day, were not following their amygdale dictates, they were following their hearts! They had a reason to live, a purpose, a meaning for their life and something waiting for them out there, away from the misery and agony of the death camps. Deep inside they knew that they would be the last ones to die, with or without that particular daily bread intake they were giving away. It is that type of *choice* I am referring to, the one that defies the crowd and the law of the masses, the one that follows the commands of your inner value system and your own definition of what is *right* in any given set of circumstances.

Following your heart is not about knowing what to do, is about doing what you believe on, what you regard as the thing you must do, right there, at that very moment, when a difficult determination has to be made. Those that can do it have to have the ability to step beyond the here and now, to raise above their own selves and project their visions into something greater than their mere existences, something worth living and dying for, a noble mission they have taken as their own, consciously or not.

WHAT IS RIGHT VERSUS WHAT WORKS

Ever since the dawns of mankind any personality trait that acts as the driver of behavioral patterns manifests itself into some sort of continuum. It is also reasonably accurate to say that the distribution across such a range follows a bell type of curve (the engineer in me speaking now). We will find a small percentage of the population on each end of the spectrum with the majority around the middle of the distribution curve and fading out as we approach the extremes. Rightness and workability conform the two ends of one of those continuums. Some individuals carry with them such a strong sense of rightness on everything they do that they can hardly think or care on whether it works or not. If they do, they would never overweight workability to the point of avoiding or compromising what they consider to be inherently right. At the other end of the spectrum lie those individuals with a strong sense of workability, those who will do whatever it takes to get things done, with little or no regard to their sense of rightness, their motto seems to be: if it works, it is valid and must be done (some may even call right to what works). The general population is neither at one extreme nor the other, they fall somewhere in between, some closer to one end, some closer to another and most of them around the middle.

I am not in favor of any extremes, they normally represent an inability to apply a balanced judgment to the situation at hand and force the person to see every situation from the same angle. Amplitude of thought is a mature skill of well-rounded personalities. That said, there are situations that clearly call for an inclination toward one of the ends, without necessarily reaching it completely. Let's for instance pick the field of sports, if you play competitively, you will want to win. Results are an important part of the game. You certainly want to do the right things, what Michael Jordan would call the *fundamentals*, but most importantly, you want to do things that *work*, things that will lead you to a winning score. You cannot ignore what is *right*, as a matter of fact, it is by doing what is right that you will ultimately pave your road to success, but focusing only on the *right* things will not take you there, you need to balance your attention on what *works* as well. Winning as many games as you can is also important if you have a desire to play competitively. Let's pick another example, parenting. The approach here is different in the sense that if in sports you will balance right and works in a 30/70 manner (30% right, 70% works), in parenting, you would rather do it in a 70/30 way, an almost quite opposite approach. While you certainly want to see your actions to work in the short term, you are much more concerned in your children's future well-being which sometimes requires you to accept difficulty and struggle as part of the game. In sport terms, you may accept being regarded as a sub-optimal coach, sometimes as the worst coach in the world (the parents in you know what I mean), eventually lose some games, as long as you see your kids getting their lives on the right path, making the *right* choices, and maturing according to their age and life stage. As a parent, you not only can but must also accept losing some of the early games to get to the Championship later in life. Doing the right things as a parent is *more* important than doing things that work, especially if *work* is defined in the context of the immediate present or near future. Unlike in sports where your main interest gravitates around winning in the current season, parenting is a long term responsibility that will be measured across a longer time span, not this season or the next, but the whole sport life.

What you ultimately want is to identify the areas in your life where to be *right* is more important that to make it *work*, or vice versa, and act accordingly. Workability is generally defined as doing what leads you to the desired results, whereas rightness as what feels inherently aligned to your value system, to Universal principles, or to those salient aspects of your life. Right and work not always go hand in hand, actually, they generally divert in the sense that rightness deals more with long term life objectives while workability is more of a short term attribute of the task, generally related to present or near future results. What may work for the task at hand, may not necessarily be the right thing to do, and it is up to you to make the call and do it or not.

In some complex albeit non-relevant circumstances you will accept the sacrifice of deviating from the ideal rightness finding some alternatives that may be right enough in the spirit of workability. We all live in a far from ideal world and picking our battles is a big part of honoring our essentials.

If rightness is an important attribute for you, you may never reach a point of doing things that are plainly wrong (in your own personal scale) just because they work, but you may accept some trade-offs, in other words, engaging yourself on things that are right *enough* if they work *reasonably* well. It all revolves around the type of situation you are dealing with, and whether that battle is worth being fought or not.

As a parent, I always lean to the *right* side, while as a sales manager, I need to carefully watch what *works* and at the same time pay a good deal of attention to what is right. As a father, I want my kids to be happy, socially responsible humans and successful in their lives which is the reason I always err to the *right* side, whereas as a sales manager, I want my business to outgrow the market in the next ten years but I need to make quota every semester, and these are the reasons why I keep one eye on what is right and another on what works. Do you see the difference? I want to be the *best* parent I possibly can in the long run but only need to be a reasonably good manager every year. As a manager, I balance right and work finding the best of both worlds, as a parent I only go for what is right with no compromises whatsoever. Simply stated, management is for me a short term life assignment, parenthood is a long term one. In the quest for answers to choosing between right and work I found the mind to be our best ally in matters of workability while the heart is indisputably our all-time companion for rightness concerns.

When trying to do right, always follow your heart!
When looking for things that work, think with your mind.

Never condition your peace of mind to the unimportant, to the short term results of your long term efforts or to what the world suggests your current contribution to the preservation of the status quo to be.

THE WORLD AND THE UNIVERSE

Throughout the subjects developed in this book, I regularly refer to the world as the symbolical entity composed by the surrounding environment, the traditional and conventional forces that make the fabric of everyday life, the people, the circumstances, the outcomes and the rules of engagement, in other words, what the *eye* can see. Alternatively, I refer to the Universe as something of a greater magnificence, lying at a much higher level of complexity where the human mind, especially the conscious side, cannot wander. The Universe operates in a non-sequential time continuum moving from future to past (and vice versa) in a split of a second and having visibility to the big picture, something that only the heart can feel. The Universe neighbors with the realms of the unconscious, individual and collective, the unknown, the ambivalent, the ambiguous, the diffuse and the unclear. You can't venture yourself to the outer world expecting complete certainty in the conventional way as the Universe operates in a dimension alien to all of us on Earth. Immersing ourselves in the Universe domain and attempting to operate in synchrony with it requires a unique set of core competencies and beliefs, capabilities very rare in the masses as they do not make crowd following behavioral patterns any easier. The general population can't even imagine a world so unpredictable where actions will have to be based on pure belief, faith, and unconditional love to our purpose and to our creator. Such a vision reflects an ideal perception of a real world force fitted in a model that refuses to be changed as if resisting following a path that should not be avoided. A world like that would be *nirvana*, a naiveté, an illusion of an unthought-of vision yet to come, a foresight of what the most pure souls would define the ideal world to be.

The average human operates in a much more simplistic level of complexity, where they can only see what their stature let them see. Defense mechanisms built in the core of our minds would try to prevent us from reaching stretches of imagination that would blow our most deeply held assumptions away requiring a replacement of the paradigms through which we operate. The same defense mechanisms are responsible for not allowing us to even pose the overarching dilemma of: *why to see more?*

The realms of the Universe will present themselves as both intriguing and attractive only to those that can break the molds of conventionalism and challenge themselves with questions outside of the ordinary, puzzling their visions of the future with theories pertaining to alternative world configurations, mental constructs that may represent nothing but a series of what-if scenarios far from reaching blue print format as long as the forces of mass thinking and mass behavior regulate the current set of affairs.

The brightest future of mankind lies in the hands of those willing to defy the status quo and believe in the beauty of their dreams to the point of living and dying to chase them!

ABOUT QUESTIONS AND ANSWERS

Why trouble the mind with abstracts conceptualizations that would lead nowhere but to a world thousands of years ahead of our time? … why worry now for things that may never come? Because nobody is given a task so big that he or she could do nothing about. Implanting the philosophical itch for answers to apparently absurd questions would be purposeless, a waste of Universe power, an underutilization of restless hearts and the derailing of very capable minds. If seemingly irrational (for the general public) but inherently right questions stop at your porch and knock the symbolical door of your-self they must be seriously considered and their meaning sought after even if never meant to be found.

The process of thinking about transcendental subject matters that will lead us to no immediate revelations or clear paths of action carries the gift of exposing ourselves to thinking, feeling, and sensing patterns we had not experienced before, namely a dynamic that will open our minds and our hearts to realizations not conceived as possible. Immersing ourselves into the unknown will fill us with future joy, something that we will only access if we dare to believe, for it will not be visible until years later, when the inner work has been done. While not all the right questions are meant to be answered they are all meant to be asked, not once but multiple times.

We came to Earth to do the right things and to do them the very best we can, it is that simple. You must define what *right* and *very best* mean for you and it is perfectly acceptable to keep changing them as you learn, as you grow, and as you evolve into the *who* you were meant to be. The closer you get to your destination, whatever it may be, your view of the world around and inside you will change and so will your own and personal definitions of *right* and *very best*. Accept your departure from the old and your arrival at the new, renew your-self, experiment with life, be a catalyst to help the best and the greatest inside you to react, to precipitate, to catalyze and to crystallize.

When you commit yourself to do the right things the very best you can expecting nothing in return, you are accepting that it is perfectly fine if the short term results you get are not as great, for at the end, results are none of your concerns and certainly not even part of your win scenario. Your purpose in life is not short term, it never was and it will never be, we are here for the long run. The key is to keep going despite the difficulties, the undesired results and the adversity that aiming at the stars carries with it.

> *When the expected comes to you, you will experience no resistance, no hesitation, no second guessing and no conflict. It is when you are faced with the unwanted that you have to reach deep inside and tell yourself: I am here to stay, and I will keep on going no matter what. Do not make lifelong decisions based on short term results.*

Like in a clock, you will not see the micro movements of the hands but you will see them at a different position an hour or two later. They move even when you don't see them moving! Our eyes and our minds are limited and can only see or think in direct proportion to the amount of information they can process, assimilate and digest. What would be the intent of teaching advanced calculus to a kindergarten child? Would he or she get it? Would he or she be able to use it? It would only bring confusion, trouble, and non-sense to his or her kindergarten-like life. The Universe operates under the premise of giving assignments commensurate or slightly more complex than what every human can handle, there is no point in overwhelming a brave spirit with challenges inconceivably above what of one can possibly do at any given point in time. A life of contribution is a life experienced through a series of small advancements in the direction we need to move, we will be asked to stretch but not beyond what we can reasonably reach, but certainly further than we may have conceived as possible. Nothing is impossible even if you think it is!

Always remember, if we are daring and willing to give our very best,
we will be challenged beyond the confines of our imagination ...
and no matter how audacious the mission, if it fits in our
hearts, it can be done, even if our minds would hesitate.

Patience and persistence will be always your allies, develop them to almost perfection, they will accompany you through your journey and provide an invaluable service to keep you going when what lies ahead cannot be seen with the eyes, when the magnificence and brilliance of a better future lies around the corner of our life, still invisible and apparently non-existent to our rational mind.

Whether our most beautiful visions of a future yet to come lie one
or a thousand years ahead of our time does not make a difference,
a thousand years are nothing but a few visionary lifetimes in
a row! ... Do not be the one breaking the chain of fortunate
events that will take humanity to places unthought-of!
Only those willing to be part of something greater than themselves
will be called upon to join a league of restless beings eager to give
it all for the betterment of a future beyond their lifetime.

Like the clock that keeps moving no matter what and even when not seen as moving, you must continue to focus and give your very best on the things you deem right! It is not our business to judge whether they work or they don't, we are here to do what we were told to do, to fulfill our life call and honor the cause we were entrusted with.

It is imperative that you raise your symbolical eyesight to see beyond the
here and now as the answers to meaningful life-long questions will not
be found overnight, you need to keep asking them times and again.

A pledge to know that keeps coming to us for apparently no reason is nothing but a blessing, a compass (although a bit blurry) to aid us in the process of finding the true north of our life. By asking the right questions a thousand times, you literally force yourself to focus on the key priorities that will make your life worthwhile. The gift of asking feeds the burning desire to learn, to know more and to ultimately wonder where is this all coming from, why is this here in the first place.

It is the blending of faith and curiosity what will bring
peacefulness to your heart, always seek to understand
even if the more you ask the less you know!

Never doubt the commands from above, whatever you were entrusted to do, you must do without hesitation, and it is perfectly reasonable to try to be aware of, to seek for answers to the lifelong intrigues that will elevate you to a higher level of complexity. A soul that knows what it must do, and why it must do it, can multiply its contribution by ten, by one hundred, or by one thousand!

Awareness is motivational power that feeds the knowledge
hunger of the curious heart. If you feel a burning desire to
know, dare to ask! ... Eventually you will be told.

The answers to your innermost questions lie within your own self and you have the power to reach them. When looking for the words of wisdom that will satisfy your itch for knowledge avoid paying too much attention to the outside world, stop listening to what is spoken in the different confines of everyday life as the rhetorical bridges that will help you cross the abyss between today and tomorrow were only built in the roads inner to yourself. When it comes to the quest for meaning, what the world thinks does not matter at all and whether other people may believe you have failed or triumphed is completely beside the point.

Those that claim ownership of invaluable knowledge, know no better
about you than a single cell in your whole body. Don't be surprised
to conclude that you have failed at times when the outer world was
celebrating your largest accomplishments, or that you have succeeded
when the outer world was condemning you for your greatest failure.
Learn to listen to no-one but your own heart!

Mind your inner dialog more than you mind any conversation with the outer world, what other people believe of you speaks more about them than about you. You have failed only when you think you did, not when the external world believes it. It is you and only you who determines when and how real failure presents itself. If you happen to get external opinions, lovingly and caringly thank for them, then peacefully move on, do what you have to do and do it graciously, the very best you can, with or without the world at your side.

When it comes to preparing for the next phase of your life journey, there is little of real value in the judgment of outer voices, kindly leave their opinion behind, pack only the indispensable and travel light, the road will be long and most everything you need is inside your own self.

You will need to be brave, spirited, determined and able to stand your ground, even if you are the only soul in the planet that thinks or feels that way.

The only failure I know of is the failure to give your very best for the things you deem right.

If after the world's largest perceived failure on your part, you can reach deep inside and say: *I believed on it with all my heart and I tried hard, really hard, giving the very best I had* … it is a huge success to me, the biggest success a human being can expect. It does not get any better than that, although the world can still think otherwise! When the world frowns at you, reach inside, and if what you see is something you like, smile back! They will not understand, and the truth of the matter is, they do not have to. You do not need their permission to smile, for the same reason you do not need their permission to succeed (although they may call it failure).

When you give your very best on the things you deem right, you are giving the Universe all you have and the Universe will not ask for more, not in a million years! Just for a moment, only for a brief moment, imagine what kind of a world this would be if every person would think hard about what right means for them and would then commit to do their very best at it, each and every day of their lives. Do you see the world being any better to what it is today? If you do not, try again!

The Universe has a game plan much more elaborated, complex and beautiful than the best plan we could ever imagine. It has to be that way otherwise it would be too simplistic, remember what Einstein said: *make things simple, not any simpler*. Einstein also said: *the solution to a problem lies at a layer of complexity higher than the one where the problem was created*. The Universe operates at a layer of complexity way higher than ours, several levels higher, which is the reason why the Universe can see the solutions to the problems we create but we cannot, unless we elevate ourselves to a higher level, higher than the level where the problem was created. To expect the Universe plan to be human-mind-like would be to force it to be much simpler than what it should really be! We can put together a giant jigsaw puzzle one piece at a time, but to picture it in our minds all at once, to be able to tell where a single randomly picked piece goes in the context of the overall frame would be impossible, such an undertaken is beyond any conceivable stretches of imagination. We can't fit such a level of difficulty in our minds and process it with our limited brain power. All we can do is to put one puzzle piece at a time having the conviction that, if we are persistent enough, one day we will finish it, regardless of exertion, effort, or length of time.

Those who attempt to crack the codes of Nature's master mind are forcing themselves into a process of excruciating mental anguish. You cannot, under any circumstance, conceive your-self as capable of figuring out how thousands of years of Universal wisdom interact to ultimately conform the totality of the human experience. The Universe has been learning and treasuring true knowledge for millennia and there is no possible way for our conscious mind to capture and manage that vast amount of knowledge, only abstractions as the collective unconscious can be eventually associated with the hosting and sharing of such an unlimited source of insight.

The mere exposure to higher than manageable levels of knowledge would drive us insane, for it would require our brains to operate in a way they are not prepared to, like asking a car to run on jet fuel and reach jet speeds would not only not work but also damage the engine structure permanently. Cars were built to be fueled by regular car gas and driven at regular car speeds, they were not built to be airplanes, fueled with airplane gas and take off the ground.

Likewise, our brains were designed to handle much simpler knowledge structures than the ones the Universe does. It is expected that human knowledge would evolve overtime in a controlled and gradual manner allowing the constitution of our brain to shape and morph into a higher octane engine capable of running at higher rpm's and use more powerful fuel types. These processes take time and must be oblivious to the conscious mind, hidden, unperceived, unnoticed, like the movement of the hands of a giant clock that we are only allowed to look at every one hundred years without feeling in any sort of urge to reengineer it at our will or desire.

It is in the spirit of respecting Nature laws and facilitating the pursuit of human kind purposes that some things are better left unknown. The Universe knows what it does and there is a reason for keeping it secret, mystically treasured in a place and a time far from the here and now.

While such a vast amount of knowledge would be unmanageable by the average mind, it is possible to conceive minuscule particles of that totality to enter the realm of our brain power and fast forward our assimilation of a reality yet to come. Having a glimpse of insight is like injecting a shot of a NOS into an engine prepared to run on NOS bumping the speed up by stimulating advanced functions of our mental machinery. You cannot give a shot of NOS to any car, first they would not be able to take any advantage of it and second, you would blow their engines out if forced to use it. If you want to eventually run on NOS, you need to get your engine upgraded … such a process requires hard work and preparation.

Once the heavy lifting has been done and you have developed your capabilities to even imperfectly decode the symbolical language in which the Universe communicates, you will be presented with signs, encrypted messages, synchronistic phenomena and serendipitous events that will help you advance in the complexity of realizing your life purpose and your role in the advancement of the world. It is not an accident of life that you will be exposed to layers of knowledge other people can't even think about. The question is not *if* but *why*. Why are you the recipient of such privileged and somewhat restricted wisdom? What is the Universe expecting from you? This is not a mistake, a casual happening, a random occurrence but something you long sought for and something meant to be. There is no such a thing as a random coincidence when it comes to Universe driven circumstances. There is a reason for everything that happens whether we know about it or not.

ABOUT LIFELONG COMMITMENTS

The best commitments are those your heart suggests you to make without you fully knowing what you are getting into.

Kwai Chang Kane was riding on a wagon with a road companion and they reached an intersection. An unpaved, gravel filled road that led to a yet to be seen destination, unknowingness in its purest and most primordial forms. In the spur of the moment, Kwai Chang asked his friend: *where does that road lead to?* His companion, full of awe and surprise by the abrupt and passionate inquiry, said: *to a town called Ninevah.* Almost immediately Kwai Chang jumped off the wagon and told his travel partner: *I must go there.* Completely astonished by the urge of the apparently purposeless decision, his partner could not help responding: *why must you go there? ... there is nothing worth in that town,* to which Kwai Chang added: *I would tell you if I knew why.*

We go through the different paths of our life flavoring the new and re-tasting the old, as if living were nothing but a paradox aimed at finding meaning in the mystical yet ordinary routine of walking explored and unexplored terrains. In both cases, we build experience, we learn, we treasure knowledge, develop skills and escalate the symbolical wisdom staircase. As we continue to scan the new and the novel, it gradually becomes more known and we feel more familiar to its company. Those that used to be strangers would eventually become old acquaintances through the passage of time. Eventually, we reach a point when we say ... *I know it,* and if the exposure, practice and effort are intense and prolonged enough we can even say ... *I know it very well.* We all carry a mission of our own, a call to action, a purpose to fulfill, and whether it ever becomes conscious or not, it does not make a difference, it is there anyway and we cannot avoid its encounter.

It is such a purpose that makes some paths more attractive, more convincing and more appealing to us than others, as if there were a rare

form of alchemy binding our existence with the very reason that brought
us here, a sort of mesmerizing chemistry standing behind the recipe of
a magic sip that enchanted our hopefulness for a life still to be born.

The inner need to align our actions with our life's utmost legitimate call can become as tantalizing as irresistible. It is through a process of discovery that we venture ourselves to make commitments about what we *want* to do and accomplish in life. There is a hidden treasure in the discovery of what we are here for and the things we can do to deliver on that purpose. Such a mystical series of events would conform both a privilege and a duty, a quest we cannot and should not refuse to embark into, a journey of growth and fulfillment by which lifelong commitments are secretively born and lived through.

Those commitments are best made when we see what we are asked
to do even without fully understanding how complex, intricate,
or challenging it may be, perplexed and blinded by the inner
beauty it displays and the enchanting charm it radiates.

The Universe operates in ways unknown to the human mind, rooted and hidden in the realms of the heart, where believing comes first and seeing comes second. No wonder the lack of hesitation that propels our inner self engine to immediately ignite its twelve cylinders and engage its high gears full steam ahead. Whatever needs to be known is already known, even when our mind is still trying to figure out what we are being asked to do.

It is in the blink of an eye and without any amount of thinking, that
the most fundamental and life altering commitments of our existence get
made, at those crucial moments when our hearts rather than our minds
have taken the lead! The best commitments are those your heart suggests
you to make without your mind fully knowing what you are getting into.

Engagements of that tenure are not made because they are easy, clear, or bring immediate comfort to our lives; rather, they are made because they are the *right* thing to do, regardless of risk, complexity, difficulty, or effort. What stands behind those deeply held promises is something that must get done, and it is our duty to give our *very best* to do it, even if it comes to the ultimate dilemma of all: *getting it done or die trying.*

> *It is at that very moment, when our heart artfully commits our will to the lifelong pursuit of our purpose, that the battle of an honorable versus an ordinary life is won.*

You will be neither jury nor judge but will bear witness to the most transcendent moment of your voyage, when the very best in you will make a leap of faith into the abyss of the unknown hoping that nothing less than the divine will be provided by the silent yet truthful pledge emanating from above. At the end, we were sent here to do our very best in the causes our life was bound to, and for as simple as it may sound, all we have to do is to submit our will to the commands of our call.

> *We were created out of unconditional love, and only such a type of love can be used to live the life we were blissfully given.*

It is my deepest belief, the legacy of half a century of intense soul searching, that a life conducted in such a manner will lead to little or no regrets, which is not to say that one would not go back and do some things differently as wisdom comes from the *doing*, and doing wrong teaches more than doing right (right or wrong in the sense of what seems to work). In this context you may, when looking in hindsight, say "If I have to do this again, I would do it this way instead" and if that thought is perceived as regret, lovingly refuse to accept it, for it is not something regrettable.

An action taken with the utmost consideration and deeply feeling it was the right thing to do, should never reach the category of *regrets*, if anything, it should constitute the basis for a wholehearted reflection, a *what-if* type of statement, a question of what would have happened should we have done some things in a way different than the way we did them, perhaps better suited for the impending circumstances as seen now, in hindsight, for it is easier to be wiser about the past than about the present or the future. No one can attest what would have life been about if what happened would have not happened. That would be pure speculation and a claim of having the ability to predict a past based on circumstances that never occurred.

The truth of the matter is that we are where we are and thinking what we are thinking because of what we went through, what our perceived mistakes have taught us and the lessons we have learned. It is because of those lessons that we can see more clearly as if we would have reached a metaphorically higher vantage point from where we can envision a world different than the one we used to see before the learning took place.

The learning, and the underlying stumbling that provoked it, was absolutely necessary to be where we are now. Never regret mistakes, for without them, we would remain stuck at the very same level of complexity we were before the mistake transpired. It is through the evolution into a higher and more complex self, something done through the process of expanding our life experience inventory, that we grow tall enough to see beyond the past horizon allowing the best of us to break free and fly away.

I strongly encourage anybody willful to embark in a life of honor to make lifelong commitments, especially in those areas of their lives that are noteworthy, essential, and ultimately a big part of what they believe they are here for!

Don't worry or rumble about how easy or difficult what you are about to commit is … if you hesitate, it's because you *can* do it! Your heart will never let you even consider, let alone commit to, something way out of your reach (and I am not referring only to your *current* but also to your *potential* reach). The things that come to your mind and pass the *heart-test* are those you should *seriously* consider as candidates

31

for lifelong commitments. You must make the commitment first, and then figure out *what* and *how* to do it …

You are not alone here … The stars align to help heroic spirits looking to do the right things. The Universe is at your side and you can't ask for a more capable or more loyal ally!

Be valiant, plucky, and persistent in your efforts, and over all things, *never give up!* This is not going to be nirvana, there will be long, cold, and dark nights, maybe a few that would seem to never end, but no matter how long, cold, or dark the night, the sun will always come out. The darkest the night, the closer the dawn … always remember it!

Every time you stumble, struggle or fail (based on the outer world definition of failure), you are one stumble, struggle, or failure closer to succeeding! Wherever you are going, you are getting *closer* and *closer*, nor *farther* and *farther!* If you are committed to a lifelong effort and to *never* give up, you will make it … or you will die trying, which is absolutely the same thing.

We are not here to accomplish anything, especially those things we believe we need to accomplish. We are here to give our very best on those things we deem as right and to never stop trying. Whether we accomplish anything or not, is not up to us to decide but to the Universe. It is the Universe who decides What, When, and How we will accomplish what we are supposed to accomplish. Don't try to play God! We can only see the tip of the iceberg of that thing called life. Don't pretend to know it all … be humble.

Make lifelong commitments and give your very best being as willing to let go of the symbolical doors that are closing as to go through the symbolical windows that are opening. This is a difficult task to do, perhaps one of the most difficult so far as some doors will only close for the Universe to see how *tenaciously* we want to go through them. Only then, when we have knocked on that door enough times with no intention of stop knocking whatsoever, they may open again. You can't ask for more until you have proven you have the capacity to handle what you have.

Obstacles are a test to your endurance and a prevention to get yourself into something that is way over your head. Doors that close are calling for you to knock at them, especially if you were planning to walk through. You have to knock at them, once and again, eventually sit down at the door step to see if it would open, and if not, go back to knocking, with as much or even more stamina than before! ... never give up on a life call! You will *not* tear the door down; brute force is never the answer. If the door is meant to open, it will open, perhaps only when you are *ready* to go through it. There is almost always something of value waiting at the other side of that symbolical door and you must be prepared to face whatever that *something* is.

Other doors will close for us to look for windows and ultimately shift our paths, letting the present and the past go off to a new phase in our lives. So ... how do you tell which door is this? Shall we relentlessly knock and forever wait until it opens, or look for windows instead? This is a real dilemma! Sometimes you will not know, at least not immediately but after knocking and waiting for a long time. Everything is part of the master plan of your life, your knocking on the right or wrong doors, your waiting whether truly or mistakenly, everything happens for a reason. Eventually you will know and you will know for sure, although it may take some time, some struggle and some stumbles.

Don't ask for anything more than the opportunity to keep trying and keep giving your very best ... and if your pledge is granted ... Celebrate!

OUR LEGACY TO THE WORLD ...

What is it that you will leave to the world when it's time to go?

Have you ever thought that we are here only temporarily? This is nothing but one stop in a longer, infinite glide, a lifetime within something larger, something that we do not know exactly what it is, an unconditional source of light and love. Life, as we know it, has to be a part, a component, a piece of something else, something greater, more meaningful, more fascinating, nobler, a sort of bigger picture regulated by the Universe master plan. Even not fully knowing where our life fits in the more holistic view of the whole, we know for sure that we once came and that one day we will have to leave. And then I wonder ... what is it that I will leave to those that will stay and come after my time to leave will arrive? What is my unique contribution to the world, a token left behind my existence as a treasure for others in appreciation for the right I have been given to live in this place called world and enjoy this experience called life?

I'll share mine with you ...

- First and foremost, I believe in the existence of a benevolent God that created us for a reason and I feel morally, spiritually, lovingly, and dutifully obliged to do what is expected from me. This is not the type of obligation you do because you are told to but because you truly, deeply and sincerely want to do it, like when something emanates from within, a sort of burning need coming from the bottom of your heart to do good for others as good has been done onto you. We can only give what we have, what we have received and nurtured, treasured and saved, waiting for the opportunity to share it with those that would need it the most. Hence, my first legacy to the world is to accomplish the mission I was entrusted to the very best of my abilities, each and every day of my life.

- Second, I was born a man, a son, a husband, a father, a grandfather maybe and I feel compelled to do the best I can on each of the roles that honor those inside my circle of love.

- Third, I married a woman that I love beyond reason and without whom my life would be unbearable. I have learned to see the world through her eyes and to appreciate a kind of beauty I did not know existed. I am wholeheartedly devoted to her and will do everything I can to make her feel loved, cared for, respected, admired, complete and happy, while striving to help crystallize some of her most beautiful dreams!

- Fourth, I have the honor of being the father of three beautiful children who I love from the bottom of my heart, they are *everything* to me and I will do everything at my reach to help them make some of their dreams come true. I will do and be all I can do and be to lead their lives by example, with no reservations of any kind, help them reach adult life in peace, in love, and responsibly. I wish them to become happy, independent, good men and women, loving and caring human beings that will in turn leave their own legacy to the world.

- Fifth, I am here to help others, those in need, those with good intentions and no means, those that need to be helped, taught, inspired, guided, and coached. I am here to be a resource, a support, a teacher, a mentor, on all those fields I have somewhat mastered and to all those that want to learn, to grow, to make something positive with their lives in accordance to their own personal purposes, and in so doing continue the hope filled work our ancestors initiated hundreds of years ago.

For those of us that believe in the existence of a benign God that created us out of unconditional love, and also in the existence of something unique and personal we and only we must do, finding out what that something is becomes one of the most fundamental and challenging questions we have to answer. Sometimes, although rarely, such a glimpse of insight may pop up in our mind as if by accident and one immediately knows what its meaning is. Whatever the case, and whether you found it or it found you, you will know that you know! If you don't know that you know or if you are unsure, then you haven't met it yet (at least consciously as you may have been working on it for years, even not knowing what it is).

> *Let things be the way they are meant to be, for there is a reason, an order, a hierarchy, a sequence of events that has to be followed not to alter the mystical creation of what Nature has in mind. Some things are better left unknown until we are able to comprehend their place in our lives and their reason for existence.*

If we have the habit of listening to our heart, it is very likely that we are doing what we have to do perhaps not knowing that this is it, that this is the one and only important thing we are here for, the only one thing we can't leave unfinished by the time we have to go. Self-awareness is not a condition to spend your life as your Creator dictated. Good will is. There are thousands, millions of good men and women that have done what they were entrusted to do without even asking themselves the question of whether or not there is such a thing called *life purpose*. Self-awareness is not a requirement but a privilege to invest ourselves more fully in the business of doing what we are here for and for some strange reason falling in the whereabouts of the unknown, some people wonder ... *what is life all about?*

> *Curiosity is an attribute prevalent in those with an itch to know more than what they already do, to find out, to inquire, to discover, to connect, to understand and to be understood.*

Looking for the answers to philosophical quandaries that may not exist at our conscious level of complexity are aimed to help us get to the bottom of our core, deep inside where the boundaries of our inner self starts to connect with that we know little about, the mysterious yet fascinating world of mythology, alchemy, and the collective unconscious.

I was curious ever since my early childhood always wondering how things worked. When I watched TV (it was black and white at that time) I wondered how come I could see and hear a person inside a wooden box in real time? It was inexplicable to me, so I wondered. Wondering about the things you can't explain will lead you closer to their explanations, even when all you may feel is that you are confusing yourself or becoming outnumbered by not easy to explain matters. It was that same curiosity what mobilized me to study Engineering and get to know how some things work. I just wanted to know if for no other reason than to satisfy an inner curiosity need. After my technical curiosity was somewhat quenched and I could explain how a computer worked, my curiosity started to shift to more complex aspects of life.

One of the characteristics of personality traits is that they never go away, they may change, morph, evolve, but they never vanish or evaporate. If you were curious as a child, you will still be curious as a senior, maybe not about the same things but curious still. When I reached my early thirties and even without even noticing it, I was propelled to study the human mind and become more able to explain how some of the basic psychological processes worked. I devoured every book of psychology I could find and stumbled with renowned authors like Maslow, Fromm, Jung, Piaget, Frankl, Skinner, Freud, Damasio, Ryan, Deci, Csikszentmihalyi, Seligman, Goleman, Rogers, etc. I just wanted to learn.

I don't think I knew at the time what I was exactly looking for but I can certainly attest that the need was strong, burning, and unbearable. Looking in hindsight, almost 20 years after, I believe I was trying to answer one question and one question only … *what are we here for?* Sometimes we do not need to know why we do what we do, it's just not necessary, not the right time, and knowing may just defeat the purpose of our doing. Some paths are so intricate and so complex that the untrained eye cannot be given visibility to it without becoming blinded by their glow which would very likely alter what we were supposed to do. Accept that you know as much as you need to know and if you think it is not enough, keep asking and you will eventually stumble with that you need to find, only when the time comes, not any earlier, not any later.

When I started reading about psychology, I was dwelling with subjects such as *why people think the way they think, do the things they do, change, don't change, etc.* In a broader sense of the effort, I was trying to crack the codes of human rationale and behavior, the dynamics behind what people think, feel, and ultimately do. I just felt a strong need to know the *why's* behind both typical and atypical desires and behaviors. While I can't tell with astonishing certainty why I was so curious about human behavior and psychology, one thing I do know and strongly believe is that whatever it was is intimately related to what I came here for, however imprecise my rationale can be. Only in hindsight I can guess that I was so intrigued because knowing more about the mind would led me to better learn about myself and in so doing be more able to do what I was entrusted to do.

It is in that trend of thought that I can come up with a thousand things I have learned throughout the last 20 years that have made a positive impact in my ability to fulfill the mission I was entrusted. Some of those things came to me as a result of asking those questions and researching in the field of psychology, other things just met me as life experiences, a sort of gift from above, signals, treasure chests left along the road I was travelling at the moment. Regardless of how much I may have oversimplified a rather complex path finding process, I strongly and deeply feel that my curiosity had something to do with finding my way in life, the Universe knew I was hungry of knowledge, willing to learn, willing to experience new things, eager to give everything back, and more. I was then and I still am committed to the purpose I was entrusted, some things are created to never go away.

After I had read enough about psychology, I eventually stumbled with the utmost difficult question in the quest for knowledge a human being can find … *what are we here for?*, which inevitable led myself to asking … *if there is a reason for our existence, then what is it?* From there, it went on and on, one question leading to another in an endless yet exciting treasure hunting expedition giving me the sense that I was digging deeper into something worth it, something that would take the rest of my life to figure it out. Over the next twenty years my mind kept asking the same questions over and over again, in different ways, shapes and forms, but the very same questions indeed. If there is a purpose to our life then ...

Are we supposed to know it?
If yes, how do we know about it?
How do we find out what it is?
Where do we start?
How do we know we found it for sure?
What do we do once we know?
What If we can't figure it out?
What if we don't like it?
What if we can't do it, or if we can only start it but cannot finish it?

I kept asking about and sleeping on life changing unknowns for years, as if trying to quench my ignorance thirst, consciously and unconsciously looking for answers to my pledge for wisdom. Not until after quite some time of reading, reflecting and debating with my own self, I realized that I was knowingly or unknowingly in the quest of my life call! I really, truly, deeply wanted to know. Over the following years I realized that my need to know was based on a strong feeling of giving something back, of contributing to this world in the best way I could, of honoring the command and the call of my Creator, a benign God that loves us unconditionally and beyond reason.

If there was something called mission, purpose, life call, etc, unique and personal for each human being, I wanted to know mine, and I wanted to know it so passionately that I would keep seeking and asking the question in all forms and shapes, over and over again until I would find the answer or would die trying. I guess I was coming out of the belief that by knowing what it was I would have a greater chance of fulfilling it, of honoring it and of never giving up! I asked the question thousands of times, consciously, unconsciously, awake, in my dreams, directly, indirectly, I tried everything. I looked for clues in Nature, the Universe, inner voices, signs, metaphors, analogies and everything that would be meaningful and out of the ordinary. Gradually my mission started to become uncovered, dusted off, brought to light from where it was since the day I was born. I had to polish my interpretation of it a few times, rough some edges, simplify it, enhance its inner beauty. Like when you find a brut diamond, the beauty is there, you just need to craft it, gently, lovingly. One important aspect about finding your purpose in life is that you will never know *exactly* what it is but can get quite close. Your mission is part of a master plan created by the Universe, something mystical that lies at a higher level of complexity, much higher than what we can reason, hence we can't fully grasp it. We can see bits and pieces of it but not the whole, not the interconnectedness of it with the rest of the overarching master plan, it is just one of a thousand pieces in a giant jigsaw puzzle.

> *... and you don't need to know it exactly, you just need to know it enough, and even this is not necessary some times as many people work on their life calls being consciously unaware. You will know as much as you can handle, this is the best that can happen to you, you do not want to know more than what you can comprehend.*

I will certainly polish my mission a bit more over the years to come and for now, it is enough to say that I know that I know, I know enough to fully engage myself into it. I know the direction I am going, the direction I was asked to go and it is my duty and my honor to make it my own, becoming one with it!

Although it is more complex than what I can write in this essay, I can confidently say that the reason for my existence revolves around helping others in ways that are both known and unknown to me. It is a key part of helping others to write about what I learned in life and what I consider of value to those willing to make higher contributions to the world in their own and unique ways. My writings are only for those that want to read them, if and only if, they believe they can benefit from my experience to enlighten the fulfillment of their own personal life quests.

I am here to help, especially those with good hearts, good intentions, and committed to do for others more than they do for themselves!

FOCUS ON YOUR MISSION AND
ITS SENSE OF RIGHTNESS

*How do you know you have found your mission? The answer
is simple, you never do ... your mission will find you!*

When the time comes, and usually after a considerable amount of soul searching work, your mission will show up at your doorway, and when it does, you will have no doubts, you will know it is *it*! If you wonder about whether something is your purpose in life or not, it is not the time for you to know yet, if you are supposed to know, you will have no doubts at all, there will be no reasons suggesting you to hesitate. It may still be a bit undefined, a bit unexplored, a bit uncertain, and a bit ambiguous in the sense that you may not fully realize its entire essence or extent, but once your life call finds you, you will undeniably know.

*Part of the fascinating nature of how the Universe has planned
each and every step of the way is that we do not necessarily have
to consciously know what our mission in life is in order for us to
work at it, many of us have started working on our calls well before
we became consciously aware, if we ever did. Self-awareness is a
gift that some people have been provided with which aids them in
the process of reaching their destinations, but it is not a necessary
companion to travel the most beautiful roads of our lives.*

In the lack of conscious purpose awareness, we always carry our inner compass, and it is that compass what guides us through the wilderness of life, pointing true north when we do not clearly know where north is. Notice that I emphasize the idea of conscious as opposed to unconscious awareness, and the reason being is we always know at an unconscious level, our heart will guide us when our mind is starting to get lost. In a broader sense, your mission always finds you, even when it may not tell you it did. Nobody is left alone without an assignment of their own, a life call to go after. All our lives have true meaning from our very first day and it is our job to reunite, join efforts, collaborate, and walk together with it, through whatever paths the Universe has asked us to follow. If you are *consciously* found, if you can feel you know what that special something you have to do in life is, an immense sense of peacefulness and love will come to you, you will feel you are finally back home, in the exact place you should have ever been and at the exact time you should be there, fully knowing what is expected from you and entrusted with a life long enough to pursue it.

You were blessed beyond reason and the Universe trusts you much more than you trust yourself. Nobody is asked to do something he or she has absolutely no possibility of doing, something impossible to do and something that will lead you only to failure and frustration. You must believe in you ... what you came here to do is far from impossible!

It is at this juncture when you must clearly know the difference between difficult and impossible. While the former may carry a low probability of occurrence, be sitting two inches or two miles beyond the farthest stretches of your imagination, and tied to the unrestricted nature of your commitment to pursue it, the latter is simply not meant to be (the Universe will not allow it to happen).

It is here when you need to break your reins loose and let the greatness you treasure inside to flourish and emerge. What you have been asked to do, whether you know it or not, may be difficult but it is certainly not impossible. The Universe does not hand off impossible but difficult assignments.

As far as how difficult it will be, enough to stretch your capabilities to the best you can offer which is generally way beyond anything you have ever imagined you would be able to do. If you feel deep inside there is something you must do and don't have the slightest idea about how to do it, you are on the right path for a life lived with honor was never supposed to be easy. All you have to see is work ahead, not a brick wall that you cannot get past it, you will move on, advance, evolve. Often times, the reason why you cannot imagine how to do something difficult is because the capabilities to deal with it lie at a higher level of complexity and development than the one you are in, requiring you to elevate yourself, to grow, to escalate the way you think, feel and ultimately act for the increased level of difficulty to become manageable (the Merriam-Webster definition of difficult is: *not easy, requiring much work or skill to do or make* ... there is absolutely no mention to impossible).

If you are willing to put the required effort to acquire the necessary knowledge, practice enough to transform that knowledge into skill and commit to turn your skills into mastery, difficult is absolutely possible. Even circumstances with one-in-a-million probability of occurrence happen once every one million times!

Working on your life call should become an overarching priority in your life. It is the most important thing for you to do and you must find the way to love it unconditionally for this is the way you are loved by your Creator. A loving mission will gradually start to morph into an unavoidable burning call to action, an inescapable urge to give your very best, a genuine and legitimate desire to leave a legacy onto the future generations and to change the world into a better place to live ... one life at a time. A lifelong commitment will inevitable spark your energy in the service of your purpose, mobilizing you to work hard on what you have been entrusted to accomplish. Even when it may be perceived as work by the outside world, work may not be the best word to describe your involvement in a dearly loved and inescapable cause insofar it will feel more as a sort of joy, a pleasure of a rare kind, far from a burden or an obligation and close to the most fulfilling endeavors you have ever entertained.

We work on our missions by choice, by desire, by will and only because we want to, in spite and not because of any strong feelings suggesting that we have to. A mysterious and captivating

> *blend of love and duty masqueraded in an irresistible drive*
> *to do what the heart regards as divine and sacred.*

The creative imagery of the future result of your work and the final product of your fully realized dreams is such a compelling proposition that one can hardly stop thinking about it, let alone wishing to be working on something else.

> *Your purpose completes you and makes you whole while embodying*
> *the primary reason why you are here. Without an altruistic*
> *mission to engage with, your life is nothing but a collection of*
> *random experiences aimed at nothing but building the extraneous*
> *illusions gravitating around a purposeless existence.*

There is a special kind of peacefulness that is only reached when you are fully utilizing your potential for something noble and greater than yourself, something intended to embellish the collective good of human kind. When you devote yourself fully (in heart, mind, body, and spirit) to such a cause, you will reach the summit of your own mount Everest, the highest peak you can possibly climb, a place where every cell of your body will be aligned with your pursuit empowering you to generate incredible amounts energy and focus, reaching talents and capabilities you were not aware you had available. You will finish your days exhausted but with the feeling that it was absolutely worth it!

Maslow's concepts around the phenomenon of peak performance and Jung's constructs of meaningful coincidences will apply to you as you will reach levels of optimal engagement and synchronicity between what you desire and what you do. Jung's individuation postulations will describe the evolution of your life experience as you would have embarked into a journey of growing your-self to unseen levels of self-discovery and reinvention. Csikcentmihalyi's flow dynamics will embrace you and make you feel one with the task, as if nothing else exists. The passage of time will get distorted; hours will feel like minutes, and minutes like hours. Living in a state of peak performance, synchronicity, individuation, and flow is something difficult to describe in words, it has to be felt and first-hand assimilated.

One common aspect of these moments of joy and fulfillment is that they tend to be brief, they come and go, interlaced into the fabric of everyday life. We are not supposed to be in flow twenty four hours a day, but when we are, the feelings are so intense and the memories so everlasting that they will leave palpable traces of their sweetness until the next time they come to visit us.

When something good that can be repeated is also brief, it is twice as good! A moment of flow can spark enough energy to ignite your engine and keep it running for as long as it would take for the next flow moment to come. Never underestimate the power of a soul in a peak performance state. When the sun of your heart shines, it shines so brightly that its heat can keep you warm for the longest and coldest night!

There is something else you need to be aware of, something that may help you prepare for the moment when embarking in the pursuit of your life call may come. Actively pursuing your mission requires courage and the ability to become *yourself* in every aspect of the word. You will most likely face circumstances that will require some degree of independent thinking and acting, moments when you will have to be faithful to your-self and accept that the outer world may not agree with the way you think or like the things you do. It is the way it has to be and you must be prepared to come to terms with the eventual disagreement, the disapproval, and the desire that you think and do otherwise, kindly and gently allowing for that space between what the world expects from you and what you must do, not to be filled as the gap needs to remain open, untouched and recognized as the price to be paid for being faithful to your own self.

There will be times when you will have to take the less travelled side of the fork on the road while letting rest of the world continue on the most travelled one. Your actions will have to be regulated by *your inner sense of rightness* and not by what the environment around you rewards or punishes. You must be willing to not only tolerate the rejection but also engage in rightful actions that may lead to episodes of world's defined failure or what others may simply call non-sense. It is all part of the business of following your heart and being faithful to what your value system tells you to do, with no hesitation or compromises of any kind.

> *Some people, perhaps many in number, will not appreciate what you do or why you do it and it is perfectly fine, they do not have to, not as a precondition for you to do what you must do. You do not need their permission or consent and for as insensitive it may sound, their judgment of your actions is simply unimportant. Show kindness to them and respect their disagreement for your job is not to get massive acceptance but to invest yourself fully in what you call is asking for.*

Some people would find life easier if everybody would agree with the what's and the why's of what they must do, but it seldom works that way and you certainly do not want to align your actions to what the outer world is able and willing to accept. Let the outer world live its life when at the same time you live yours … judgment will be inevitable. Have the fortitude to do what you have to do in spite of the eventual lack of acceptance and approval, in those moments when the world's expectations will diverge from yours.

I will make only one exception where you need to make a special effort to align your purpose, those you love and love you, they deserve that special stretch from you to explain what you do and why you do it. It is in such an alignment process that you may also learn something about them, their *what's* and their *why's*. Be open and sympathetic to them, they are a big part of what you do and why you do it. If what you must do will eventually result in a rather massive lack of understanding from the world around you, it may well be because what you must do is not only ahead of the world's time but also perceived as unnecessary, unjustified, unexpected, difficult, non-sense or nearly impossible. That was the case of recognized heroes and heroines in the history of mankind, people like Mahatma Gandhi, Martin Luther King Jr., and Mother Teresa just to name a few. Remember that for every one thousand souls that oppose, reject, or are simply indifferent to what you must do there may be another thousand or another million that would like, enjoy, or benefit from it, whether they know about it or not. If what we must do will *truly* help one soul and one soul only, even at the price of disappointing the world's status quo, it was well worth it! Sometimes your followers or the beneficiaries of your good deeds are not those around you but those you have never or will never get a chance to meet (conceive the possibility that what you are doing will not be appreciated or utilized in your lifetime or by the people you will ever know).

Worthy causes require no company or external encouragement to be undertaken, if the Universe and your heart say go, you must go … now!

Something important to note about rejection or ignorance from the outer world is that when such a dynamic shows up, you are certainly not doing what is expected, which generally represents a good sign and something that would suggest you are following a cause for reasons other than mere crowd acceptance or external recognition (since you are clearly not getting it). This is a counter-intuitive process and you must become familiar with it … *when everybody around you is in agreement with what you do, there is something wrong!* I have only rarely, if at all, embarked myself in something absolutely worth doing when at the same time, those around me (at work, social networks, people you relate with, etc.) were in absolute agreement with what I was doing. The most positive reaction I have borne witness was skepticism and that look indicating they had no idea about what I was doing or why I was doing it, and I was fine with it. Accept that you are different, actually everybody is except that only a few are brave enough to recognize and embody their uniqueness.

I was never a believer of defying crowd behavior for the sake of contrarianism but as a result of doing what I must do. What you must do has to be done, regardless of what the world thinks. The Universe is at a higher rank than the world and what you must do has been dictated by the Universe chain of command. The Universe is wiser than the world and cares about you in ways you cannot imagine … it is your moral responsibility to care back! When that crossroad comes, stand tight and choose wisely, go in the direction you have to go, with or without the world behind you.

Do not become resentful or angry if you are singled out, casted out, or regarded as an oddity, you may deserve those qualifications for having dared to oppose conventional wisdom and swim upriver, against all odds and with a probability of success low enough that only one in one hundred will make it (which by the way, that may be you!).

I would even suggest you get mentally prepared for it, sooner or later you will have to face it. Those who may criticize your actions, object what you do, ask why you do it, or expect you to do otherwise, simply can't visualize the beauty you envision as their vantage point is rather different than yours ... the world they see is not the same world you envision (you may be able to see with due clarity what is not there yet, the masses can't). Albert Einstein introduced the suggestion that a problem cannot be resolved at the same level of complexity it was created and I would not be surprised if those that are against a noble, yet not easy to recognize purpose, would still remain at the complexity level where the problem that such a noble pursuit is trying to resolve was created.

Without the burning, passionate, and wholehearted call emanating from the inside, no one can just defy the odds of conformity, venturing into the unknown and embarking in a battle that many would consider lost even before started.

Entering battles that were, from the world's point of view, *impossible to win* to finally prove the world's definition of impossible wrong by winning an unreasonable low number of them, is not a farfetched endeavor if your heart tells you to do it. What most people would consider a waste of time and a waste of a life, daring souls would regard as the most important cause to which a life can be devoted.

You must learn to think in non-conventional terms, only by being able to find your own inner compass and steering your life based on its reading you will be able to be who you came here to be. If being yourself seems hard, you do not want to try how demoralizing, devastating, and agonizing being somebody else can be!

The thinking and acting patterns characterized by a strong sense of self-determination based on greater-than-the-self purposes have been behind the life stories of those that made outstanding contributions to the world as we know it. It is now easy to recognize their role in the enlightenment of today's quality of life but back then, when what they were trying to do was just an idea, an extremely low probability cause, something nobody had done or even attempted to do before, nothing but a burning vision of a different future only existing in their hearts? ... back then it was anything but easy! All they had was an idea, an obsession, a beautiful dream they could not stop thinking about ... and a whole world telling them "it can't be done!" Difficult battles are not always won, at least not the first time around and you must be resilient, willing and able to keep going and keep thinking that the best is always yet to come.

Winning is not the ultimate purpose of your efforts but the feeling that you played your very best games and lived a life worth lived! At the end, winning or losing is of no importance, and quite certainly not something you must worry or be concerned about, score keeping is not your job but the Universe's. Your job is to give your very best each and every day, laser focusing on the priorities that were assigned to you from above. At the end, you will win only those battles that were meant to be won, and lose those that were meant to be lost, and in the process of winning and losing you will learn and grow!

One final comment about losing, my investment coach always teaches that when it comes to investing like a professional we must learn to lose right. What a great concept! ... if you did what you were supposed to do and it did not lead you to win, then you have lost right, you have done everything you were supposed to do and that loss was part of the game, a mechanism to teach you a lesson and something that increases the probability of winning the next time around.

It would be unrealistic to expect that everything will go well in life, that there would be no bumps, no setbacks and no disappointments. While healthy stock market uptrends are formed by a series of higher highs and higher lows (prices zig-zagging in an overall upward direction), healthy lives are constructed by a series of success stories intertwined with episodes of *perceived* failure that would represent some sort of retracement to a previous point in our long term journeys. I qualified failures as *perceived* because what we frequently see as failure is not necessarily a mistake but an opportunity to learn. The external world may regard it as a flaw but this is the external world's interpretation of it and not the absolutely truth (actually, what the world thinks about non-conventional actions is generally quite imprecise).

The only failure is the failure to keep trying. When things did not go as you expected, learn something and try again! The confidence that a strong sense of direction provides will empower you to plead guilty of disobeying public opinion, a charge that would not worry those in the quest of their life purpose. The voice of the crowd only matters when you do not have an inner voice loud enough to silence anything that comes from the outside, and the irony is that such inner voice has to be as loud as a whisper, loud enough for you to hear it!

Follow your heart and you will be ruled by your core, your values, your principles, your inner sense of self and direction, your true North. You will not need to look around for others to tell you what to do or where to go, you will know better!

Life is a magnificent journey, the most beautiful ride you can ever imagine. There is however one requirement for you to enjoy such a voyage, you have to find ways to be comfortable with your-self. This is all you will have, you and only you will be your all-time travel mate. Others will come and go, stay for a while, lend you their loving company and then depart. Everyone has a journey of their own and no two journeys are exactly alike, not all the time, not from beginning to end. Don't look around for reassurance, you will not find it there. Don't look around for love, you will not find it there either. Look around to see how much you can do for the Universe, how much you can give to others and how big of a legacy you can leave in the field of your life call.

Life is about doing, about giving, and about being all you can be … and such a path requires courage and determination!
Do not condition your thoughts, feelings or actions to public acceptance, you do not need any type of reassurance to go where you must go and to do what you must do. Just do what you have to do and enjoy every bit of it, ultimately accepting the fact that the few and not the many would eventually understand.
You are here to be the best human being you possibly can, with or without the rest of the world cheering for you. There is so much to do and so much to give, don't get distracted!

WHAT YOU ARE MEANT TO DO AND WHO YOU ARE MEANT TO BECOME

Whatever the reason you are here for, you did
not find it, it rather found you!

The Universe has a container full of dreams, of all sizes and kinds and is
always on the watch for dreamers to adopt those dreams as their own. It
is in this process of "matching" a dream with a dreamer that the Universe
finds a home for the noble and altruistic tasks humanity needs to get done.

Whatever it is you are here for, you do not find it, it finds you and all you have to do is become one with it. This essay was inspired by the movie *The Legend of Bagger Vance* who found me in one of the many walks through the paths of everyday life.

We travel through the entirety of our existences with the illusion that we discover treasures along the way, rare gems that may eventually change the course of our lives. In reality, we only find what was placed there for us to stumble with in an almost inevitable manner, crystallizing an encounter that has long been meant to occur. In a sense, those meaningful events that have crossed our paths were waiting for us to get there, miraculously meeting us at the right time and at the right place, as if it were a coincidence, a meaningful coincidence built around a shared and secret purpose. This is one of the central aspects of Jung's Synchronicity theory, the postulate that some thoughts or events seem to get attracted by the likeness of their meaning representing a unity that is neither causal (meaning that one thing is the cause of the other) nor random. One of the postulates in Jung's synchronicity theory revolves around the notion that there are three main underlying ways to relate the occurrence of psychic (thoughts) and physical (events) phenomena: cause, chance, and meaning.

Where the general population has seen nothing but a random coincidence between non-caused or correlated circumstances, Jung saw, not once but multiple times, what he referred to as meaningful coincidences, apparently randomly connected situations linked by meaning or similarity of purpose. In all these cases, the probability of a chance occurrence was unreasonably low and the coincidence could only be explained as being part of something mystical, mysterious, or simply beyond the reaches of conventional logic.

It is not uncommon for self-determined individuals, those who carry a mind of their own, to think that whatever happens to them is a product of their own creation, a consequence of the decisions and actions they have pursued. Such a mental construct has reasonable validity as they were, in one way or another, the initiators of such a behavior and they could have decided not to invest themselves on such a course of action.

What they are not accounting for is the fact that there seems to exist a more encompassing law of attraction that tends to link individuals with their ultimate life call in such a way that they would be led to believe they decided to do it, instead of being gently biased towards it as when a magnet attracts iron objects or twists a compass hand to point north. I am absolutely convinced, although I have no scientific proof of any kind, that for individuals determined to follow their life calls, there is no possible outcome other than to sooner or later do what they came here to do, as if the possibility of not doing it were simply inexistent. A sort of self-fulfilling prophecy operating at a subconscious level of abstraction.

Think this way, we believe that as humans we have free will and that we can do as we want, true but with one minor exception. What we *may want*, in other words, the extent of our free will, is *not unlimited*, it is rather only part of a somewhat restricted set of options, not a true *free* pick where you can decide to go in any possible direction or to move without boundaries of any sort. In essence, the so called *free will* is not completely free but *reasonably free*. You could *theoretically* decide to go in any imaginable way, and at the end, if your underlying motive is to follow the very reason why you are here, you will submit your choice to what you deem to be right, and hence limit the number of options available to you (limit by desire not by external imposition).

It is when the self follows their inner guidance (either consciously or unconsciously) that synchronistic phenomena start to shape up and catalyze the alchemic reaction of like-minded meaningful coincidences.

Not too long ago I was engaged in a rather philosophical conversation with a friend that holds a rather different cultural background and to whom I was trying to explain the notion that, as humans, we all have a mission to fulfill and that we are all meant to be somebody and do something in life. I also explained that, based on my beliefs, it was that somebody and that something what we will ultimately become and do, whether we want it or not … and that this is what we call fate or destiny. My rationale was founded on the premise that, at the end, everything and everybody are part of the Universe master plan, an overarching governance model simply meant to be.

When I was articulating this construct to my friend, I felt puzzled by a comment he made as a result of his evident and respectful disagreement with the conceptualizations I was presenting to him. His argument was centered around the notion that, if my theory was to be believed, then all those individuals whose lives were wrong-headed and hurting instead of helping humanity (criminals, murderers, etc) would also be part of the Universe master plan, what he could not accept as a truthful statement. His reflections suggested that such a plan would be somewhat flawed and defeat its underlying purpose.

He definitely got my attention and during the time I was listening to his argument, I sensed that a piece of my analysis was missing, I was not seeing the whole but only parts of it. How come the Universe, representing a Higher Power, God, or otherwise would make such a foolish mistake? There was something I was not considering, something that would make the whole premise of the Universe guidance to make perfect sense, even with our limited understanding of it. My friend was right in his observations and I knew that if my beliefs were to be valid, they would have to sustain the test of his disagreement. Finding an alternative definition of how the overall Universe ecosystem operated started to bug my curiosity and fuel my inquisition into a quest to decipher such a philosophical riddle.

Humans have choice, this is the ultimate freedom Viktor Frankl postulated in his logo therapy theory and it is by the virtue of such self-determination that every person can decide to be who they were meant to be or be somebody else. As to whether this ability to choose is a right, a duty, or both, it requires a more in depth discussion, but regardless of what it is, we cannot deny the fact that humans can indeed exercise choice, especially at the crucial times of following or not following their life paths. Although my confusion was escalating, I sensed I was getting closer and closer to the feeling of truthfulness that comes when light overcomes shadow. I was on the right path, even when I could see nothing but feel everything.

If humans had the ability to choose, what was it that differentiates those whose lives seem to have been predetermined to follow a behavioral pattern aligned with their purposes from those that would exercise free will regardless of what the Universe expects from them? Why would the Universe pick some souls and grant them with a life of fulfillment while leaving others left to their own devices to eventually choose poorly and never go where they were expected to go? It was not too long after reflecting on this dilemma that an epiphany about self determination invaded me.

The gift of choice, if properly understood, is both a right and a duty, and ultimately something that must be exercised with due responsibility. Only after choice has been wisely utilized, the right doors will open for us to go through them, still not knowing what lies ahead but enlightened with a sense of correctness strong enough to illuminate a seemingly inexplicably uncertainty.

That was the missing link, the puzzle piece that I needed to bridge the gap between my friend's rationale and mine. Unlike any other animals which operate partially or entirely on instinctual drives, humans were provided with choice because they possess the ability to use it wisely and for the reason it was intended (although the possession of an ability does not mean the proper utilization of it).

> *Ignoring, neglecting or simply refusing to exercise choice wisely with respect to our life meaningfulness is a crime of incredible proportions and a waste of a lifetime that could have served humanity advance to further levels of evolution.*

If we arbitrarily remove or never see the *duty* component of self determination, only exercising the *right* side of it, choice becomes nothing but a mechanism to please ourselves in any way our stretch of imagination would allow. If that were the case and our ability to choose would be nothing but a *right* without any regard to its *duty* part, free of any moral responsibility or obligation, one could literally make decisions as one would wish and then face (or let the world face) the consequences of the perceived rightful (and not dutiful) choice.

> *It is the sense of duty, purpose, and commitment to do what one feels right what empowers the gift of choice with its ultimate meaning, the ability to transform the world according to the individual and collective missions we have been entrusted with. Only when choice is framed in a context of both rightfulness and dutifulness it can elevate itself enough to enlighten its significance and steer us through the paths we are meant to follow in the fulfillment our own prophecies.*
> *Choice is not an entitlement but a privilege and as such, it carries responsibility.*

I have absolutely no doubt that every person on Earth has a mission so unique and so special as he or she is. I also carry the belief that such a life call can become visible or remain hidden, which is specific to each of us and our stage of maturity at any given point in our quest. If we would carry an unstoppable sense of inner rightness about what we are here to do *and* if we would allow such a driving force the authority to dominate our decisions, our future would be significantly more predictable that only the passage of time would separate us from becoming who we were meant to be.

This is the essence and the context in which synchronistic phenomena is more bound to occur, when there is a connection between what we are pursuing and the ultimate purpose of our life, when the sublime meaning of our daily actions converge with an indisputable vision belonging to a future yet to come.

Time and space relativity are key attributes to the dynamics of synchronistic events which are connected by their similarity of purpose, mystical attraction, and overlapping intent. Our unconscious is the gateway and the communication media by which our limited conscious mind can access ancient wisdom and connect with the Universe, that same Universe that devised the plans we are supposed to follow and complete.

For those that choose wisely, respecting and honoring both the right and the duty side of their self determinations, life is regulated by its inner sense of meaningfulness and in one way or another we are pre-determined to conform what we are here for. My friend was correct, there are a number of individuals who, consciously or not, have decided to ignore the *duty* side of choice and entirely focus on the *right* component of it, feeling entitled to make decisions as they wish and with no further interest or regard other than pleasing their selfish needs and desires while ignoring, neglecting, or refusing to fulfill the missions they have been assigned with (which is inherently linked to the *duty* side of choice).

Plainly stated, this is a simple way to live an irresponsible and purposeless life, one that stays away from the commitments that mature and highly evolved beings make when they (consciously or not) choose to walk the paths their lives are expected to follow and in so doing individually contribute to the collective embellishment of human kind.

In the dialog with my friend, I was only addressing a segment of the population, in a sense blindsiding myself from seeing those individuals that care little or nothing about what they are here for. In reality, it is actually a bit more complex and not simply a black and white type of distinction, there are not only those that follow their purposes and those that don't, human traits and behaviors fall into continuums and not into extreme positions with no activity in between. I am confident enough that if we were to plot a diagram of how self determination is used by a statistically valid and well diversified number of people, we would find nothing but a bell type distribution of their choice styles and underlying motives. While some people would be more selfish and care little, if anything, about their fellow humans (these are the criminals, the murderers, etc), others would be extremely selfless and compassionate, almost always thinking about how they can do more for others and for the world. It is in between these two ends of the continuum that the remaining majority of the population falls, displaying signs and traces of both camps depending on the circumstances (self or selfless centered choices).

What fascinates me about the opportunities to work for the betterment of the world is that, if we work on the right priorities and put enough effort into it, we can always move the media of the *choice* bell curve to the right making it asymmetrically oriented to the altruistic end (again the engineer in me speaking). Such opportunity is right there, waiting for us to choose more wisely about what we do. I acknowledge that this is a higher level of choice, something I would call *meta-choice*, namely working to help human kind be more conscious and more responsible about choosing so the number of people aligning their life with their mission would be higher in number, reducing the percentage of those solely inclined or more geared towards doing as they please, with no regard of any kind to what they came here to do.

*There is a countless number of people that have the latent intent to
do more good with their lives and do not know where to start. It is
to them that I would like to lovingly advise that the place to start
is nowhere but right inside them, in the bottom of their hearts!*

*Listen to what your heart has to say, it may whisper at times
and you will have to make a real effort to listen to it. Take
that time and make that effort, what you will hear will
change your life in ways you have never imagined.*

*Every worthy transformation of the self starts by listening to our
inner voice, for it is emanating from the core of our deepest self, the
numinous place where everything starts and everything ends ...*

CHOICE THEORY REVISITED

Nature is wise and there is a place for every being on Earth, living or not. Everything *is* something and at the same time *evolving to become* something else, a more developed form of that initial being. A dog is a dog and is meant to become a more evolved form of what its species would allow, always operating by instinct and through an animal-like brain power, and so is an apple tree, or a piece of marble. The life of an animal is not expected to be that different across their life cycle only because they are created to conform a peculiar type of life whose behavior and contributions are limited to their mere existence and the role they play in the Nature's ecosystem.

Humans are different creatures, more complex, more developed and provided with a superior brain, able to choose their responses from a wider set of options, including the neglect of their nature and their reason for existence. While humans are also meant to be similar and share common traits, they are not expected to be exactly the same and adopt the same type of behaviors at every given point in time, not from a superior functional level. It is true that there are some commonalities that all humans must adhere to and live by, which represent the most basic and primitive set of needs (described in full detail by Abraham Maslow). These needs are related to survival and the preservation of our species. Only after you escalate over the basic and into the superior human needs you can start to perceive the uniqueness and the differentiation among individuals. Self-Actualization, as Maslow would describe it, is the cultivation of our unique talents and the pursuit of our ultimate purpose in life. Viktor Frankl referred to the same concept in his logo therapy foundations and the constant search for meaning. Intrinsic Motivation, Flow, and Peak Performance are also states of being that are, more often than not, associated with the superior (as opposed to the basic) human functions and the quest of the person's life meaning.

Unlike most animals, humans have a wider scope of possible behaviors and it is the exercise of the gift of self determination what Viktor Frankl called *the ultimate human freedom*, our ability to choose our response in any set of circumstances. It is in that response where our ability to adopt the life we were asked to live lies, and in so doing become the *who* we were meant to be. Can we choose otherwise? Of course we can but this is not something we are supposed to play with. Just because we have the freedom to pick our response does not mean we must choose poorly, we were given the gift of choice because we inherently carry the ability to choose wisely! A dog does not get to choose which type of dog it will be, most of their life is spent in the basic needs realm, neither an oak nor a rock get to choose either but humans do!

Have you ever wondered why? Why were humans given the gift of choice?

What we must do requires bold and principle centered self determination, we must select our paths and what we do at the time we walk them in order to fulfill the reasons why we are here, only by exercising choice wisely we will be able to advance in our journeys and conquer the summits related to the missions we were entrusted with. It cannot get any simpler than this ... *to fulfill the purposes of our lives we must exercise choice wisely.*

Self determined action (aka choice) is like a hammer or any other tool as it was created to be used for the specific function it was meant to serve. It is a basic principle to use things for what they are, and not for what they are not. Choice was given to us to be used wisely and it is in this simple yet extremely powerful statement that the key to a successful and honorable life lies. Nobody can avoid choosing, even if you choose not to choose you are choosing anyway. Inaction is a form of decision making, an active or passive decision of *not to act*.

Choices like what to wear or what to eat may be seen as irrelevant, and for the most part they are, especially when other more meaningful aspects of our lives are considered. There are however some choices that play a determinant role in the unfolding of our lives and must be carefully examined before making them. These choices are structured inside the answer of two of the most fundamental questions we have as humans:

- What are we here for?
- Who are we meant to be?

It is in the exercise of choice to fulfill the response to those two questions with determined and responsible action that we will show the world how serious we are about doing what we came here to do. Life is not an entitlement but a privilege, a heavenly crafted command to assist our Creator in the betterment of the human experience. A Life lived with honor is a solemn business and a commitment passively accepted by us when we were born. It is through the years to come when we need to renew that commitment and replace the passive acceptance of life duties by the active self-determination to do what we came here to do. Choosing wisely is a mandatory requirement to rightfully conduct the business of our own lives and something that has to be exercised with rigor and discipline as soon as we possibly can.

At the end and in the overarching scheme of things we do not find but are rather found by our life call. Only after that first meeting takes place, whether it is a conscious or an unconscious encounter, we can decide to follow or not follow the lead of what our life was expected to be. That choice is the trigger of what will follow next, namely a series of self-determined decisions daisy chained to provide continuity to our first and most important commitment, to become who we are meant to be. That first choice is crucial, choose wisely and stick to it!

For those that have chosen a life full of meaning, following their inner paths became so natural, so second nature that they may not be able to imagine how life would be without it. Nature is wise and does not make mistakes, humans do, but we can always learn and make it better the next time. Never give up, keep always trying! Whatever your talent, gift, or uniqueness is, was not given to you by accident, there is a reason for it and you must honor it.

We do what we are, either we are born with a talent or learn it along the way. Whatever it is you do it, and if we don't we betray ourselves ... and it is sad – Dr. Cross (from the movie Along Came a Spider)

ANYTHING GREAT HAS TO START
IN YOUR MIND FIRST

If we go as far back in history as our mind can reach to find the most meaningful creations of mankind, we will realize that most of them started as an idea first, a thought, a what-if, a dream, in one or a group of audacious individuals before it crystallized into a final product, an event of some sort that later became a milestone for the future generations, a before and an after of what was brought to life, something born out of nothingness and into fullness.

It is of paramount importance that you become acquainted with the idea that however marvelous or magnificent that creation was, it was nothing but an idea at its origins, perhaps a novel and extraneous theoretical postulate nobody else believed in, another close-to-impossible dream that no *reasonable* man or woman would pursue. Whatever was about to happen had not happened yet, mystically staging the vision holders as the only ones that could see beyond the obvious, synchronistically connecting the dots of a future yet to come, as if secretly building an unconceived world configuration that struggled with a present refusing to be altered and defied.

Nothing great in the history of mankind happened by accident, even if it was perceived as a random outcome of unintentional causes (and there are numerous cases of these phenomena), chance occurrences are not part of the Creator's plan, each and every major advancement has been carefully crafted almost to perfection before it came to fruition and it all started as an idea, perhaps a very low probability notion mysteriously implanted into the heart, mind, and soul of a courageous human willing to defy the odds of failure in the quest of the impossible, fueled by nothing but a burning desire to do what one came here to do.

A myriad of great things have happened since the dawn of time and another myriad will come before dusk. Whatever the number of monumental achievements still about to occur is, they will start in somebody's mind as an idea first. If and only if, somebody gives that idea a chance to grow stronger, eventually proving its theoretical validity and legitimacy, then that future outcome has a chance to emerge. It is the unconditional love and the strong sense of duty to do what we came here to do what will help us volunteer to be part of *out of the ordinary* idea beholder communities, a group of gutsy humans determined to face the unknown and fight the dragons of complacency as part of the arduous and fulfilling task of becoming who we were meant to be and do what were asked to do.

It is rather the origin and not so much the pursuit or the realization of such paramount accomplishments what intrigues me and provokes a great deal of self-thinking, fueling a curiosity beyond the ordinary about the process by which life altering visions of a future yet to come are born. It all starts somewhere as if a mystical and synchronistic connection of an unrealized future would be knocking on the door of a visionary soul able to act as the medium for such a meaningful coincidence to take place (or as a dear friend of mine would say … *it is as if we would be antennas receiving a broadcasted signal from an astray place and time*). Whoever the Universe picks to be the beholder of such a magnificent vision has been entrusted with the monumental task of being the carrier of a hard to convey message, a circumstance ahead of its time, a theorem that questions everlasting proven formulas successfully used times and again. Mysteriously enough, those accepting such a call, have been previously embodied with an incredible amount of belief, a steel determination, an unshakable conviction, and the ability to keep going in the face of external disapproval and rejection. The Universe will never send a soldier to fight a battle he or she has absolutely no chance to win, such a pursuit would be a mistake of incalculable proportions and a sacrifice worth avoiding. Those that were picked have a chance to make it, even if one in a million, but a chance still! To fully comprehend this assertion, it is necessary to realize that some causes will range across multiple generations, refusing to believe that a lifelong unfinished business is a failure to the overarching enterprise we were entrusted with. The Universe will ask us to do what needs to get done as if we were nothing but micro pieces of a giant puzzle planned to be built one lifetime at a time.

It is such an unbendable set of beliefs what will sustain the test of time and the questioning of the masses empowering the beholder to trust his or her visions with astonishing clarity, when they are nothing but embryonic forms of a grandiosity yet to be born, way before it is even a project, an undertaking or a materialized pursuit. In its initial phases, great transformations are nothing but a blueprint of a different world configuration, something that may, in a seemingly arrogant way, flout the current state of affairs as if a hidden yet extremely powerful driving force would be propelling the visionary mind to look at the status quo and confidently say ...

> *I don't believe this is the only way things can be,*
> *and quite certainly not the best one either!*

For greatness to emerge, some people have to have the courage and the humbleness to stand up for what they believe, out of unseen levels of conviction and determination, in a sense making the bold and irrefutable statement to live a purpose-led life, silently telling the Universe ...

> *I believe on this vision that I hold true, which has been given to*
> *me for a reason and representing a quest that conforms a purpose*
> *handed to me from above. I hereby make a lifelong and honorable*
> *promise to live and die for that cause and forever chase it with*
> *all the passion and the hope that my brave heart can give me!*

Some people may call the statement above a sort of self-sacrifice, I would call it a beautiful devotion, an honor in its truest form, and a divine opportunity to do what our Creator has asked us to do with a perfect mix of *love* and *duty* aimed at becoming the *who* we were meant to be. At the end, and after everything has been said and done, our life calls are something so magnificent in the context of our existences that we would be puzzled to find an alternative path appealing enough to undeniably engage ourselves with.

While fewer in number, there are countless of brave hearts that every single day and in an anonymous manner display the courage to stand in front of a human race that seems to accept the current state of affairs, and seriously think …

This is not right, there has to be another way in which the world can operate, a better way, one more aligned to Universal principles, something that can take the world to a brighter and more appealing state of being, a higher stage in the evolution of mankind. Not only that, I should also be able to help make a difference, be part of something greater than just myself, to work in the quest of such a vision in whatever field or domain the Universe and my Creator need me.

When you seize humanity as a whole, there may be a rather small army of daring souls that has been silently and relentlessly working for the creation of a better tomorrow, embodying the courage to feed the fabrications of a different future to the point of turning them into dreams, fantasies and illusions forcefully converted into so strong of a belief that it may have a chance, even if only one in a million!

All we have to think is that even one-in-a-million type of circumstances are likely to happen once if they are tried a million times! When the call for action is coming right from the bottom of our hearts, in a compelling and burning enough fashion to make every cell in our bodies to vibrate at unison, no probability of occurrence, for as low as it may be, will stop us, we are in motion and with the Universe's army behind us. No strong-willed spirit fighting for a right cause is going to be left alone!

At the end, when all bets are off, it is not about making or not making it, it is rather about giving one's very best to chase it and in so doing show the world that there is another way, a way worth living and dying for, even if we can only show this alternative path in the form of an unrealized dream, so vivid, so enlightening and so full of passion and determination that others could not ignore its existence.

I was always attracted by the difficult, the almost impossible, those things others would leave aside or behind either because of complexity, low probability of occurrence or simply lack of vision. What attracted me was not the complexity or difficulty per se but what generally lied behind it, something absolutely worth creating, a life altering type crusade in the utmost positive sense of the term, a breakthrough in the conventionalism of our daily lives.

> *While I recognized the charm of such an altruistic proposition, I could not ignore that for as glowing those inner creations may be, to become a true beholder one would have to embody the strength to face an almost impossible call to action, to deviate ourselves from the way of the masses and take a detour from mainland and into the woods, armed and equipped only with the hope that whatever we believe in, can become true.*

It was never easy for me to think in terms of the rationale used by the self-called *realists* that would weight their pursuits based on how probable their perception of the outcomes is.

> *Why in the world would I keep myself from doing something that, even when difficult, was absolutely worth doing? The mere thought that just because the odds of such an enterprise becoming a reality do not seem to be in my favor, was so farfetched as a thought pattern that I could not even entertain the time to distract my conscious brain from what it had to be done. Who said that life was meant to be easy and free of difficult crusades worth living and dying for?*

Do you think we are alone? Do you really think that when an idea of such magnificent proportion is implanted in your mind and in your heart is because a random wind blew that seed from nowhere to *accidentally* land in your inner backyard? Moreover, do you think that worthwhile causes and pursuits are regulated by the easiness of realistic enterprises?

Noble and altruistic life missions defy the laws of probabilities and require brave hearts daring enough to face the dragons of complacency with the intent of slaying them, even if with nothing else but wooden swords!

If you believe that accidents of that magnitude happen, please open your mind and get past what your eyes can't see! There is a world a thousand, perhaps a million times bigger than the one you know just an inch above everything you can see, touch, and believe at the present moment. There are no accidents big enough to tempt a fearless spirit to chase dreams that can change the world, even if what you are about to do will help one soul at a time. Please *believe* ... first in you, then in what you see, not with your eyes but with your heart.

Believing should come before knowing, and even if you will never know ... You need no proof to believe in something, beliefs are born out of faith, knowledge out of proof. Be brave enough to believe and you may eventually be able to create what the world will one day know.

Somebody has to start at the belief level and make that belief so powerful if not more powerful than any knowledge, thinking about it day and night, not doubting, not hesitating, not clouding the blue sky of your vision with what is realistically possible, not even for a moment. Whatever it is, you must believe it can be done, accepting it will only happen if it was meant to happen, despite any high or low probabilities, but strongly tied to our effort, passion, persistence and resiliency. In the movie Soul Surfer, Bethany Hamilton's father was trying to explain Bethany how un-easy going back to surfing with only one arm was going to be, to which she responded ... "Dad, I don't need easy, I just need possible."

Why go for the easy, the highly probable, the undemanding, when there are still so many possible, worthy and life changing causes out there waiting for someone brave enough to say: *I'll take that one ...* like picking children wishes written on paper ornaments hanging from the branches of an orphan's home Christmas tree!

I never understood the value of living a life of easiness and lack of meaning. At the end, what is life if not an opportunity to give our very best for a cause worth living and dying for? Why would you let such an opportunity pass by your side without extending your arm and grabbing it so strongly that your arm would have to be detached from the rest of your body before you let it go! Do something significant with your life! This is the way it was supposed to be, you came here for a reason, a noble, magnificent reason!

Don't just live, control cruising the paths of fate and playing the *least-amount-of-effort* game and in so doing turn what could have been a life of honor into a life of pleasure and need gratification. *If there is a need to be gratified, make it the need to live an honorable life!*

Look around, look inside, it does not have to be something heroic, not all of us came here to become a legend but all of us have worthy dreams to chase, dreams that will help change the world and turn it into a better place to live, even if one day or one soul at a time. I will say it again and again, do for others more than what you do for yourself, think about the collective good, the embellishment of our future generations, the prosperity of those in need, of those that have the right to have a better life and for whatever reason, they can't. Forget about those that can and don't want to, they have what they need and maybe more, they have just decided to ignore it.

All of us were given dreams for a reason, not by accident, not by a random act of life or fate. Your dreams call for the very best in you and will challenge every cell of your body, not once but multiple times. Stand up and live up to the challenge, defy the odds of probability and pursue your most beautiful visions of a future yet to come.

The greatest creations of mankind started in a dream as beautiful and as far-fetched as the one you hold near and dear to your heart, just give it a chance, give it all you have!

WHEN THE UNIVERSE ASKS YOU TO DO SOMETHING

The best leaders of all times are those with a burning desire to help and serve those they lead.

... just help and serve? Yes, help and serve those they lead and the ultimate purpose of their lives.

In one of the many paths that Eli had to walk to fulfill the task he was entrusted, he said ... "do for others more than you do for yourself" (from "The Book of Eli" movie). Those who follow the inner voice of their hearts have no desire other than to fulfill the missions they have been assigned, entrusted and honored with. They are *humble* in nature and *bold* in character, they need to, they have to, and they ought to as they will be asked to slay dragons and give all they have.

At the very least, we are all leaders of our own lives which is a task that requires moderate to large doses of humility and boldness, vehemently knowing when the dosage is just enough, not any larger or any smaller than what the impending circumstances would require (this is a self-administered medication, prescribed from above).

When the Universe asks us to do something, we just do it, no questions asked ... and we do it the *very best* we can until the last day of our life! You do not argue with your Creator, especially if you believe in the existence of a benevolent God that loves us unconditionally. If you don't like what you are being asked to do, or you don't get to the bottom of why you are asked to do it, it's because He knows some things you do not ... it is as simple as that. Children do what they *like*, adults, especially responsible adults, do what is *right*, what they are supposed to do. We are here on Earth for a reason, and it is an honor to have a mission to fulfill ... *honor it!* When you look at your life as a whole, not with your eyes but with your heart, you don't do what it feels like doing, you do what your *heart* tells you to do, easy and hard alike as there will be plenty of both! ... and in that mix lies the beauty and the spice of life!

The things that come easy are those you already mastered, simple or complex you already found a way to get a handle of them and quite often they may feel as second nature. Generally speaking, the *knowing* comes from the *doing* and when you have done something over and over again, you will eventually master it. Doing what you already know, the things you have mastered, poses no challenge on the know-how side of things although it may still be motivationally challenging if you don't like or you don't know why you have to do it. Whatever the case, you are not at a steep point in the learning curve and not advancing in your development in an accelerated manner, however you maybe discovering some nuances, perfecting your style, or becoming more proficient in the art and the science of doing it. Your advancement has flattened out and if there is any progress it will be in the long run. This is not a bad place to be, especially since after so many years of struggle and growing there has to come a point in your life when you start mastering what you have so painstakingly learned throughout the course of your lifelong school-work.

I like mastery but have to confess that it is struggle my favorite learning stage and you may know why. When you struggle with something and try to figure out how to do it *right*, you feel puzzled, challenged, defied, and you have to create something that was not there before, at least not in a form you could easily see it. We keep reinventing ourselves when what we are doing seems not to work, at least not in our conventional definition of the word work. The bigger the struggle, the bigger the learning! Be brave!

By saying I like to struggle, I am not suggesting I would put myself in situations that will call for trouble just to learn out of it, and like my father used to tell me, *you don't want to look for trouble, trouble will find you*. No matter what you do, there will be times of struggle in your life, even if you do the *right* things every day, the *very best* you can. Actually, if you do *right*, there may be more and not less struggle, but of the *right* type. Why? Because you will not do a single thing to *avoid* struggling, you will do what needs to get done, to struggle or not to, is not a question that crosses your mind at the time of deciding what to do, although there may influence the way or the pace at which you do it so you face an amount of struggle that is manageable.

I am a big believer that there are two main camps of people in this world, those that *avoid* the things they are afraid of or don't like and those that *go after* what they believe in, refusing, neglecting, or ignoring the possibility of failure … and we all have the choice to join one camp or the other, indistinctively and in all shades of gray. I could have avoided *lots* of problems and confrontations should have I done things I decided not to, or the opposite, shouldn't have I done things I decided to do. I have never done what others expected me to do, say, not-do, or not-say, only because they expected (or even demanded) me to behave in such a way. I plead guilty of that charge and dutifully accept the sentence.

> *In the central aspects of life, I have never done what others expected or even asked me to do only because I was asked but rather because after thinking about it, I decided it was something I truly believed in and wanted to do. The fact that something was expected of me (and regardless of any rewards or consequences) was never as a strong of a motivator to mobilize my inner drive in such a direction. When it comes to the most important aspects of my life, I do not compromise my judgment, I only do things in what I regard to be the right way.*

> *To struggle or not to struggle should always be a consequence of doing what you believe to be right and not the result of acting like the world expects you to act. I would rather fail a thousand times because of my own reasons rather than succeed only once because of somebody else's.*

This is not to mean I do not listen to others, especially those I love, respect or are recognized leaders in their fields, to learn from them and eventually adopt their actions or recommendations as something of value to adopt or imitate. Actually, I listen to those significant others all the time, but not after I have a chance to review their opinions and have them go through my *rightness* test I decide to embrace and pursue them. Learning from others is an ability of the advanced learner, he who can not only experiment things himself and learn from his own experience but also from the experience of those others that have proven to be successful in their fields, in ways we can honor and respect.

For those of you that like to play any sports, and regardless of your talent level, the way to mastery is through learning the basics and putting them into practice, tons of practice. This is not only applicable to sports but also to many other life disciplines, however it is more visible in competitive activities. You practice routinely, you follow your coach's advice and you do your homework, day after day and with no protest or hesitation. You will get tired, exhausted and then you will rest. You do this long enough and you start to get better, you can feel it, your skill level increases and so your self-confidence.

One day you make a bad turn and you pull a string, you inadvertently and involuntarily hurt yourself and what comes next is six to eight weeks of physical therapy and a gradual come back. You have retraced, pulled back in your advancement, a stall in your development path ... right? Not true! As long as you can learn something out of that episode in your sport life, something you did not know, it was a *win* and not a *loss*.

Bad things happen and even when we can try to avoid them, we will never be able to eliminate them completely (although we can learn not to stumble with the same stone twice) and this is a *good* thing. On your way to mastery, struggle will teach you things you did not know. I love the comment of a seasoned professional that when discussing his joining a new venue, he was asked: *what do you bring to the table? ...* and his response was: *20 years of mistakes.* I love it! It is through mistakes that we *can* learn the most, especially if we are focused on learning something valuable from them. With the right mindset, mistakes will not stop us but push us forward with more strength and determination than before! Mistakes are a blessing in disguise.

Failure to do what one wanted to do must be capitalized and reflected upon, not just ignored, neglected and blamed to someone or something else outside of our control. Be mindful that this view and treatment of mistakes is counter intuitive as our first reaction is to think of mistakes as something undesirable and to get rid of, a waste of time, something to be eliminated and forgotten.

*If we do that, if we think of mistakes negatively and wish them
to never happen to us, we position ourselves sub-optimally,
unconsciously stop trying, and start to get in a state of avoidance
rather than in a state of action. Remember that mistakes
are a key part of the evolution process and the real failure is
not to make mistakes but to learn nothing from them.*

After a mistake takes place, we can always do something different, better, wiser, not only to avoid the error but to also benefit from similar circumstances in the future, in the utmost positive manner and in alignment with our life purpose.

Back to the sport injury example, you now know how to be more careful and avoid risky movements that can hurt yourself. You have evolved as a sport professional, reached the next level, aggressively and consistently training but now with safety in mind. This new knowledge will not slow you down; to the contrary, it will help you move faster, with fewer interruptions, in a more holistic and consistent manner. Professionals know how to train without getting hurt, amateurs do not. Once you are back on the field, you will proceed with the wisdom you did not carry before, aware of what can happen, more conscious of the possibilities and their inherent probabilities. You start slow and gradually increase your pace, acting with more self-awareness, controlling the risk of further injuries and being more open to what can happen as you have expanded the repertoire of possible circumstances. Time passes by, injuries decrease, you start to get to the point of how to practice hard but injury-free, you are approaching a pro-level domain, you are advancing, thanks to the mistakes and the learning that followed them.

As a professional, you will have both winning and losing games. While winning games will pump you up, losing games will frustrate you, make you feel the struggle. Refuse treating defeat as something negative, it is not, you need the losses as much as you need the wins. Find holistic ways to *celebrate* instead (just be careful to show your excitement so explicitly to your teammates and coach as they may not understand ☺) striving to decode the writing on the wall, the one or two things you can learn from that experience that will make you a better player the next time around. Defeats give us the opportunity to learn something we did not know. Notice I wrote *"opportunity to learn"* and not *"lesson."* It will be up to you to transform that opportunity into a learned lesson, only *you* can get yourself together after the defeat and say: *I am going to learn something out of this and I will become a better player!*

If you do nothing, or even worse, if you start blaming others, the other team, the surrounding circumstances, etc, for what happened, you will block your learning gates and justify the failure as something that was completely outside of your control.

> *You can only learn when you are convinced you are in control of your actions and to a certain degree to what happens to you as you grow, when you feel you are in charge of steering your life to reach that beautiful future you always dreamed about.*

It is true that the other team could have been better, but that does not mean you cannot improve, learn from them, or learn from your mistakes. Avoid getting into a downward spiral of negative thoughts as nothing good will come out of it. My investment coach always said *negative thoughts release neuro-inhibitors, rather than neuro-enhancers, which are released by positive thoughts, we certainly learn more and better when we are in a positive state of mind.* Think positively, reaffirm yourself and your team, assume there will be winning and losing games and think whether or not you did your best, your very best ... at the end, that is ultimately what really matters. If you do your best each and every time, and keep learning from your mistakes, sooner or later you will get it, your brain and your body will figure it out! This is the way you transform an *opportunity to learn* into a *lesson learned*.

Be open to redefine what *best* means to you, in your own language, in your own way. Gradually and as you learn, what used to be *best*, will no longer be, as a new definition of *best* will come into place. This is the natural progression toward becoming who you were meant to be. The definition of *best* for you today is not going to remain stagnant, unchanged, static, as time goes by and you get to experience life in a more profound and holistic manner. As you change and evolve, your definitions of best will also change and follow you in your journey. Whatever your direction in life is, you cannot think of somebody that has mastered what you are after without going through the struggle-learning process that mastery brings along, not once but several times.

Si te postran diez veces te levantas
Otras diez, otras cien, otras quinientas ...
No han de ser tus caídas tan violentas
Ni tampoco, por ley, han de ser tantas.

Almafuerte (Poesías, 1942)

Be prepared to fall ... and to get back up! Not once but a thousand times! You do not focus your thinking on how many times you have fallen, whether you will fall again, or even how much it hurts when you do, you just get your attention around how to get yourself back on your feet once more, and keep trying. Every fall will make you stronger, wiser and closer to the *who* you want to be, the *who* you are meant to be. Get always back up!

It is the reflection that follows the fall, what will help you grow. Your vision of what is *best* will gradually change and with that, your actions will follow a new set of patterns, alternative habits learned as a result of the fall. Be also open to accept that maybe you did not give your very best, it is fine, it is not a crime ... if that was the case, regroup, recommit and try harder the next time around.

When it comes to the doing, or the lack thereof, the only crime you
can commit is to consistently fail to do your best, time after time,
fully conscious of what you are doing and what you are not.

We are all humans and no matter how committed to do and give our very best we may be, we will occasionally fail to do what we must do. If you find yourself falling in that category, you are like all of us, human beings *striving* to do the best we can! ... just learn from your mistakes and try harder the next time around. It is all part of the learning process. A missed opportunity to do our best because we failed to do something we now know is important is an extremely powerful motivator to catch the next one coming and not let it pass us by again! It is part of our nature.

PARTNERING WITH THE UNIVERSE

Lili and I always expected our children to learn the values of giving, of sharing, and of helping. We told them enough times that they were tired of listening the same saying ... *you were given two hands, one is to give, the other to receive, and you have to use both hands for the reason they were given to you.* This is of special importance with those still transitioning a narcissistic stage and as a parent you may feel compelled to address it after seeing your children, generally at an early age, to be focused almost entirely on not only receiving but also on asking (or should I say demanding?). Children, particularly in their teen years, have a tendency to take what they think they need, sometimes with both hands, forgetting they have the *give-hand* purposed to give.

It is our role as parents and care givers to help our children grow wiser, socially responsible, more sensitive to others, more compassionate, and to foster the development of their self-awareness, a blissful gift that a caring heart has to possess to sense the way in which we are spreading the love we have received and nurtured inside.

It is of paramount significance that children learn, as soon as possible in their maturity process, that we are here not only to enjoy our own life but also help others enjoy theirs, in a sense leaving a legacy to those around and after us. It is through this process of education and leadership by example that we teach our future generations values such as kindness, consideration, compassion, forgiveness, inclusion, and in so doing gradually displace their age related self-centeredness to allow the *others* part of the world to start coming into the radar screen. I hereby and by means of firsthand experience, acknowledge that such a task is anything but an easy undertaking, something that even when far from light weighted is well worth the effort and the acceptance of being labeled as *not being cool* (beware of being called a *cool parent*, it is not a good sign of responsible parenthood ☺).

The future of our children and the future of the world lie on our ability to craft universally accepted values and morals into the daily and piece mail labor of building our children's character. It is also true that no one can give what one has not previously received and we, as parents, caregivers, and educators, have to always give first. It is only after they have received love, care, and affection (also limits and boundaries) that they can little by little start to accept that the cycle of life includes the receiving and the giving parts, not just the receiving or the demanding. We parent them to help them grow, become fully functional adults, happy, adjusted to the societal norms, responsible, and caring. Simply stated, we help them build the foundations of the *who* they were meant to be, nothing more and nothing less.

We all need a partner, a mentor, a coach, somebody to look at with admiration and respect, somebody that would inspire us and help the best inside of us to come out. What we came here to do is so glaring that it may blind us to the point of not seeing what lies ahead, incapable to conceive anything and everything that we can possibly be and become. It is there where our mentor, our life sponsor comes into play, to reassure us of everything we can be and in so doing develop the gift of self-awareness and self-confidence. Do not try to do this alone, whatever it is we have to do, it is always better if we can find someone that has been there before, someone that that knows the road, the rules of engagement, how to navigate through the difficulty that will come, because it will certainly come ... perhaps when it is least expected.

Such a gracious engagement is something that would bring fulfillment to both the coach and the coached, for that what it is given shall be received ... Blessed are those that have something to give and are willing to give it unconditionally for their altruism will charm a tender heart in the need of the warm embracement that the selfless intentions of the eternal giver will graciously offer. An honorable life advances in circles, what goes around comes around, good karma reigns and regulates the way in which the Universe operates. Those that give will receive and those that receive must give so the circle of love gets circumvented times and again.

The practice of giving heals the soul and serendipitously morphs both the life of the giver and the receiver into a holier and more enchanting way of conceiving our existences.

*Anything given to you straight from somebody else's heart was
a heavenly sent gift, expected to be nurtured, treasured, and
embellished beyond its original form with the sole purpose of being
shared with somebody else, for there is no other reason of having
something than to make somebody else the new recipient of it.*

It is by the loving and caring act of giving that we extend the love of our Creator onto our fellow humans and build a numinous constellation of selfless beings eager to do something for those in need. Such a connection with somebody else through the kindness of unconditional giving, makes us partners in the celestial communion aimed at doing what we came here to do, something unique and special to each of us sitting on the overarching essence of the greatest purposes of all, to spread love and help build a better world.

There is a different kind of partnership, a sort of mystical connection with the Universe and its all-encompassing transcendence, the plan behind all other plans, the very one reason we are all here. Such a blending with the yet-to-be-known mysteries of the greatest sources of wisdom, love and compassion represent an unavoidable stop in the journey of our life, something that after fully experienced will remain in our memories as an encounter of magnificent proportions, both an end and a beginning, a reunion of what should have never been separated.

When we wish to be part of things greater than ourselves, our needs and personal interests expand and become more collective in nature to the point that we almost inadvertently start to wonder about the common good, the betterment of others and the embellishment and enlightenment of the present circumstances. Our circle of interest expands, we see beyond the mundane, we elevate our concerns to a higher level of complexity and in so doing we see what was until then invisible to the eyes. Our attention fades away from the self and starts to notice those in need, those we could potentially tender a hand and those whose lives could be touched and changed by acts of synchronistic kindness and graciousness. Our attention is redirected from our-self to those out there that either need us or can simply benefit from a loving hand.

I generally name *Universe* or *Nature* to a sort of Higher Power, a God-like figure that regulates the flow of life and the occurrence of significant coincidences aimed at guiding our lives in the direction and the confines of the paths we must follow.

While the existence of such a Higher Power only resides in the inner faith of the believer, far and away of any kind of scientific statement sustained by undeniable proof, I find it difficult to conceive the world operating in such a harmonic manner without the charming oversight of such a divine force enticing the best of us to emerge and become attracted to altruistic pursuits like a magnet pulls minuscule pieces of iron closer and closer into the realms of its force field and towards its core.

Such a Higher Power, the Creator of the Universe, operates at a different and much higher level of complexity, one that gravitates light years away from us, in a dimension that no stretch of imagination can even ponder, visualize, or conceive. All we can do is accept that whatever it is, it is well beyond what we can potentially rationalize and we must accept His superiority and love-fullness, subduing our will to what He has planned for us. This submission requires the ability to conceive a benevolent God, a sublime and omnipotent figure of authority, miraculously glowing and radiating love in its purest form, the Creator of all creations, the Father of all fathers, an enchanting source of positive energy that is only looking for the wellness of the world, the prosperity of human kind and every form of life. Such a noble, philanthropic and selfless superior force is geared toward helping us evolve, mature, grow, and in so doing steer our earthly experience to contribute in the utmost positive and honorable way.

The passage of time along with the cumulative collection of the ordinary experiences we happen to find ourselves in, teach us that life moves in cycles, that there are moments of happiness and moments of sadness, moments of glory and moments of struggle, times of excitement and times of anxiety, if there is a white there has to be a black for there is no yin without a yang. Accept that such a balance must exist, it is part of our human nature to also expect the net sum of our overall life experience to be positive, in other words, that the moments of joy should outnumber the moments of pain, our fulfillment outweigh our void, and that tears of joy would come more often than tears of sorrow and in so doing tilt the equilibrium of life towards the desirable. It is the hypothesis that such a positive balance exists what gives hope in the quest of our ideals and the realization of our most treasured dreams, profound and blissful visions of a future yet to come.

Fighting for what we believe in gives meaning to our lives, an inner and unavoidable reason to get up every morning and say: *I have something meaningful to do, worth my effort and my struggle, my joy and my fulfillment, something I cannot leave this world without giving my very best to it!* Some people are born with a need to set high standards for themselves (and often for those others they are responsible for), others develop such a need along the way, pursuing what will not come easy, that which will stretch every muscle of their selves and inevitably embody a need to try hard and resist the temptation of giving up. The stopping of the eventual agony of trying a hundred times without certainties of any kind will arrest you and you must prepare yourself for it, accept your weakness and respond with strength, you carry inside more than you think you do and there is nothing, absolutely nothing a courageous soul cannot do with a loving heart behind. Believe in you and in your mission beyond reason, for reason alone will not be enough of a driving force to make you do what you have to do. When reason falls short, faith and belief come in to help ...

Those that carry the inner and irresistible desire to live their lives according to the scripts of their missions will be guided to persist, to stay, to not perish in the face of what the masses will call a cause of lost hope, something unimaginable greater than what the average person can reasonably do. Indeed, what a daring soul is pursuing defies the confines of reasonability and conventional logic, diving into the depths of the inexplicable, the perplexing, the mystical, the alchemic, what cannot be dealt with a scientific mind but with a faithful heart.

The realms of the impossible only exist in the whereabouts of the mind, the heart knows no impossibilities, knowledge regulates only what the mind can conceive, restricting any attempt to fly astray and skydive into the universe of the beliefs, where only faith and not knowledge can empower a free spirit to emancipate itself from the governance of humanly created boundaries.

The kingdom of heavenly life calls cannot be found on earthly manifestations of driving forces, sources of insight, wisdom, or the like. To embark in a divinely created cause, one has to surrender oneself to the enlightenment of superior forces, the mysterious yet captivating domains of the unknown and in such a devotion step forward into the nebulousness nature of a heart led path. When it comes to fulfilling your purpose, there is no need to see with the eyes, let your heart take the lead.

Finding the algorithms to crack the code of a non-conventional life, one solely regulated by the dictates of our call, will give us the ability to stay focused on what we must do, avoiding the distractions that the average person being carried away by the busyness of daily life is exposed to.

To get where we need to go, will require us to pay little or no attention to the unimportant, the inconsequential, and the mundane, even when those contingencies maybe highly regarded by a world close to us and subject to adverse consequences intended to impose a pseudo submission to man defined life standards aimed at dictating what the masses are supposed to do.

The inner conviction necessary to break out from such a compliance force field cannot be found in the land of confusion that a mind insisting on following crowd behavior normally wanders. Breaking loose from the ties of a conventional life will be only possible if you are willing to devote your life to the very reason why you are here, graciously deviating from the path that an easy life will suggest. Doing what you came here to do will challenge your innermost beliefs and lovingly corner you so you can demonstrate whether or not you are ready to stop at the next station, disembarking the train of life as usual. Such an assignment is intended to be the first of many steps to prove that you can navigate through the turbulence that will come, without giving up at the first windfall, out of disbelief and lack of commitment to your own purpose.

Those that move forward with steel fortitude were not born that way but developed and nurtured such a character through years of practice, struggle, and the reinvigorating fulfillment that doing what one regards as right provides. It is only by following the dictates of your personal and unique crusade that you will serendipitously carve the shapeless marble you once were to uncover the hidden sculpture of who you will one day be.

The rhythm and balance of their movements is so magically coordinated that they seem to dance on water with the lightweight enchantment that walking on rice paper and leaving no visible trace would miraculously create. Their movements are flawless, even when the judgment of the outside world may condemn them to a life of ostracism and solitude, a sentence largely undeserved and irrationally sound. Deaf to such an unjust and primitive verdict, they continue to walk the less traveled roads as if the price to be paid for civil disobedience would not be worth mentioning compared to what they are experiencing in return, namely the inner peace of mind resulting from a life fully and honorably lived, as what they are here to do does not need to be understood, approved, or consented, it just need to be done, utilizing every bit of commitment, talent, and stamina available to the self.

A DRIVE FROM WITHIN ...

I feel morally obliged to pay tribute to the work that Deci and Ryan have so beautifully crafted in the field of intrinsic motivation as their research and postulations are fundamental to the underlying dynamics of a life driven from *within*. While the field of inner drive can be approached from a purely scientific perspective, it simultaneously follows and responds to the archetypes of ageless traits deeply ingrained in the mysticism of unconscious insight. What we know of and about our minds is much less than what it is indeed capable of, and the fact that we are unaware of its totality and its powerfulness is nothing but a rational proof to the theory behind our conscious ignorance.

Based on the cumulative research conducted on intrinsically motivated people, it can certainly be attested that they are so engaged on the task, or the final outcome of it, that there seems to be nothing else required from the outside world to push them in the direction they have chosen to go, all their drive, stamina, vision and desire comes entirely from within themselves and they are willing to do whatever it takes to stay on it. When it comes to that particular endeavor they happen to be engaged with, they are literally *self-driven* individuals. If anything, the world will have to stop them or they will keep going, and going, and going, until they can go no more or get tired of doing what they are doing, in which case they will get some rest, take a break and then go back to it with renewed energy and ideas. Difficulty is their ally, resting at their side and covertly fueling their creative engines, for the larger the challenge, the higher the fulfillment.

They love pushing the envelope and getting things done through effort and by putting up with any fights they may encounter along the road. They do not shy away from difficulty, quite the opposite, easiness is never among their first picks as the very best they have to give and develop will not be called upon. For as counterintuitive as it may feel, they seem to be possessed by an enigmatic craving to be challenged, to be defied by the intricacies of complex enterprises and undertakings well beyond their current (but not potential) stretch of imagination. In simple terms, *easy* is a synonymous of underutilization of their potential, a common type of stagnation disorder presented as a massively rare disease involving the deprivation to leave as marvelous a legacy as possible, something inherently rooted in the mysticism of self-discovery and reinvention.

Wherever they are going requires constant moving, they must be on the go each and every day, there is no time to lose, no energy to waste, and no good deed to leave unfinished. They know they can do better, more, escalate to higher levels of complexity and they are not pleased when they are deprived of the opportunity to contribute with their very best, which rests on hard to accomplish tasks pushing them to stretch and reach out.

> *For a selfless and contribution based personality, there is*
> *nothing worse than the feeling of having fallen short on*
> *what they could have done to fulfill their life calls!*

Falling short on what they *could* have done represents a missed opportunity and a clear form of betrayal to their highly set standards. Underperformance means nothing more and nothing less than the settlement for something less than the best they could have come up with.

> *Self-driven individuals defy the odds of probability each and every*
> *time, pushing themselves full steam ahead into the doing of things others*
> *would not even consider thinking about. They just don't mind stumbling,*
> *falling, and hitting themselves hard, a circumstance for which they have*
> *a simple cure: get back up, learn, and try again! If someone can do it,*
> *so do they, and if nobody has ever done it, there has to be somebody*
> *able and willing enough to try and do it for the first time, nothing is*
> *impossible unless you think it is (and even if you do, it may not be).*

Perplexity, whether they found it or are found by it, is their true ally and despite of its company, they will go to bed tired and feeling they have done their very best. Winning or losing does not matter if they have truly given everything they had to give and picked a battle difficult enough to challenge their potential on those meaningful aspects of their life. It is in those battles where they have already won in their own terms, despite what the world believes. Restless and unselfish souls have already redefined the concept of winning and the world's traditional definition means nothing to them, they can think better, higher, larger than the conventionalism of the masses. When most people feel defeated they feel victorious, when the masses feel uneasy they feel excited, rain is nothing but the anticipation of sunshine and they can't help living in the future when their bodies are still in the present.

They have made an upfront commitment to refuse feeling frustrated with immediate results, if they are going to be successful at putting their very best on the table, they must learn to ignore the superficial aspects of the here and now since what they are doing will not thrive until later in life. They are working on the roots of something much greater than what the average person can think of and root caring requires incredible amounts of blind trust on what one is doing. This is the only way to become what they truly have to become, which lies in a future yet to come. Every intermediate feeling of inadequacy has to be first lovingly acknowledged and then forgotten, it is the radiant glow of a beautiful tomorrow what will melt the clouds of an overcast here and now.

The secret to a worthy life lies in the mastering of the ability to escape the contagiousness of flimsy crowd behavior and become able to think, feel, and act in individual terms about what one must do. Such a dynamic requires a sort of conscious and unconscious abstraction of both past and present to laser focus the self on the vision of the future that best serves our call.

Past and present are of value insofar they can help us picture the forthcoming reality we are after, the one that needs to be built, created and rescued from the unfortunate fate of neglecting or ignoring what we came here to do.

We should only look back to see how far we have come and how we can utilize the experience we nurtured in an effort to move beyond the present time and circumstances. We should not regret on what we did wrong, what we could have done differently, or even what we failed to do, there is nothing to regret if we always gave our very best ... whether the world liked it or not ... and whether it worked or it didn't.

Redefining the perception of *winning* is an extremely important step that can be attributed in part to Star-Trek captain Kirk's affirmation that there is no such a thing as a *no-win* scenario. In order for you to think in those terms, the problem and what winning ultimately means for you will have to be redefined, regardless of what the outside world or conventional wisdom has to say. Applied to the discussion about becoming who we are meant to be and the process of partnering with the Universe to chase a *higher-than-the-self* cause, winning is redefined as *following our purposeful paths and giving our very best each and every day.* If we do that, we will win each and every time, and in so doing provide testimony to the disbelief in *no-win* scenarios, win or lose is nothing but a matter of definitions and compliance to them. You are not forced to accept what the world's definitions for win or lose are, *you can and must create your own*!

> *Regardless of what your mission in life is, if you follow it with enough love and duty, aspiring to engage in the required complexity it will call for (so you don't sell yourself short), and give your very best, you will always win! Don't listen to the world's loudest yells, listen to your heart's whispers instead!*

Let me close this essay by going back to the theme of partnering with the Universe. Once you know what you are up to, or even if all you have is a sense of direction, a guess of what you are here for, a hint, a hunch, a sort of intuition of what is expected from you, then partner with the Higher Powers, seek their guidance, their advice, their counseling, their support. Most importantly, if and when you get the answers to some of your long-sought-for questions, do as you were told, have faith and venture into the unknown with bold determination and courage.

The way to communicate with the Universe is to ask, in our waking moments and in our dreams, once, ten, a hundred times, until we get some clues, signs, or metaphors pointing us in the direction we were looking for. Often times all we will get after reflecting on what was handed to us may be nothing but a set of higher complexity questions aimed at elevating our thinking to a higher level of understanding. Those who ask the right questions will get the right answers! Ask, listen, and act. There is no point in asking if you are going to do nothing with what you hear. Commit yourself to a life of service, of contribution, of collaboration, of doing the right things and of doing as told. This is winning in Universal terms, this is the way you break the no-win scenario mental barrier no matter what it is you have to do. *Be the captain Kirk of your own Enterprise spaceship … and call it Life!*

FOLLOW YOUR HEART!

Do not underestimate the value of unexpected blessings. The world you know could evolve into something different, better, more glowing, more enchanting and most importantly more conducive to the spreading of unconditional love and care. What the farthest reaches of your imagination can conceive is infinitesimally smaller than what is possible, we are blinded by the immensity of Universal wisdom, something necessary to avoid the inevitable confusion of escalating to a level of complexity we are not yet ready to comprehend. However far our sight can reach, the horizon of what our eyes can see is truncated by our ignorance, a purposeful unconsciousness required for us to effectively do what we are supposed to do. No matter how bright we may think we are, some dynamics of the overarching underpinning of our life experience are better left unknown.

Everything that could be potentially known has much lower life altering power compared to all that can be believed (even without knowing), the mind will not be allowed to enter the realms of the heart, stop trying to know and start trying to believe!

Your analytical brain will discount the power of the unexpected, defense mechanisms aimed at simplifying our view of the world will remove anything that has a low probability of occurrence and guide us to concentrate our attention on what is more realistic, more possible and more likely to happen. Our mind will turn us into prisoners of the present and the linear projection of the past into the future. Just because our logical mind has been commanded to ban remote possibilities to the point of not even thinking about them does not mean they cannot crystallize themselves into a reality not consciously thought of. Even if we cannot imagine it, cannot confirm it and has no prior history of occurrence, the unthought-of, in whatever shape or form will come to us if our heart is open to what has been planned for us, a serendipitous and synchronistic series of connected events residing beyond the realm of the conceivable.

This is why you need to trust your heart, your eyes and your mind (especially the cognitive side) cannot see what your heart can feel, they just simply operate at different domains. While the heart wanders in the land of the unconscious, the unknown, the diffuse, the ambiguous, the unclear, the unthinkable and the unimaginable, the mind operates in the whereabouts of the reasonable, the predictable, the expected, with as much latitude as the confines of a limited set of events pictured from a realistic and conventionally accepted view of the world.

If you want to reach the full realm of possibilities available to you, enticingly attracting what may have been completely outside of any stretch of creative imagery, you must entrust yourself to the guidance of your heart, you cannot under any circumstance know any better.

Trusting yourself to the dictates of your heart will require the rigor and the discipline necessary to learn and master any new endeavor, gradually and incessantly building the courage to blind trust what your eyes cannot yet see let alone believe. You will have proof of no kind, guarantees of no form, missing certainties in a land of confusion surrounded by plenty of world-accepted reasons to misbelieve what the whispers of your inner voice is suggesting ... resist, do not give in! As you pave the road leading to your true self, you will get progressively exposed to traces of unconventional thinking, mystical signals, strange hunches mysteriously connected in the form of apparent random coincidences that no chance theory would support, unresolved mysteries *believable* enough to the beguile and the faithful but *absurd* enough to disenchant the non-believer.

Living a life led by your heart and the domains of the unknown can be stressful and somewhat anxious for the untrained mind, but you can learn to turn it around and slowly start to feel acquainted with the ambiguity of not knowing but believing in what *may* (but not necessarily will) happen next. Even the term *next* has to be redefined as it may be another *next* than the one you originally imagined, a *next* in another time dimension, after a new set of circumstances unfold and a new vision of the world has been developed. Just because you want, expect, desire, or consider something to be the best right now, does not mean it is the best for you or your mission on Earth, all things considered. Life state of affairs can and will be different than what you envisioned and with such a change your definition of *best* will evolve as well. Be open, be flexible, allow yourself to be carried away by what has been planned for you, a place, a time, and a set of circumstances you may know nothing about, and quite certainly a *where* and a *when* you must absolutely meet.

The world you are about to enter is new and novel, no self-growth and no self-discovery will be born and nurtured if you always walk the same paths, over and over again, never exposing yourself to aspects of your future life, things you will be familiar with and eventually master only if you allow yourself to be introduced to them, perhaps initially failing at, struggling with, or disliking them. There are no promises that what lies ahead is a path paved with rose petals, as a matter of fact it may most likely not look like so rosy at the beginning, but you will want to stay, the Universe will test how committed you are to follow its command and tolerate what does not seem the best you can get at the moment.

... and there lies the key, what you are after is not going to the best at every juncture but the best at the end ... only your heart can see the myriad of possibilities that are awaiting for you beyond the immediate suffering of befriending the unknown and what at first sight may seem not for you, only because it is unfamiliar or difficult to manage and predict.

Remind yourself that you are not here to succeed at anything except the purpose you were entrusted with. Any need to be in control of the outside world and the rules of engagement that run it is an illusion set by the primitive sides of our brain to feel more secure in the business of preserving our life. True control if we were to have any, would not extend our existence a single second, we just can't handle it, the Universe and what we came here to do is way more complex than what we can conceive and trying to control it would be absolutely beyond our current capabilities. What we have and what we truly and deeply need is only the *illusion* that we are steering our life in the way we want, an illusion that will ease the troubles of a mind relentlessly trying to overpower its heart, for at the end, there is no such a thing as *free will* for the obedient soul.

Break yourself loose from the restrains emerging out of your short term vision of a long term life. Be brave, be calm, be wise, reach inside and find the inner peace that comes from becoming one with yourself and your own Nature. Honor the life you have been given, lovingly doing and being nothing more and nothing less than what was thought of you.

THE LONG TERM FUTURE WILL BE DIFFUSE

The road was stony and there was nothing but squared granite around. All of a sudden, Lili sees a wisteria sinensis vine growing tall from the tiny space left in between two stones laid to pave an ancient road, giving birth to handfuls of enchanting purple flowers hanging as if they were suspended rain drops miraculously defying gravity laws. Such an awe was enough of a surprise for Lili to charmingly break the silence of our peaceful and contemplative walk. ... "look, they are growing from nowhere!" There it was a beautiful Nature's masterpiece emerging from the nothingness of minuscule particles of entrapped soil and into the fullness of a world mysteriously showing up.

Only a few moments ago, I was thinking about our financial situation and the likelihood of recovering from everything we lost in Argentina, a thought that took prey of me and temporarily distracted me from what was supposed to be our second honeymoon, a long-sought-for trip to ancient European places after more than 20 years of a enchanting marriage. Even when only half self-aware, I was a bit demoralized and under the spell of the guilty ignorance that was ruining a supposed moment of joy and pure love.

The beautiful wisteria sinensis vine growing out of cracks in aged and worn out stony roads was a sign of hope, pointing that even after everything is lost and apparently dead, beauty can still grow from nowhere, like the Phoenix bird that emerged from its ashes. It was a symbol, a message from above that came to show me the need to trust in the existence of a better future past the confines of an *apparent* stony present. That future had already happened, I could just not see it due to my *time* shortsightedness! Flowers, especially wisteria sinensis, which is among my favorites, symbolize beauty, life, and the intervention of Nature to bring order to chaos. It was during that trip to an ancient civilization that I recognized the incontestable presence of beauty in imperfection, a thesis that I have held true and dear to my heart for many years.

The Alhambra Palace, where the sign was presented to me, was a vivid example that ruins carry a sort of hidden beauty resting way beyond human reason, sustaining the passage of time and the decay of centuries witnessing what was once built. In its majestic timeless intervention, Nature was doing nothing to preserve what would eventually die to then be reborn, a life cycle miraculously crafted for mankind to contemplate the embellishment of mysterious world wonders. There are times when we have to step aside and let Nature do its part, even when that doing may be nothing less than creating beauty out of decay, a sort of magic enticing the trading of places between the old and the new, the mundane and the sublime, the earthly and the divine, a sort of mystical connection between the known and the unknown, a stubborn beauty incessantly trying to wake us up from a lifelong sleep keeping us from seeing everything that is to be seen.

The mix of the remnants of a once magnificent thirteen century palace eroded by the hand of Nature was the perfect blend of life, death and re-birth blissfully engaged beyond the confines of any possible human comprehension. That day, wisteria sinensis flowers came to set free the hopelessness of the stony road that would had not been beauty enough to get my attention if not because of the magnificent purple candor of Nature's creation. Interestingly enough and in metaphorical terms, I was myself under the mistaken *spell* of walking a stony type of road, apparently absent of beauty, and far from hope.

> *Nature will come to the rescue when highly hoped humankind*
> *efforts fall short and reach their help-required thresholds,*
> *when a certain level of imperfection and decay show us that*
> *we are only just a piece of a larger context master plan.*
> *When such a trigger point is reached, hope is always on the way,*
> *and Nature will bring it to visible levels. The dust of everyday life*
> *can symbolically bury anything but not deep enough for the power*
> *of Nature's winds to dust it off, polish it and make it shine again!*

What I call Nature is an allegorical perception symbolizing the *help* of the Universe, with whom we partner in the quest for meaning throughout the course of our lives. The notion that Nature and Universe are one and the same was created to facilitate the wisteria sinesis metaphor by merging the two concepts and simplifying the understanding of the way in which the Universe *talks* to us. You need to learn the sign language the Universe uses, it will not get too much clearer than this! Expect no text messages, no e-mails, no phone calls (no instagrams or tweets for the newer generations), nothing surging from the conventionalism of our lives as the Universe is old fashioned enough to ignore the greatest advances of technology and state-of-the-art communications.

I will be forever indebted to Nature for teaching me that I will never receive conclusive and scientifically proven messages informing me that my long term financial future will be warranted, but I can quite certainly read the signs by which Nature is talking to me, the writing on the walls, and the metaphorical images I am mystically forced to stumble upon.

The Universe will talk to you in symbolic language and if your wish is to learn it, you need to become knowledgeable on how to crack its code, solve its riddles, decipher its scriptures and in a rhetorical sense figure out how to separate the important from the mundane (or as my investment coach would suggest, amplify signal and reduce noise). Forget about everything you learned at school, this is different, this type of knowledge is above and beyond any realm of logic or science for it borders the line of ageless archetypes and alchemical phenomena, intimately related to hidden sides of your-self, your unconscious and the collective unconscious of the entire human kind.

You will never be able to learn and speak the language of the Universe if you insist on revolving around conventional wisdom, what you are up against is something resting far and away of anything the masses will ever comprehend. You need to allow yourself to think differently, to fly away from the "reasonable" world and into a higher level of abstraction, of complexity and of openness. You will labeled as weird and sometimes become casted out, accept and pay the price, it is worth it!

There is more to it, your interpretation of the message is *part* of the message. In other words, since your interpretation cannot be confirmed by any means other than your confidence that you are faithfully reading it with reasonable truthfulness, your ability to decode the message is part of the message itself. You need to assume that a certain level of uncertainty and ambiguity will always be present making it impossible to know *for sure* if what you see, feel, or intuit is completely true. It will be as true as you regard it to be. This is not math where 2+2 = 4, this is a different type of domain knowledge, a non-scientific version of math. You can still put it in mathematical terms and it will be something like this … your vision is blurry enough that you have to make an educated guess, hence everything you see seems to suggest the first and second numbers to be 2, you have reasons to believe the sign in between them is a *plus* sign, and based on what you believe but hardly see, the answer is 4. You don't know for sure and you never will. Your equation cannot be more exact then the blurriness of your vision but can be deeply and strongly felt beyond any need for certainty.

What really matters does not lie in the inherent ability of the belief to be proven, which would violate its own definition (a belief is called belief because it cannot be proven), but in what you trust to be true and the power it gives your inner confidence and the feeling of rightness it creates. In the world of logic, you think, in the world of faith, you believe.

Your ability to interpret the message is also part of the master plan as nobody will be given a message complex enough not to be *reasonably* understood if sufficient unconditional love and duty are offered in return. Be bold and find the ways and the means to befriend uncertainty, neighbor with the unknown, and welcome the new and the novel without asking that everything that happens to you is pleasant and joyful. There are no one-sided coins and all the two-headed coins I have ever seen are fake and worthless. Your wisdom and your conceptualizations of the worlds inside and around you will increase in direct proportion to your ability to face that which you know little about. If you are afraid and remain in *known-land* you will not grow, not learn anything new and remain stagnant. This is not what the Universe expects from you.

Be brave, get out of the cocoon and face the unknown, spring your wings and fly away … your life as a caterpillar has already come to an end!

Our limited understanding of the holistic process of life, both on Earth and beyond, forces us to live in a world ruled by probabilities of occurrence. For every one thing we know, there are a thousand we do not, and only a handful of those thousand will reach the attribute of belief, faith is not endless, not in human terms. In a world of uncertainties, nothing is for sure, guaranteed, eternally granted to us in a way it cannot be taken back, all we know is that some things are more or less likely to happen than others as qualified by our assimilation of the complexity of the impending future circumstances and our ability to control them. In such a real world, ruled and regulated by human knowledge, there are no absolutes, all is relative. In a world of probabilities, all you can expect is to know with the highest possible certainty what is about to happen, and accept that you will be sometimes right and sometimes wrong as any effort to predict the future with absolute certainty is futile. It is no different with being able to read the signals of the Universe, the probability is part of your ability to read the code, the scripture and the ultimate the message you will get. At the end, nothing in life is certain, not even the past as you can always get different reads of what happened and reprocess your memories in alternative ways creating a new version of a past you were not aware it existed.

If you can come to terms with the idea of living in a world ruled by probabilities, then reading the signs of Nature will help you tremendously, if you cannot, signs will confuse you more than what you may already be (even if you think you are not confused). Sign language is meant to give you high level guidance about what could happen based on what you are sensing from non-conventional and extra-ordinary sources. It is your way to hear what the Universe has to tell you. As in any other language, learning to read it will take time and practice and in this case, since your conversational partner is a Higher Order entity, you will have to trust you are communicating. When talking to the Universe, you can't simply ask a question and expect a conventional *yes* or *no* answer, it will just not happen, at least not in the traditional way of the word but you can get a sign, a symbolic clue that can help you connect the dots and guide you in the direction you must to go. It will be up to you to translate those signals into the insight you need even if it means reformulating the question so as to better match the responses you are being given (at the end, what makes you believe you have asked the right questions to begin with?).

I wish I would have the wisdom and the eloquence to explain with words the mystical and abstract revelations that only exist in metaphysical structures, shapeless ideas that come to us in the form of hunches, strong feelings, unspoken and unwritten commands from above to do some things and not to do some others. That which cannot be explained with words can only be felt, perceived through our faith and suggesting that something greater than ourselves exists, something we are infinitely indebted and grateful to, an unlimited source of love and compassion, a God-like figure to which our existence was come to bear. The language of the Universe is the same language your inner, deeper and unconscious side is using to communicate with you, you learn one and you have learned the other. Reach in, go deep, explore the *who* you are, you will grow wiser. All the answers to the questions your life depends on lie inside you, there is no need to go outside of yourself. You carry with you the best college you can ever afford, where the secrets of your past, present, and future are taught, treasured and nurtured. All you need is inside the confines of your-self and your ability to connect with the Universe is nothing but empowering you with the tools that your treasure chest has carried ever since the day you were born, embellished, sharpened, and improved throughout a life of self-discovery and reinvention.

> *If you wish and desire to learn the Universe language,*
> *take your time and do it right. Open your mind to the*
> *unconventional, the unreasonable and the unexpected. Signs*
> *are everywhere you just need to let them come to you!*

There are hope signs when you are becoming hopeless, warning signs when you are entering dangerous zones, strength signs when you are in the need of endurance, the Universe will talk to you about what you need the most, whether you consciously know it or not. Although the nature of the sign is different, they all have something in common, they give you clues about things that have not yet happened to help you prepare for them (in whatever form of preparation is required). Signs are meant to assist you at visualizing things you do not see with your eyes, clues and disguised messages that only the wisdom of a loving heart can decode. The Universe will talk to you ... learn to read its signals and be willing to listen what it has to say.

If you decide to embark in the enterprise of learning the secret language of the Universe you will uncover a world you did not know existed, something completely outside of any stretch of your prior imagination. I can confidently say that once you have mastered the art of communicating with the Universe you will not be able to imagine life without it ... you were blinded and now you can see!

FEELING THROUGH YOUR HEART

*What your eyes can see is only half of the truth, to see the other
half you must close your eyes and feel through your heart.*

*We live in a world dominated more and more by scientific
knowledge, technological advances, and a myriad of fragile
distractions that threaten to draft our attention away from
the meaningful and the truly important aspects of life.*

Let me share a personal story to illustrate this point and paint the
picture of how my life was changed by the unexpected intricacies of a
cultural shift. Back in the 90's when I still lived in Argentina I started
feeling the need to capture my thoughts in paper format, learning
and reflecting about life. I wanted to become wiser, know more about
myself and ultimately my purpose on Earth. Every Saturday and Sunday
morning I would wake up early and go to a coffee place called *La
Barberia* where I would spend two or three hours, drink a latte with
croissants, read for half of the time and write for the other half, it was
just me, a book, a personal journal and a pen. I enjoyed those Saturday
and Sunday mornings a lot, I felt revitalized, renewed, reinvigorated, I
was growing strong roots inside and although it was the same me who
entered and exited the coffee place two or three hours later, I could
tell I was slightly changed by the insight dose that the whole breakfast
experience provided. I followed that routine for years, seven or eight
at least, it was a time of renewal and reinvention. I voraciously read
everything that caught my attention, from psychology to philosophy,
including some sound books on motivation and behavioral science.

I was always fascinated by how things work and the human nature
was not an exception, I needed to better visualize how we operate,
why we do the things we do and whether or not this is what we were
supposed to do from a more mystical and philosophical perspective.
After reading for a while, novel thoughts would come to mind and it

was time to capture them in paper, what in essence gently induced me into a sort of creative mood where a rare form of mysterious inspiration would imprint a call to action and demonstrate what it can do to entice an eager hand-paper-pencil triad to get moving.

Living in Argentina was not easy, there was barely any technology around, societal rules were either non-existent or not followed, predictability was an item present on most people's wish lists and planning for the future was limited to the next 24 hours. The fabric of everyday life was challenging in many respects but every coin has two sides and the flip side of that coin was that there were no things that would break (and require me to fix them), no bills to pay (only 2-3 utility bills that I had with automatic debit from my bank account), no lawn to mow, no retirement planning to worry about (I did not know what retirement was until I came to the US) and nothing else to do on my spare time other than think about my priorities and enjoy family time. It was life in its plainest and simplest forms and we had weekends and evening time to fill with nothing but relationship building and self-discovery. Lili and I entertained lots of chats and spent quite a few hours together in the ten-by-eight kitchen space where we cooked (should I say *she* cooked), had dinner, hand-washed the dishes, and shared a cup of tea while recounting what happened during the day. Like every family in every third world country, we had good and difficult times to go through, life was quite unpredictable there and we lived one day at a time with no formal planning for the future as there was no reasonable way we could figure out what tomorrow would bring. We were at the mercy of our destinies, feeling helpless on the outer side and fully empowered on the inner side.

Suddenly the turns and twists of fate offered us a *once-in-a-lifetime* opportunity to change the course of our lives and the lives of our future generations, even those not even born yet. It was a juncture we envisioned ourselves at for about a couple of years, as if we would have synchronistically known it was coming to knock on our door. It was certainly a fork on the road with two completely different alternatives, would we stay in the comfort zone created by the old and the known, even when we knew it was not what we wanted and something far below our expectations or would we go with the new, the unknown, the uncertain, but with enough signals suggesting that it *could* be a better match to our personalities, our view of the world, and what we hoped for our future generations?

It was not an easy decision in any respect and we made it putting first things first, a beautiful future, even when still in vision format was worth any try and the risk of failing to reach it. It was not until after long reflections and deep soul searching that we decided to leave Argentina and move our family to the United States of America.

For those that have never gone through an international relocation where the culture you leave behind and the culture you get into are diametrically opposed, imagine a jump into the unknown with no guarantees of any kind that you will find anything familiar, other than the most instinctive human conditions and basic character traits (deep inside, people are people anywhere you go). Most everything we had to experience for over two years was different in almost any respect to everything we knew and lived through for over forty years.

Moving our family to the United States was the most difficult, stressful, and defying experience our family had to go through, a real test to our endurance and our vision of the future, yet, it was the most fascinating adventure we had ever embarked into.

My heart knew it was going to be worth the price, although my eyes could not see how big of a stretch it would finally came to be, it was a challenge of gigantic proportions and quite certainly something we strongly underestimated. I have to confess though that a part of me knew (perhaps an unconscious part) and mobilized me to tell Lili that it was going to be so difficult that to really understand whether or not it was for us, we would have to withhold any judgments until the first three years would go by, assuming it could take up to three years to adjust and adapt to the new world. Something inside me was saying ... *hold, it will be worth at the end, but it may take longer than expected and it may be more challenging than what you imagined.* Even when I did not hear those words in that exact manner, the feelings I had insight were suggesting such a concept. This is a key aspect of listening to the voice of your heart, it is a rhetorical voice that many times comes in the form of a feeling, a hunch, a gut feel, an instinct or a difficult-to-describe extra sensorial perception. Your heart is connected to the unconscious and will not speak to you in plain English language, you will have to decode its message and its meaning.

I knew we had to do it and I knew it was going to be puzzling, although I had no specifics, just a bunch of shapeless feelings. Should have I believed my eyes and the myriad of challenges we had to go through, we would have never left Argentina or leave it to only come back soon thereafter without fully realizing what our future would have brought us in the new land. Our daughter Naz, who was eleven years old at the time, cried every single day for over 6 months until one day she came to us and said, *I feel that if this did not kill me, nothing will, I now know I can live anywhere in the world, the worst part is over.* My eyes were immediately filled with tears of sadness and joy, listening to a child state she has outgrown what was the worst nightmare of her life gives you peace but at the same time the chills that come when you realize that you purposely albeit unintentionally created those nightmares, even if for a noble and worthwhile reason.

Lili also cried for several months, although nobody saw her crying (she was so loving and caring that she would cry in solitude to prevent us from witnessing her suffering and her mental anguish), and had butterflies in her stomach for over a year, a byproduct of the anxiety she was undergoing.

Despite the strong mental anguish and the clear evidence that a psychological disorder of magnificent proportions was taken place, no doctor would treat her condition as it was not a medically typified disease … a strange sort of homesickness in its purest forms. Despite the fact that the doctors we consulted did their best, they did not know any better as none of them had gone through something like this in their lives.

> *Lili had to learn to cope with her sorrow befriending her*
> *butterflies until the day they decided to fly away.*

For over four or five years I barely had any time to read or write, there was a void in my usual weekly reflection process, I can now, and in hindsight, see that the inner dialog was taking place at an unconscious level as I was drinking from a fire hose and did not have any mental bandwidth for the philosophical weekly routines I was used to engage into. Life in the United States was overwhelming, busier than I ever imagined, with lots to do and lots of experiences to digest and process, we were learning at such a high pace that most of the new realizations that landed into our fields were doing it in an oblivious manner, we were learning much more than what we were consciously aware of.

It was true that we almost immediately gained access to a better quality of life but it was not without a price. We paid our dues dearly and without regrets, we somewhat knew what we were doing, although we were not fully conscious of its grandeur and the myriad of ramifications that such a decision would create over the years to come. On a personal stance, I really missed my Saturday and Sunday mornings, and they came back, but not until seven or eight years later, when the dust of the unknown settled and we gained some control of our lives back. Looking back at the all encompassing dynamics our family had to go through, I can certainly attest that I purposely (although not consciously) turned my attention away from my eyes and into my heart.

> *The United States life experience was so mind blowing, so full*
> *of awe and so unmanageable that it took me over five years of*
> *struggle to decode some of the basics dynamics of our new life to*
> *the point of comfort where you can allow yourself to return to*
> *where you always belonged, to symbolically come back home.*

From the first day of the move and almost without noticing it, I started seeing more through my heart and less through my eyes. As a matter of fact, I was seeing through my eyes all that was to be seen and realized that there was more, much more than what the eyes could see. The irony of it is that as long as your eyes remain open, letting the outer light blind you, you will involuntary let that blindness reach your heart. In order to see beyond, you have to inevitably come to the point of regarding what you can see, no matter how glowing and breathtaking or frustrating and depressing, as only half of the truth, only the visible part of it.

Not until accepting that there is an entirely different world beneath the surface, you will be able to turn your attention inward and start reaching deeper for the true meaning of your life experiences, the source of your joy and your sadness, and in so doing empower yourself to answer the complex set of questions that have remained holy and untouched as if they were part of a sacred legacy beyond any stretch of effort or reach.

Learning to see through our hearts is a process that can take years to develop, not only because of complexity or difficulty but because it requires us to trust what our eyes cannot see, to venture into the unknown and be vulnerable to what we can or cannot find there, to become one with Nature and the innermost parts of ourselves, the very place where our true essence lies dormant and waiting to be awaken. Our heart is the guardian angel of a source capable of radiating an immense amount of light, a place where all the quests find their true meaning, the mysterious and charming realm where it all starts and where it all ends.

Only when you are compelled to see beyond what your eyes can see, when you can no longer deny that there has to be something else, something above and beyond the evident and the mundane, something regulated by forces of a higher order, divine in their own way and offering you a love as unconditional as you have ever imagined, you are opening yourself to take that leap of faith and venture past the point where your eyes can lead the way, a new phase in your spiritual journey where your heart will be your only compass. Your heart will start to guide you only when your eyes can see no more … allow it, you have to trust your heart to do its job.

If you are in a stage of your life where the most beautiful things you have ever seen came through your eyes, you are not ready yet, you have not seen it all, and you don't even know it. Not until after being puzzled by what your eyes can see and after questioning yourself "is that it?" you will consider other possibilities beyond the mere rational and logical and immerse your conscious mind into the sea of the unconscious, the unknown, the mystical, the inexplicable and the nonsense, what your kids would say ... Dad, Mom, this is ridiculous.

If all you trust is what your eyes can see, I am afraid you have seen nothing yet! There is an entire world out there invisible to the sharpest eyes! You will understand when it comes time to, in the meantime, keep working on your priorities and do not be afraid to face the unknown, the most beautiful life gems are there, where the reason and the logic fall short and are not allowed to get in. The world of the unknown cannot be rationalized with our current brain power, we just don't know what we don't know. The most beautiful treasures of life are secretly hidden beyond the farthest reaches of what the eyes can see ... in a place meant not to be seen but to be felt.

Allow yourself to be carried away and led to where you always belonged, Heaven on Earth, a place and a time where all dreams come true, where the only fear is the fear to not do what one is supposed to do, the fear to live an empty and meaningless life.

It is in your hands, nobody can take this away from you, and by the same token, nobody but you can make this happen. Either you make it or fail to ... be courageous, be brave, you are not alone!

If the legacy of an ordinary man striving (and struggling) for over fifty years to live as extraordinary a life as possible is to be considered, do not lose any minute, immerse yourself into the depths of the mysterious and fascinating paths of your heart expecting to find the unknown and the unfamiliar, the never seen before, a beauty beyond reason, a blissful fracture of the perception of life, and a rare kind of peacefulness that can temper the troubles of everyday life. You will be asked to trust your feelings, your intuition, your inner voice, your sense of rightness. You will have to do things you may not fully comprehend, not only from a *what* but also from a *why* and a *how* perspectives and as long as they feel inherently right, you would want to do them, to the best of your abilities and even if you sense you will not do them proficiently.

The intriguing and mind blowing aspects of following the inner guidance of your heart is that once you truly, genuinely, and unreservedly devote yourself to it, things start to make sense and you start to see (should I say *feel*) what was not visible before. When you embark yourself in the simple yet monumental task of becoming one with Nature, one with the Universe, and one with yourself, the stars would align and show you the way, lost or not, you will know where you are and most importantly, where you are going, if nothing else in a blurry but confident manner. Chances are you may feel asked to do things without having been given enough information, not carrying the required skills or experience and yet you are expected to do your best with what you have and what you don't. This is exactly the way it is supposed to be, so if you feel that way, celebrate, you are on your way to uncover the mysteries that your heart has been treasuring for you!

It is true that the world within us is not as certain, as specific, and as tangible as the world around us, which is the reason why we must make a radical paradigm shift and adopt a different mindset towards life. Conventional wisdom may not be of much help, neither science nor technology as the inner paths of our hearts are ageless and ignore advancements of any kind, all that matters is our ability to practice unconditional love and to do for others more than we do for ourselves, in whatever form or shape our life call requires.

Accept your ignorance and if you do not know where to start, start by loving those that need to be loved. The most beautiful gift you can give another human being is the gift of love, especially when they need it the most. And even if with this advice you still do not know where to start, look around, it won't be too long before you find a soul that has gone through so much adversity that is in a desperate need of being nurtured, cared for and unconditionally loved. Open your heart to them and let love winds blow back and forth. Gradually you will start to see what was until then, unseen.

There are no secret formulas or magic recipes to get immersed in the practice of seeing through your heart. Open your-self to the simplest and truest forms of love and the rest will come to you. Accept that even when someone cares for others more than he or she cares for himself or herself, only good things can happen in the world, long term. If this is a principle you can live by, you are about to experience immense fulfillment at doing whatever the Universe is expecting you to do. As far as others are concerned, everyone will have to make their own choices and decide how to best lead their lives to find the inner peace that comes from doing what is inherently right, those deeds that embody the spirit of worthiness that emanates from following the commands of our hearts.

Life was given to us with a purpose and within that purpose is contained the reason for our existence. Honoring it is not optional and must become the only one task we cannot leave unfinished.

WHAT YOUR EYES CAN'T SEE

If you have questions without answers then you are on the right path. Based on Albert Einstein's approach to problem solving, we could say that the answers to life's most important questions will be only found at a higher level of complexity than the one where they were created. You will have to escalate to that level of complexity first, humbly accepting that such a leap of faith to reach the unknown and the uncertain could be painful, growing generally is. Whatever the struggle, the difficulty and the pain, make the promise to never give up! It is in the heartfelt and steel forged determination to always stay that your fortitude and endurance will be engendered.

When it comes to rising to superior levels of maturity and for as puzzling it may sound the deeper you go the higher you get. The answers to your most earth shattering questions are nowhere but inside you, if you are looking around, in the outer world, you are searching in the wrong place, turn back, reach in, there is nothing of significance far from your heart. It is there where the eyes see no more that the golden gems lie, dormant, peaceful, calmingly waiting for you to unlock the treasure chest that has been protecting and preserving them all along, all the way to the day you were born … and even before.

It could have been a longer or shorter journey until this point and it does not matter, you are here now and have to be audacious enough to look at your fears in the eyes and say: *Yes, I am afraid but I will not stop asking questions until I get the answers I am looking for; if I fall, I will get back up, always one more time until I listen what I came here to listen, so it is up to you whether this is going to be a short or a long conversation.* If you can think it, you can say it, and if you can say it, you can do it. Many of us have been there, gone deeper than we had ever imagined, almost to a point of no return, maybe not by choice but handheld there, kindly but without our permission or consent. True may be that should had we known what was it going to be all about, we would have never given our approval, which was the reason we were not asked in the first place.

*The first few steps of a thousand mile walking trip will not
reveal the wonders still to come. Only those indomitable
enough to venture into the unknown will bear witness of the
majestic and indescribable beauty of what lies ahead. If you
are living your purpose, the best is always yet to come!*

To do what we came here to do may require us to gain strength or wisdom in extraordinary doses, intakes that will not happen through ordinary prescriptions or treatments. To emerge astronomically stronger may require us to go deeper than what may have ever imagined as only when we can face the worst in the eyes, and witness our survival, we will return knowing who we really are and who we can truly become. For as paradoxically as it may sound, to go higher may require that we go lower first. We are all stronger, wiser, and more capable that we think we are and it is only by putting those qualifications to an endurance test that they will have to emerge and become visible. While our heart always knew who we truly were, our eyes only saw the façade of what lied beneath …

*The Universe will make some decisions for us, especially those
decisions we would never make ourselves, not because they will
not lead us where we need to go but because they open a path
so full of uncertainty that we can't see what lies ahead.
If we are about to fall prey of our fears and let them take control
of our lives, we will most likely be removed from decision making
duties. The best of us starts right after where our fears end!*

*Courage is the gift of doing what one has to do, not
in the absence of fear but in spite of it.*

Your eyes will at times involuntarily and inadvertently lie to you as there is way more beauty past the horizon than what your eyes can see before it. Acknowledge and accept that to fulfill your life purpose you may need to be carried away from many of the things you are familiar with, far from your comfort zones and to a land you know nothing about. Things happen for a reason even the things we believe have absolutely no reason at all. If you cannot explain an aspect of your life you deem crucial, wait, it may not be the time for you to be given such an answer, keep working at it, keep asking the right questions. The day will come when the wisdom to integrate the until-then-mysterious will be handed to you, perhaps when you least expect it, when other matters have taken control of your attention and you are fighting other battles. It is true that the more we ask a question and the more we work at it, the closer we will get to the whereabouts of its answer, but what it is not true is that we can shortcut natural cycles and get those answers before we are ready to handle them.

The Universe knows what it does and nothing happens by accident or before its time. Your heart also knows and it is able to talk to the Universe, they have their own secret encounters where they reconcile their differences and align their agendas. As far as *why aren't you invited,* it is simply above your pay grade! But this is what you can do, you can listen to your heart, it will tell you as much as you need to know and most importantly as much as you can handle at the moment. When your eyes see no more, turn to your heart, there is much more than what the eyes can see. If you are not yet in the habit of talking to your heart, get started as soon as possible, it is one of the most beautiful life honoring investments you can ever make!

> *Your heart does not speak the outer world language, it has its own codes and symbols custom made to communicate with you and assist your at following your own purpose. There is no one that can help you learn the way in which you heart will talk to you, no one else speaks your heart's language and no one else can learn it but you.*

So how you will do it, how will you learn to do something without help of any kind, something you may have no idea of even how to get started? You will be helped but not by someone else, you will be helped by your very own heart! Ask a question and listen what you hear, listen carefully and without excuse. You did not hear anything? Ask again, and again, and again, until you hear something, even if a whisper, then try to listen what it says. Your hearing abilities may be put under test. When it comes to listening to the heart, the softer it speaks to us, the more attention we need to pay.

Do not discount the fact that the loudness of the outer world may be overruling what your heart is trying to tell you. If there is too much symbolical noise coming from the outside, you need to move to a quieter room, a room where you can listen to nothing but what comes from within. It is only then when you will begin to hear life changing inner bound messages, perhaps some things you were told for years and you were not ready for them. Today is not any better or worse than yesterday, and yesterday not any better or worse than tomorrow, you will be able to listen only when you have the desire and the ability to understand. Not a day earlier not a day after. Wherever you are, there you go!

YOUR EYES WILL KNOW, YOUR HEART WILL BELIEVE

There are two extreme camps of human beings along the see-believe trait continuum, those that believe before they see and those that have to see before believing ... as far as the rest of humanity is concerned, they fall somewhere in between.

Human kind does not follow a black-and-white type of distribution on any personality profile but conform more of a bell curve type of pattern. The masses normally fall in the middle of the trait with extreme cases spreading more into the tails of the curve. By definition, you *know* something when you have proof of its existence and you *believe* something when you regard it as truthful with no proof of any kind. The field of knowledge is covered by science and the field of belief by faith. Science and faith have always been presented as apparent opposites, sitting at different sides of the road and subject of clear discrepancies. Since all opposites reconcile at a higher level of complexity, let's revisit the relationship between beliefs and knowledge in more detail and look for possible overlapping areas.

Believing is more of a feeling and is related to your heart, to what you regard as right and true. Knowing is more of a thought and is related to your mind, to what you or someone else has proven to work or exist and that can be replicated (this is a scientific requirement). The apparent opposition of the *believe-know* dilemma can be over extended and related to a few more dyads such as right-work, heart-mind, conscious-unconscious, known-unknown, etc.

*When we see through our eyes we say we know, when
we feel through our heart, we say we believe.*

As human beings, we are all unique and special in our own ways and while some people have a preference to trust their hearts, others have a preference to trust their eyes. Needless to say, there is a large portion of human kind that seems to have similar preferences for one or the other depending on the circumstance and their life stage. Those that lean more to their hearts are the believers, the dreamers, the visionaries, the early adopters, the risk takers, the more optimistic, and the more daring. They are the ones that can conceive future world configurations, clearly envisioning them before they come to fruition, if they ever come to fruition. Actually, many of those *still unrealized* alternative world configurations will never materialize should they not start in somebody's vision first.

> *It is the visionary who believes in beautiful yet still latent dreams who will chase the not impossible and slay dragons left and right to prove his vision truthful. Even when the road to succeed can be full of struggle and disparagement, making them fall more often than the non-believer, their stamina, conviction and faith will get them back on their feet to always try one more time.*

Those who need to see first to then believe are the spectators, those that will follow the leaders once a way has been found or made. They will want to see which of the many tried attempts have worked to then pick those *safe bets* and not the hundreds of *perceived* failed trials. They cannot envision anything different to what they see and can only believe what is now known.

> *Believing before seeing is a gift and whoever the carrier is also has the responsibility to do something with it. If nobody would believe before seeing, then how come the world would eventually evolve and transform into something different? Somebody has to be fearless enough to dare the status quo and envision a different reality, one with better and more opportunities for the embellishment of human kind and the development of more altruistic life contingencies.*

Having the ability to envision a *better tomorrow* is a privilege that only strong and spirited hearts are given. Such a gift will require the beholder to chase that vision and give his very best to make it happen, with absolutely no guarantees that it will work other than his inner and burning set of beliefs. They will have to follow no lead but their own and they will fail (as perceived by the external world) more than they will succeed (again based on the external world's definitions). What awaits at the end of a compelling vision, whether fully realized or not, is worth a thousand lifetimes of chasing it!

> *There is no other fulfillment of such magnificent proportions than the one that comes out of leading a noble life entrusted with a cause greater than ourselves. It is only after we find what we are here for and give the Universe our unconditional commitment to relentlessly work on it that our life finds its natural place in the overarching constellation of human kind.*

It is at such a juncture and not before that we find complete harmony of body, mind, heart and soul. Everybody has a dreamer inside, it is not the absence of dreams what makes people hesitant and sometimes reluctant to try new things, what really kills dream-chasing ventures is the lack of commitment to acknowledge those dreams as your own to then chase them as part of your purpose in life, vigorously, with no reassurances that they will work, only with the vision and the legitimate desire to give everything you have in their pursuit. The beauty of partnering with the Universe in what we came here to do lies in the acceptance that all we are asked to do is to give our very best each and every day of our lives. As far as results are concerned, they are not something we should worry about, we can only control our actions and not the outcomes of them, especially in the all encompassing circle of life. It is the Universe who will determine how successful we will be at attaining the results we *think* we should attain (many times the ends of our journey are far from where we think they are, not yet having faced the many twists, turns and forks in the road which will take us to places we never thought we would go).

Be able to live in the apparent ignorance of not knowing many of the things that would be required by others to mobilize them in one direction or another. *Be perfectly fine with just believing and not knowing, calmly floating in the blissful ambiguity of an out of the ordinary 'outer space.* Some people experience quite a bit of difficulty at differentiating beliefs from knowledge insofar their belief system is so strong that no proof of any kind would turn them more believable, trustable or energizing than any piece of rock solid knowledge. They believe what they are supposed to believe, and they know what they are supposed to know, and when it comes to the most substantial aspects of their lives, knowing and believing are nothing but the two sides of the same coin. Proof is only needed by the unbelieving self who needs factual reassurance before committing themselves to any vital enterprise inadvertently trying to force fit beliefs into knowledge molds.

How will a still-to-be crystallized vision come true if it does not start as a belief first? Somebody has to believe on it so feverishly and so desperately to turn the odds of fate in its favor, only then and if the belief turns true, the proof that the masses need will come.

The knowledge of the many is born out of the beliefs of the few.

I could not stress more the power of believing. Human kind would have not advanced if not because of the many beliefs that, after unconditionally loved and nurtured were eventually turned into knowledge. It goes without saying that for every one vision that ascends to the summit of its original conception there are another thousand that have never left the ground to reach significant heights. Blessed those that gave everything they had for the unrealized dreams, their battles were not in vain, humanity could have not reached the few symbolical summits without the many apparently failed attempts that ended up not too far from the ground. Dream chasing is not a high probability venue but something that embodies the most enchanting visions of a future yet to come at the price of dying with the feeling that all we have left is a magnificent unfinished business, only hoping that somebody will take over from where we have involuntary left.

Strong beliefs have knowledge power in the hearts of the beholder, when their hearts speak, their minds listen, attentively. We are all expected to believe on something, it is not just the same something, that's the only difference. Whatever you believe on the most, even if you are a bit uncertain about what it is, stands at the center of your life for a reason, it is your call to action, not a choice but a duty and you must learn to love it. Only by following your beliefs and by trusting them as the ultimate truth, whether they will be ever proven or not, you will have a chance to live your life to its fullest extent and in the utmost honorable way.

Whoever you are meant to be is intimately related to what you believe on, never neglect to see it, never refuse to chase it and never pick a life that does not gravitate around it. Turning your back to your beliefs and refusing to transform them into dreams that will be passionately chased is the biggest crime you can commit and the most straightforward path to become somebody else other than the who you were meant to be!

HOW MUCH CAN YOU IMPROVE
THE FUTURE IN A LIFETIME?

A bridge goes nowhere but let thousands, millions of people cross-over and reach their desired destinations, as far or as close as they need to go. A bridge sacrifices itself to perpetual stagnation for the collective good of the souls it allows to cross-over and move on.

Like rhetorical bridges, many noble beings have decided to sacrifice a big part of their lives for the betterment their future generations, for their well being, their progress and their lessened struggle. They really don't care too much about themselves as they see through their children's and grandchildren's eyes, walk through their legs, breath through their lungs. The vision of future generations getting over the hills of struggle they had to go through to ultimately reach places they have never imagined for themselves is so comforting, so convincing and so inspiring that any stretch of effort seems minuscule when compared to the beauty that such a glimpse can elicit.

The sheer thought of a better future is so exhilarating that it becomes almost impossible not to embark in such a journey, knowing well that it will be filled with discovery, reinvention and immense doses of both joy and adversity. There will be happiness and sadness all around, hopefully more of the former than of the latter, and whatever the case, there must be no stopping us, no second guessing, no hesitation, no fear of failure, no regrets and most importantly no expectations of success other than the one emanating from doing what we came here to do.

Why us? ... because in every genealogical tree, it comes a point where a generation has to do something momentous for those coming after to have a better and more profound life. It can't be scientifically predicted but it happens in a pseudo random format, synchronistic phenomena disguised in a chance occurrence custom. Circumstances like these tend to happen more often when world contingencies drastically change, either for the worse or for the better, laying an enticing wondering worth being explored and nurtured, if nothing else to help humanity advance. Such a remarkable fracture in the way life was projected is not to remedy a problem but to reach out to a new world of opportunities, a place and a time resting peacefully beyond our present circumstances, far and away of everything we can possibly reach. Unless we turn ourselves into bridges, allowing those that will come after us to continue with our legacy, crossing over the wonders of our time, leaving the old behind and venturing into the mysterious domains of the still to be found, the realization of such a realm of unseen possibilities would stay as distant from them as it was from us. We have a once in a lifetime opportunity to shorten the path to the advancement of humanity, to allow others to outpace us and capitalize everything we have learned and experienced in the quest of a better world.

Courage will be required, not only for those serving as the bridge but also for those crossing over it. It takes two or three generations to go through a radical change in the genealogy of a family and before stability arrives for life to go back to normal. Two or three generations of vigorous souls determined to put an end to the opaque fabric of a suboptimal present and give a symbolical birth to a startling chapter in the future of those to come. This is a decision made with the hope that the future will be better than the past, perhaps the distant future and the distant past, as the immediate future may not be too much enchanting than the immediate past.

When these pivot points in the history of a family or mankind in general arrive, somebody has to pay the price of such a change, nothing major carries no cost, some self-sacrifice will have to occur. Being a bridge, or crossing over it (both acts require faith and courage) carry honor and duty. You have to see it as the privilege to help change the history of your loved ones, of diverting the course of life for the better, of creating opportunities never thought of, never conceived, beyond the reach of conventional wisdom, an act of grace, serendipity and synchronicity.

When you turn yourself into a bridge for future generations to cross-over, you are redirecting the life experiences of countless of human beings, creating new and unthought-of opportunities for those that will come after you, both alive and to be born. You are investing your present for the future of hundreds and thousands that will outlive you, it's not even a question you need to answer, it is a command to act and do what you were expected to do.

If you happen to be that *one*, the chosen, the knight to fight the dragons of complacency, fill your heart with pride and get started, the sooner the better! *Why us?* ... is not the right question and if you happen to feel inquisitive, ask yourself: *Why not us?* Some people have the desire and never get to have the opportunity!

Having lived in an emerging country for over 40 years, I became a living testimony and have borne witness of a countless number of individuals who could have done so many good things and just did not have a single chance to put those noble intentions into practice unless they really stretched to create the opportunities that were not handed to them by the outside world. Others have the opportunity and not the desire, the symbolical opportunity train stopped at their stations only to leave without them. Having the desire and not the opportunity or vice versa represents a crime to human kind and whether it is imposed by the outside world or ignored by the person does not make a difference, it is a crime anyway. Only a selected few have both the desire and the opportunity, a close enough and impossible to miss chance to change the future and make the world a better place to live. If you are one of them, feel honored and do what you must do!

There are plenty of bridges still to be built and everybody is special in their own way. Nothing happens by accident, there are no coincidences and no mistakes in the Universe's master plan, you are supposed to be a bridge, the most beautiful bridge you can possibly be ... feel blessed and honored. Others are waiting for you, they need to cross-over and get beyond, you are their hope and their only way to go where they are meant to go!

The future of generations yet to come lies in your hands, you need to realize it, to visualize it and to believe on it! No matter the price, no matter the sacrifice, no matter what you must leave behind, it is always a privilege to be a bridge. If by the time you must leave, breathing your very last breath, all you can say is "*I was a bridge and nothing but a bridge*" you could rest in peace, the type of peace that only the few among the many can taste, the peace that comes from doing right, from doing your very best at every juncture of your path, the peace that comes from becoming the who you were meant to be.

It is of absolute and imperative importance that you seriously think about adopting these visions as early in life as possible, it won't be any earlier than it can be (you have to nurture some wisdom first), and as soon as your heart tells you it is time, you need to start working on it, day after day, year after year, until the last day of your life. Do not shoot for perfection, just do it, it will get better as you go.

Throughout the course of our lives, we are given a small number of trials to make or initiate out of the ordinary changes to the world around and after us and the irony of the process is such that when the opportunity comes, it does not look as a life-changing one. Rather, it looks as one more choice among the many we do every day in the survival side of things. Your mind sometimes does not see it, it can't tell the difference between a horse and a donkey a thousand feet away but your heart can! Some things are just not visible with the eyes. Listen to your heart, it will tell you, advise you, whisper you, eventually push you, gently, softly, lovingly. If you really have to do something, you will feel a sense of unease if you don't listen to your heart, you don't do it or you try to ignore the subject altogether.

Failing to act on something relevant will carry a price, a high psychological toll even if you have not consciously realized the full extent of it … and the Universe will find ways to let you know, just listen to what you will be told! It has to be like that, a lettuce seed is not too different than an oak seed, they are both seeds despite the fact that one leads to a plant a hundred times taller and thicker than the other. Some things are just not seen by the untrained eye until the point they reach their full maturity and completeness. It takes a dauntless soul to grow a hundred feet tall oak as for every one thing that goes well there are five to ten things that can go wrong. It takes resilience, persistence, patience, optimism and endurance to face the unknown and venture into a lifelong journey of dream chasing with the only hope that if we do our part, the Universe will be at our side witnessing our conviction and collaborating with the crystallization of what was meant to be.

There will be cold, long, dark and lonely nights but the sun will always rise afterwards and its warmth will soon erase the most troubling memories of the night behind. There is no wound that would not eventually heal, no tired heart that would not have time to rest, no hunger that would not find a piece of bread, no thirst that would not be quenched by some fresh water, just stand still and never collapse, strong bridges never do!

CAN YOU KEEP RAISING THE BAR FOREVER?

Some people find it easy and pragmatic to plan their lives and their future in such a way that they can do most of what they came here to do in however long or short their stay to be. Others live on a more day-by-day basis, enjoying and struggling with whatever comes to them; they just deal with what they are presented with, the catch of the day. Regardless of which camp anyone belongs to, there comes a point in the life of a man when you need to look back and compare what you have done to everything you wanted to do in life, all the way back to the earliest memories you can recall. This mental exercise will require effort and may not come naturally. It requires rewinding and fast forwarding our entire lives to do a kind of all encompassing assessment of where we are compared to where we wanted to be, and to make things a bit more complex, there is not one but many places we envisioned we would eventually be at some point in our journeys.

An introspection of this sort may also take us through a mix of feelings ranging from joy to sadness, from excitement to frustration, from pride to guilt, from bravery to anxiety ... be tolerant and compassionate with you. Whatever it is, it is and you will sooner or later have to accept it, denial of something you regard as truthful will only delay the inevitable, whatever was done or not done is part of a past that belongs to you. Both the action and the lack thereof, if it was the very best you could do given the circumstances, is all you can ask from yourself.

Part of what we may regret or wish we would have done differently is generally associated to things we knew were not the best at the time we did them but for some reason we did them anyway, moments of spiritual weakness, when a flawed vision was leading us, or simply times when our faith fainted or vanished.

Accepting what happened does not mean doing nothing about it and despite the fact that you will not be able to turn the clock backwards and change what you did you can always decide what you will do in the future, should similar or related circumstances arise.

Some events in our life have a meaning and a purpose
beyond themselves and were laid in our paths only to provoke
further actions we would not entertain otherwise.

This is a fundamental building block in the fascinating yet mysterious and paradoxical way our life unfolds, as if following a script we were not part of creating, secretly hidden from us for a reason. In a broader and holistic sense, it all gravitates around a more complex definition of learning, one that makes it an imperative the going through apparently undesired events only to evolve into a wiser and more experienced being, integrating something else for the future appearance of unimagined events, a key insight that will make us do or not do what we would have or have not done should the unwelcome circumstance have not occurred.

The meaning of certain (wished or not) life experiences lies in the
message they imprint on us and what we can learn from them for
what will lie ahead, some things are nothing but stepping stones laid
in our way for us to keep moving in the direction we have to.

Most all of us have involuntarily done things that have caused pain or discomfort to others, especially significant others, those we love and love us. Almost all wounds would eventually heal if enough love and care is gently offered. If you realize you have hurt somebody, whether intentionally or accidentally, it is your responsibility to offer a sincere and heartfelt apology without expecting that apology to be accepted. You apologize to let the other person know how sorry you feel for their pain and to acknowledge that you wish you would have not caused it. It is up to them to decide what to do with your apology. Some wounds may be deep and acute enough to not heal immediately, if ever, and you must accept it. The unconditional and genuine nature of an apology are the two most important attributes of it. When you offer an apology, it is for them, not for you, although it may relief some of your grief and guilt. Being patient and sympathetic with those we may have hurt will give us the kindness and compassion necessary to restore the peace we used to have.

If you want to repair past mistakes and truly make up for those you have hurt, apply enough amounts of unrestricted love and care to the relationship, expecting nothing in return and only offering your love to them. Depending on the depth of the wound, some things may never be the same and you need to accept it. It is important that you realize that even when some things may never be what they once were, they can certainly be better than what they are now and you can be at peace with yourself knowing that you made a mistake and also your very best to repair it or offer your most sincere and kindest apology. Nobody is perfect, accept the price of living a life of good intentions and some failed attempts.

Going back to the assessment exercise, when you compare what you have done or not done versus what you wanted to do, go through it in small increments, may be mini-assessments every year, the big bangs start to come after we get past the middle of our lives, when we realize that what it is left to do is less than what has been done, in other words, when what we have still to live is less than what we have already lived. The fact that we are now in the latter part of our journey is not something that should worry us, time is not all, we now have more wisdom and tranquility than ever before and we can use it to enhance the quality of the life experience … not only ours but most importantly that of others!

We started this essay with a differentiation in personality types, the future and present preferred profiles (we all think and act with both present and future visions in mind, it is nothing but the degree of energy we spend on one versus the other what differentiates us). If you find yourself to be more future than present oriented, you may have a tendency to always adjust your plans, eventually adding actions or raising the bar once you have reached that last milestone that was once ahead and is now behind. It is perfectly fine to do that, it is actually the best way to ensure continuous improvement and growth, especially when done in conjunction with regular assessments.

While raising the bar constantly will bring the best and the greatest of you to the surface, it has a slight downside as it also carries a hidden sense of imperfection and the potential feeling that you have not done enough (the bar is always higher than what you can reach, except for the short span of time between reaching it and raising it again).

If you keep hitting in the bull's eye to only move it further away, missing the window of opportunity to make regular assessments of what you have done, failing to compare where you are to both where you were and where you wanted to be, you are at the risk of getting lost in your own life quest, feeling disappointed for nothing but a job well done!

Your regular assessments will keep you honest and self-aware to the monumental summits you desired to go after, which were not of your own invention but milestones in the purpose of your life. If you have accepted the causes you were entrusted with and did your best every day, following the commands of your heart you will be able to tell yourself:

In the process of doing as much as I could and delivering on the dictates of my mission, I have gone farther, much farther than I have ever expected to go. It is for that reason that, if this is it, if I am reaching the end of my time, I am perfectly fine with it, I am packed and ready to go, whenever the call comes.

The key is to *not stop* growing or setting higher standards because of the realization of how far you have gone. You must keep pushing and learning because you never know how far you can get, but do it knowing how far you have come! In a metaphorical way, this is like looking ahead for new places you can go, never forgetting all the places you have been to, never forgetting the beautiful and joyful journey you already had, and if this is it, you have no regrets, no missed expectations, you have done more than you ever imagined (although you continue to envision new things).

Do you see the apparent dilemma? Should you feel contempt and happy for what you have done and symbolically retire from your purpose filled duty (at the end you have done more than what you ever thought you would do), or continue to raise the bar and go for more, always pushing yourself another notch into higher grounds? This is a three-part question and the answer is *yes, no, and yes*. "*Yes*" to feel contempt and happy for everything you have done well, "*No*" to retire, and "*Yes*" to continue raising the bar and going for more.

For those more focused on the present, on living the here and now to its fullest extent, you may also want and benefit from making the assessment. While you may not have a conscious need to raise the bar (there may not be a symbolical bar to raise as life may be just a process of interacting with what is being offered to you) you may still want to do right and more as you move along, it is just not in a plan of record, written in a journal or thought in advance, but it is in your heart and in your desire to do right, one moment at a time. If the exercise turns out to be quite demanding only because you are not accustomed to tracking progress or planning future objectives, you can certainly try mentally traveling back and forth in time revisiting some of those early dreams in life and see what you have done so far. Even if it sounds difficult or a bit abstract, just try doing it anyway, once you do it once or twice you will realize it was not that cumbersome ... and who said it has to be perfect from the first time, let it just be what it is. Despite the tears and the laughter, it will be one of the best times of your life. We all treasure golden gems, raw diamonds, precious trophies worth contemplating every few years to fuel our stamina to keep travelling the roads laying ahead.

There is no better way to know where you stand in the course of your lifelong journey than to do a recount of what you did to then compare it to what you wanted to do ... and whether you like what you see or you don't, it is certainly something you do not want to avoid knowing!

If you are past the middle of your life, you are technically living the second half of it and there is no such a thing as a third half of life, the second half is the last (I was always skillful at stating the obvious!).

The best way to live whatever you have left, whether too much or
too little, is to align what you always wanted to do to with what
you will do, regardless of what you have done. Use what you have
done to learn from it, but do not condition yourself in any way
or shape to it, what you have done or not done is part of the past,
look at the past only to rescue your dreams and realize how far you
have come, then look at the future to continue chasing them!

Where do you start? Grab a paper and a pencil (sorry I am old fashioned) or your iPad if you are technologically savvy, and start to think back. Once you get in the creative mood necessary to redraw the picture of your life you will realize it was not that complicated. Here is a quick and simple recipe:

1. Divide the page in three columns and name then *Old Dreams, Accomplishments, New Dreams*
2. Write your childhood dreams (realized or not) on the first column
3. Think openly about anything you are proud of and write down what you have accomplished in the second column. Whatever comes to mind as sizeable and above the ordinary is a valid entry.
4. Also on the second column write the things you are still working at, those you have missed, and those you still want to get done. Put WIP (for Work In Progress) next to them
5. Finally and on the third column, write any new dreams you now have that you did not have before (this is a product of bar-rising for years after the initial set of dreams were handed to you).
6. Now compare the first and second columns and draw lines connecting related dreams and accomplishments (regardless if they are done or still a WIP)
7. Do the same between the second and third column. You will be surprised to see how many things you have done or are still working that relate to *new* dreams.

I doubt that once you get in the rhythm of doing this exercise, which will take two or three trials, you will not get a full page of 3-column writings and connecting lines! Does it ring any bells? It does to me!

Repeat this assessment at least every 3 years (you do not want to do this exercise every 3 months as it may not be any different). Take time to celebrate the well-done-before-the-bar-was-raised-again type of accomplishments for once the bar is raised, you will be under it again. The current or new dreams are to be compared with your deeds and results in the next five, ten or even twenty years, once you have had enough time to chase them.

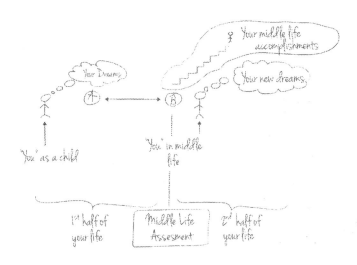

In the graph above you will compare A to B, not B to C (C would be the end of your journey and is not in the chart yet)! Doing this would be unfair to you as C was probably envisioned as you were climbing the ladder from A to B and after you realized that B was no longer such a challenging objective for you in the long run (there will be several moments in your life when you will feel that unless you raise the bar, you will be selling yourself short and you would be underutilizing your talents). That bar will continue to be raised until you get to it and feel it to be no longer high enough, at which time, you will raise it again, repeating this process until your last day on Earth.

LIVING IN THE FUTURE ... THE POWER
OF STRONG MEMORIES

I had always a passion for envisioning the future, especially a beautiful future, and many were the times I wondered why. While I do not know for certain what the origins of such a curiosity are, I can hypothesize a couple of possible theories. Living in the future, especially a better future, can sometimes act as a conduit to escape a not so great present. It can also be the result of the unconscious mind knowing that the future holds something so worth thinking ahead, something that one needs to spend present time preparing oneself for it. Remember that the unconscious does not operate in a *sequential* time continuum like our conscious mind does, the linearity and sequentiality of time is an artificially created model to contain the complexity of time travel and the possibility of creating alternative parallel realities. The unconscious mind operates in a domain beyond this limitation and can jump from present to future and back.

I may probably never know for sure why the future and everything that it can bring has been so appealing to me, nevertheless it has always been a strong motive and a medium to keep my life focused on what will come next, more specifically, what I can create, influence or in any way help build. I am also a big believer that the *best* is always yet to come, as long as one gives all that one has to give in the pursuit of what we came here for. If you ever heard the saying *perception is reality*, you may have given it some consideration and whether you agree with it or not, it seems rather factual to me that there is no one single reality but as many as human beings are on Earth. We see through our eyes and not through anybody else's. At the end, what we see is what we believe to be truthful ... and what we believe to be truthful is what we see. We live in a world of perceptions taken at face value and regarded as truthful which is a brain mechanism to reduce the complexity of the world around and inside us to something simple enough to be managed without troubling our minds beyond the necessary.

The time continuum and its sequentiality perception is one of them. We believe to be true that the future is unknown until it becomes present, passes by, and turns into the past. We also believe that the future occurs after the present and that the present unfolds after the past. I adhere and subscribe to the first statement (future unknown-ness, at least consciously), however I have a rather different view of the second, namely the sequentiality of the past-present-future triad. This is one of the many necessary illusions that the limited human mind needs to fabricate and adopt to avoid trespassing the confines of what we can regard as realistic and scientifically proven. We can't handle certain conceptualizations that *only* belong to the Universal wisdom domain knowledge, our brains can only process information that makes somewhat logical sense, is aligned with our prior set of accepted facts avoiding ambiguous or conflicting constructs that will simply raise too many unanswered questions and disturb our mental peacefulness. More complex states of maturity can manage opposites, conflicting ideas that may meet at higher levels of multifaceted thinking patterns along with the ambiguity that emanates from them and in so doing distance themselves from the average brain that craves to have closure to elemental dilemmas before moving up another layer.

The mere acceptance, even as a remote and rather unlikely possibility of a non-sequential time continuum, will infer the possibility of time travel, of moving from past to future and back with the subsequent notion of altering future as well as past events at our discretion, wish and desire.

Such a construct would imply empowering human beings with super-natural powers and the ability to control more than what we are able to comprehend. We can't be allowed to play God without sentencing human kind to an inevitable extinction. Things happen for a reason, even when such reason is not visible with our eyes.

In layman terms, the future has technically *not* happened yet, which at conscious level represents an acceptable and undisputable truth. There is however a way to elevate our thinking to a higher level of complexity and imagine the existence of a Higher Power, a God-like figure that can *see* the entire time continuum at once, past, present, and future. Such a Higher Power, to whom I will call a loving God, knows what will happen next, when and why, even how. Whether such a God has the ability and desire of altering that literal future is a more complex subject that I will leave up to theological scholars to discern. The thought and subsequent belief that there is a God that can see the entire time continuum suggests that it does exist a way of visualizing the future, even if such a way would not be made available to us (at conscious level).

If you can, even just for a moment try to imagine this hypothetical scenario where the future as well as the past have already occurred, as if we were part of a *movie* already recorded and now being played, a movie that has already been casted, burned into a DVD and watched multiple times by the Universe and our Creator. We are just characters in the movie of our lives and we believe we are *recording* it as we go, rather than *watching* a pre-recorded version of it. In a mystical sense, we are both watching a prerecorded and recording a new movie, creating an apparent dichotomy of premises as simple logic would suggest that recording something new and watching something old are mutually exclusive actions. Remember, all opposites meet at a higher level of complexity ... learn to stand in between conflicting notions and tolerate the ambiguity that such confusion would create. Confusion is nothing but the anticipation of clarity ... a blurry thought cannot keep its diffuse nature forever, either it gets clear or vanishes from the confines of our mind, and it is all up to us to decide.

We can decide to eat lunch at 11am or at 12pm or skip it altogether, we have the freedom to choose and that is part of the context that creates the illusion of *free will* in the first place. We have the ability to alter the present by exercising choice, however and if we have made a commitment to run our lives according to our purpose, that *free will is not that free*. There are predefined limits, boundaries, stretches of imagination we should not violate, especially when it comes to the most notorious parts of our lives. Lunch time is unimportant but doing what we came here to do is not, doing what we are expected to do is among the most radical life matters and we must follow the dictates of our heart, not thinking in terms of doing as we please … free will should not be considered an option when it is not.

Our ability to choose our response in any set of circumstances, something that Viktor Frankl called the ultimate human freedom is indeed a discretionary attribute that has to be managed with due respect and consideration in the context of our life calls. The capacity to make our own decisions should not be unlimited and open to any possibility we could conceive, free will is not completely free if we accept our life call, there are certain things we must do, no questions asked. It is at this juncture when you need to start increasing the complexity of the model to elevate your thinking to the next level. A framework for decision making needs to be adopted and whatever its shape or form, it has to be intrinsically linked to what we came here to do.

We all came to this world to be somebody and not somebody else, to do something and not something else, and it is there, at that very point of choosing what is intimately related to our nature, individual or collective, where the high probability of our choices should lie. Right there, in that sense of predictability relies the inner magic that forges the limitedness nature of our free will.

On a more holistic and broader context, *what* we came here to do and *who* we came here to be is different from our neighbor, our best friend or a simple stranger we cross down the road. If we have a true and burning desire to respect Nature's order and do what we are supposed to do, the higher probability outcome is that we will do and become what we came here to do and become.

It is in these cases that the future is set, has already happened and while you can theoretically exercise free will, you will only pick from a limited number of choices as some paths will never be considered. Your commitment has narrowed the possibilities and made the future so predictable that it has already been set, recorded, and burned into a DVD.

Imagine that you have accepted to walk a long, winding and reasonably wide road leading to the place you need to arrive. That road is your path and you are allowed to make regular stops, even walk backwards if needs are, to then resume your journey. You can even move from left to right and right to left, walk in the middle or on the sides, look for the shaded or the sunny spots, or find refuge under a tree during a rainy day. You can do all you can imagine as long as you stay within the confines of that road you have accepted as yours. This is the extent of your free will …

For those that commit to a life of purpose, the future is set and already happened, we just can't see it with our conventional eyes, but what about our hearts? They have a much deeper and broader reach than our eyes and are connected with both individual and collective unconscious realms. To see through your heart you have to first close your eyes as what you see through your eyes may cloud what you see through your heart. Lao Tzu's famous quote … *"A man with one watch knows what time it is. A man with two is never sure"* helps illustrate the confusion that arises when we pay similar attention to the visions of our eyes and our heart. To see through your heart you must first close your eyes! Your eyes will only see the here and now, eventually a projection of the past into the future, most likely influenced by the linearity by which our analytical brains operate. Your heart is the closest link you have to your unconscious and the collective unconscious of the entire human kind. It is through your heart's symbolic eye that you will see beyond the here and now and in so doing become able to imagine future circumstances somewhat or totally unrelated to your present life. Your heart can feel things that your eyes can't see!

On ne voit bien qu'arec le Coeur. L'essential est invisible pour les yeux – Antoine de Saint-Exupery (from the book "The Little Prince")

When it comes to the fundamental aspects of our lives, never trust your eyes more than you trust your heart! Your eyes are like reading glasses, use them for the immediate, the close, the right here, and the right now. When you need to contemplate Nature, a landscape, the entirety of your life (past, present, and future) take your reading glasses off, close your eyes and look through your heart instead!

Back to the start of this essay and to my passion for mentally living in a better future when my body is still here at the present moment, and even when I acknowledge my ignorance about why it happens, I carry a strong belief that whatever the reason, it was part of the Universe master plan and what my contribution to it is concerned. If such a reason was the existence of a sub-optimal past, who am I to say that such a past was not placed there on purpose? If it was the need to work on beautiful future possibilities, who am I to say that those visions were not given to me with the hope that I would do something positive with them? Whatever it was, it was meant to be and I was simply not supposed to be told why or asked for consent, the Universe can and will act with permissions of no kind. We all need a motive to do what we do, whether conscious or not and those motives (the hope of a better future for instance) will drive us through the intricate paths of life in the search of that we envision.

For one reason or another, I always carried inside a relatively strong tendency to imagine different world configurations and mentally jump into that envisioned future with the conviction that it was there for me to grab it, stretch it into the present with one hand while stretching the present into the future with the other, like if acting as a bridging spring of a rare form connecting two realities laying at separate although related dimensions. I never felt helpless or too far out from that envisioned future state of being to the point of believing that becoming wiser, applying consistent effort and being both patient and persistence would not take me there. All I needed was to work hard for what I truly and deeply believed, letting the Universe do its part, for at the end, it would only be if it was meant to be.

Even the strangest life circumstances do not happen by accident, everything is meticulously connected by the Universe's synchronicity. Faith and persistence are keys to fulfill your purpose and you must believe that whatever you came here to do is possible! Do you think it is a coincidence that some people are always immersed in a world of glowing but challenging visions, difficult but possible calls and at the same time they are given the talents, the persistence and the patience to go after what they believe on?

There has to be a reason for the uncommon, the unreasonable, the one or two things that make you special in your own way, able to do things that others would be unwilling or unable to do. Beautiful things are waiting out there for those that are determined to live the life they were entrusted with and utilize the gifts they were given.

Work hard for those things you truly and deeply believe on, those aspects of your life that matter the most, lovingly passing and paying minor attention to those circumstances that matter the least. There is only so much time available and you must use it wisely for the noble causes you are here for.

My mystery has been resolved, it was neither my past nor my vision of a better future alone what kept me engaged and living in a time yet to come, it was the combination of both, mystically blended and crafted together in a master piece plan. A plan I knew nothing about ... or maybe I did?

WORKING FOR THE LONG RUN

I always found it easy to give my unconditional commitment, lifelong if necessary, to those things in life that I deeply, truly and unquestionably believe on. If you do one thing in life and one thing only, start by knowing yourself, get to know and befriend who you are, and most importantly who you are meant to be. That is not all, but whatever that all is, starts there.

The business of knowing yourself is a lifelong endeavor, something you start but never end. There are no limits as to how far and how deep you can go, it all depends on how much you want to uncover and when enough is enough. Knowing too much can be overwhelming at times. Strong and powerful medicines are best if taken in small doses ...

I decided to start my life quest perhaps without consciously making that decision twenty some years ago, writing in my diaries, journals, thinking about life and reflecting on my priorities. When such an introspection enterprise begins, sooner or later you start to realize what you are doing, the patterns you follow, day after day, month after month, year after year and without even noticing it you are thinking about the way you think (which is referred as meta-thinking). Overtime and if you keep yourself engaged in the discovery of the attributes that make the who you are, you will start to perceive some common denominators, things you do, like, dislike, avoid, pursue, etc ... and in spite that you may or may not know the reasons why you do what you do, which requires a deeper and more complex level of understanding of your nature, you cannot avoid increasing the degree of self-awareness at which you operate. Whether you decide to get yourself into the *why* or stay at the *what* level, it is a good start anyway. Some things take time and it helps little to dive into deeper waters if you don't know how to swim on the surface. Get to know what you like and what you don't and the time may come when you will be ready to start seeking for the *why's*. If the *what's* are the tip of the iceberg, the *why's* are the iceberg itself.

You certainly don't want to overwhelm your-self by chasing knowledge before you are ready to handle it. You will know when the *what's* are not enough and getting to know the *why's* becomes an imperative, something you cannot postpone any longer, just wait for the right time, you will know when it comes!

In my case, knowing that I like something generally carries a strong sense of rightness, the feeling that the liked is something absolutely worth doing, no questions asked. It is more than that, it is not only what I do but also when I do it, how I do it and most importantly why I do it. It's a simple yet difficult to describe feeling, where a few factors have to converge to give me a sense of higher order peace and the feeling I should be doing nothing but what I am doing (or what I am about to do), like if all the starts were aligning to show me a path I would not see otherwise. This rationale is not for the everyday side of things, things such as what to eat, what to wear, what movie to watch but it is indeed for the most influential decisions of our lives, which also happen to fall on a daily basis. I am referring to things like spending time with our loved ones, helping others, working for a future and noble cause, taking care of those that depend on us, writing a book, etc.

> *Perhaps the best way to portray such an overarching sense of rightness is to say that it is the feeling of peace that comes to visit and embrace you in those moments when you feel you are doing exactly what you are supposed to be doing, the right things, at the right time, in the right place, when you would change nothing or be doing nothing else but what you are exactly doing.*

From a higher level perspective, it is nothing more and nothing less than the act of doing what you are supposed to be doing, at that juncture of your life and at those particular circumstances you happen to find yourself in. That inner sense of rightness is heaven to me. It completely drives my actions and I would still do what I must do even when other signals emanating from the outer world would dictate or expect from me to do otherwise.

*You need to accept that there will be times when a price will
have to be paid, defying the crowd and the conventional flow of
things carries a resistance that you have to face and be accountable
for. Accept it, pay the price. There is no price high enough to
be paid for allowing yourself to do the right things, when they
ought to be done and in the way they must be done.*

I also like to think and act long term, to literally invest in the future, to envision multiple *what-if* scenarios that may take today's reality to a completely different level. In order to successfully embark in those enterprises, you must be able to do things today knowing that they would bring positive results in the months and years to come regardless if they will be in your time or not as many noble causes take several generations to mature and crystallize. Learn to be perfectly fine with either starting or providing continuity to a change wave that may spark positive energy across many lifetimes to eventually be handed off to your successors, future holders of daring dreams aimed at changing the world one life at a time. All great accomplishments of mankind started first in the mind of someone, maybe more than just one person, well before the first rhetorical brick was laid down. Let's dare to believe!

The ability of creating, holding and nurturing positive visions of a future yet to come is essential to turn this world into a better place to live. Everything starts with a thought, a dream, a *what-if* statement deeply and passionately held with the spirit of creating something that belongs to the future and is needed in the present, crafted by those intrepid souls of all times who are brave enough to think about a different world configuration, to believe that what the outer world regards as impossible can be done and to invest their lives in causes that others would rate as unconceivable, totally unlikely and highly unreasonable.

Probability of occurrence is nothing but a way to measure how vigorous you are, how big you can think of your contribution to the world and how large of a gap you are willing to fill. Even a probability of one in a thousand will likely happen if you try a thousand times. Think BIG! How big? As big as your stature would allow you!

Climb the mount of your life and put a flag at the top, let the world know you were there! Go up, rise your body, lift your spirit, if you are afraid to fly, use the staircase! Refuse to confine yourself to a life of complacency where everything you do is assured, guaranteed, predictable, reasonable and expected. The safety and comfort of predictability is for the weak and the fearful. Life's fulfillment is not contained inside the incremental nothingness of the known but into the mysterious fullness of that we know little or nothing about.

Venture yourself into the unexplored and mystifying paths of self-discovery and reinvention. Do what feels inherently right, difficult or not, impossible or not, guaranteed or not. Pay little attention to whether you can finish it or not, all you have to do is get it started! Let the Universe be your coach and your partner, you are not alone even if you feel you are! Leave your fears behind, fight the dragons of easy living, be willing to lose what you have if only to gain the feeling that you did what you had to do, to work on what your heart keeps telling you to work on. Go at your own pace, but go … please go! The Universe will wait for you but you have to start moving and keep on going, you have to show you are doing your best, that is all the Universe expects from you!

Life, as I know it, was not meant to be easy, if it is, you are wasting your time, your gifts and your potential. Life was meant to be fulfilling, joyful, beautiful and at the same time challenging, difficult, perplexing and filled with sporadic moments of struggle and uncertainty. You were expected to grow, to evolve, to learn and to mature. This is not going to happen if we pick the easy way of life, the path of least resistance, if we join the crowds and stay with the flow, warm, fuzzy, out of the trouble of doing what your inner voice tells you to do, having absolutely no idea about how to do it, and regardless of the consequences it may bring.

There is no everlasting punishment for those embarked in the business of following their hearts and of doing nothing but good deeds. True it is that they will not be loved by everyone around, expect some resistance from the outer world, especially if you intend to change their status quo, oppose what it is expected from you or do things that will be regarded as weird, unnecessary, unlikely or plain non-sense. At the end, whatever you do, it has to make sense only to you, give you peace of mind and the feeling that your life is being honored. As far as the world is concerned, it may think otherwise and you must learn to accept it, walking your own path will require you to be complete with nothing but your own company as you need nothing else to do what you must do; you need no external reassurance, approval or consent of any kind ... and you certainly do not need to look for love in the wrong places.

A newborn grows into a toddler, then into a young child, a teenager, a young adult, an adult and finally an elder. All phases of life carry their own complexity, beauty, happiness and struggle. You cannot and should not try to avoid it, you must live the stage of life you are in, with pride, with honor, with love and with an inner sense of duty. You cannot be a fully functioning adult and live a teenager life without sooner or later paying the price and facing the consequences of your choices. There are no shortcuts in Nature. At some point in the course of your life you will have to balance your accounts and get your blessings in right order ... living and leaving in peace require responsibility and wise decision making.

Thinking long term has worked for me, I always start with the end in mind (thanks to Stephen Covey for the concept) and work my way backwards. I never do it the other way around. When it comes to my life priorities whatever I do has been thought about, meditated and carefully considered. It is not that I do not engage in spontaneous behavior, that literal creativity spark that can break the routine of everyday life and put some spice into it but it is generally in a framework of well considered thoughtful choices. Long time ago, I used to look at Brisa, my little six-year old princess and out of the clear blue say "let's go play the Memory Game!" after seeing her sitting on the couch watching TV for a couple of hours.

It is a spontaneous spur of the moment built on the foundation that *playing with your kids is a great thing to do.* You have to define frameworks on which you can make spontaneous decisions that can surprise those you love (those of you married for over twenty years know what I mean) and break routinely held habits and behaviors. Repetition and predictability can become a double edged sword for those that like spontaneity and some degree of novelty. When I think long term I do not have any specific limitations of how long it could possibly be, a few years or the rest of my life makes no difference at all, time is irrelevant in the land of the meaningful, the magnificent and the supreme. I have absolutely no problem in devoting my life to causes that are worth living and dying for. When you embark yourself into something that you respect, something you want to honor and succeed at, you may want to offer a commitment as unconditional as possible for at the end, it is most likely a big part of what you came here to do. While we all have different ways of giving our truest intent to a cause worth it, there may be ways to express that commitment in similar and likeminded ways. This is mine and I would gladly share it with you in the hope that it will inspire to create your own (feel free to steal bits and pieces of mine if it helps) …

I will stay on my purpose filled path and never give up. I will give my very best each and every day of my life to either make it or die trying, and either way I am fine, for my job on Earth would have been well done and according to what my loving Creator expected from me.

I acknowledge that depending on personality styles, past experiences and the particular life stage the person may be transitioning, it may not be easy to make lifelong promises, especially without a strong sense of fulfillment supporting your feelings and pushing you forward. If you can't do it right at this moment, keep working on it, a time may come when you will have the desire and the conviction to do it. Many people cannot commit to lifelong causes if it is too premature for them in their journeys, lifelong pursuits require preparation and sometimes will only happen unnoticed, in the background of our lives and never reaching conscious levels of thinking.

*Just because you do not make a formal promise to spend your
life on something you deem worthy does not mean you are not
covertly working on it, self awareness is a rare gift to find and
something that helps but is not necessary to embark in purpose
filled missions. Lifelong commitments have to start in the bottom
of your heart, if you don't feel the burn yet, nurture the things
you believe on the most and the urge may come with time.*

Making lifelong promises (and keeping them) is not something that the masses do regularly; it is a privilege that only a few courageous hearts are able to exercise. It is a gift, a right, and a duty. Making a lifelong commitment will ask for the best and the greatest in you to be given to the Universe and to a cause greater than yourself, postponing immediate gratification, thinking more in the future than in the present, doing more for others than you do for yourself, being willing to give it all if required. Your life may become an act of grace and service, of love and care, of placing your life call first and your self second. You don't have to do it if everything inside tells this is not for you, if this is not the way you want to live your life. Whatever you do, always listen to your heart, it will keep you honest and point you where your true north always is.

If you indeed decide to embark on making a lifelong commitment to your purpose, I can promise you nothing but one thing, you will have a life full of joy, peace, and love in ways beyond anything you have ever imagined! There are no stretches of imagination that can come even close to describe the inner fulfillment and glow that a purpose minded life can bring about, it can't just be described, it has to be first-hand felt. Becoming one with Nature and honoring your mission was something meant to be, like the dog that becomes nothing but a dog and the oak that becomes nothing but an oak, seek to understand who you were meant to be and what you came here to do … then do everything at your reach to become and do that you were sent for.

I have also the moral obligation to tell you it is going to be as glorious as uneasy, you may live a life of constant stretch, effort, fulfillment and growth. You are defying the crowds and partnering with a minority, a very small part of the world that believes in the power of their hearts to guide them through the intricate and fulfilling paths of a purposeful life.

Many of these trails are paths nobody else walked before, they are future roads that presently exist only in your heart and while you can picture their whereabouts with uncanny conviction, they will still have to be made visible as you go and throughout the process of growing into the one you will one day be. May the wilderness of your life open up for paths to be made, paths that others will walk only after you have made them, proving the impossible possible.

There will be sunny days and long nights, tears of joy and tears of sadness, you will laugh and you will cry. You will have to face your fears and keep going, you will learn about yourself more than you ever imagined and most importantly, you will do what you deem inherently right, not because of the lack of fear or difficulty but in spite of them.

There is something else, a blessing of sorts, a serendipitous gift of your lifelong commitment to purpose. You will be at peace with yourself, a type of peace that is hard to find. The tranquility of a committed soul will ease most of the troubles that your fellow humans ignoring their life calls may eventually go through, a type of peacefulness that emanates from the sense of rightness that comes from doing what you came here to do. This gift is yours to keep, a blessing from above in appreciation for your gracefulness, for your commitment and dedication, for your love and compassion.

WHAT YOU HAVE TO DO IS WORTH LIVING AND DYING FOR!

If the most important things your life revolves around do not seem to resemble a glowing magnificence along with the imperative and undeniable feeling that you would live and die for them, look for your path somewhere else, you are not headed in the right direction. Do not accept mediocrity as the companion of your life quest for meaning!

We all, without exception, came here with a noble mission to accomplish. How noble? ... noble enough not to doubt about its meaningfulness and radiance. The mere thought of it should give you goose bumps and make you feel honored and privileged to the point of flooding your heart with feelings of worthiness and significance. We did not come here to waste a lifetime by filling it with matters of least importance, things that can be ignored, forgotten or simply benefit nobody else but us. We all came here with a purpose greater than ourselves, something the Universe needs us to do, a life path that would make our parents, our children, our loved ones and our Creator proud of. I cannot tell you what it is for you, nobody can, only you can figure it out, only you can know what it is and it will be up to you to decide what you do with it once you know.

Humans are the only living creatures empowered with the gift of choice. We need choice to do what we came here to do and there lies the challenge, choice was given to us for a reason and to be used wisely, not to be used for reasons it was not planned for. Decision making is not the ability to operate at free will but a mean to an end, a way to choose the twists and turns that will take us where we must go, sometimes creating the paths if they are not there to begin with (for a path to be followed, somebody had to walk it for the first time, making it on the go). We were all made different and expected to make different determinations. Any other living creature you can think of, a plant, an animal, they all share an incredible amount of common traits and similarities particular to their species, except the gift of choice. While humans also have common denominators and similar needs, such commonality occurs more at the basic and primitive need gratification level (see Maslow's needs pyramid).

Once you start to get higher and higher in the individual uniqueness ladder and enter the realm of self-actualization, the desires, motivations and drives for action come from places of unquestionable significance and the individual differences start to be more evident. It is at this juncture when human kind differentiation prevails over human kind similarity.

Every person is meant to be somebody and not somebody else, to do something and not something else. It is different with any other living creature, dogs are thought to be dogs and nothing but dogs and so do oaks or dolphins. Nothing special or unique is expected from them other than to conform to the dynamics and genetics of their species, to be what they were born to be. It is different with humans, we did not just come to be plain and simple beings, we are all special and unique in our own ways, with a path of our own, a mysterious yet mesmerizing way to be the one we came here to be.

Not even for a moment you dare to think that the Universe could be the same should you choose not to be and not to do what you were meant to be and to do. The Universe needs you to be who you came here to be and do what you came here to do!

Those of you that have been found by that something you are supposed to do, that unique and special assignment carrying your name on it, know exactly what this mysterious yet fascinating disclosure is all about. As for those that are still in the quest, keep trying, your heart knows exactly what you must do and who you must become, you may not be ready yet for that meaningful inner conversation that one day will take place. It is important to realize though that just because you have not been officially notified does not mean you are not working on it or you are not getting closer to it. As a matter of fact, you may very well be involved on those matters with undue diligence, love and passion, even when consciously unaware of them.

> *If you have a will, a genuine, true, and unconditional desire*
> *to do everything you possibly can to fulfill your purpose in life,*
> *you are getting there, every day a step closer, whether you know*
> *what it is or not (you always know at a deeper, more holistic and*
> *unconscious level). Self-awareness is not a requirement for you to be*
> *who you are meant to be and do what you are expected to do.*

Viktor Frankl called this process *the search for meaning* and built his logo-therapy constructs around the notion that all humans come to Earth with a reason for existence, something that stands as the meaning of life, a source of energy that will fill us with joy and represent the very reason why we are here for. I must state again, at the price of repetition, that choice is not to be exercised to decide whether to follow our life path or not but *to discern how to best follow it!* There are some aspects of our life for which we should see only one choice, duty and love to the task (or its ultimate aim) should drive us to action, with as much passion, energy, enthusiasm and commitment we can pull from within.

> *Powers come with responsibility and we were all given special and*
> *unique talents. We are all expected to use them wisely and for the*
> *reason they were given to us, not ignoring, neglecting, or abusing*
> *them. Our paths in life are not filled with optional assignments given*
> *to us to be discretionally exercised if the circumstances favor doing*
> *them. Our purpose, whatever it is, whether we consciously know it or*
> *not, must be fulfilled and pursued with every bit of stamina we have,*
> *from the day we are born until the day we die … unconditionally.*

> *There's a difference between interest and commitment. When*
> *you're interested in doing something, you do it only when*
> *circumstances permit. When you're committed to something,*
> *you accept no excuses, only results – Art Turock*

149

When it comes to the business of our own life, we cannot accept being interested, we must be committed! Commitment also requires revisiting our priorities to make sure they are properly aligned with our purpose. Let's not make the mistake of thinking that just because we are engaged with an endeavor, it is the right thing to do. Throughout the course of our life we will find countless opportunities where we are indeed doing what we should be doing and it is in those circumstances when we need to continue doing it, refining and enhancing what we do in every conceivable way. Conversely, there will be a good number of times when we will feel deep inside that we are not in the right path, not necessarily because it leads to terrible outcomes but perhaps because it is far from optimal, not aligned with our life call, or something that just does not feel right for us in that phase of our life we happen to be in. This is even so if we are good (or great) at whatever it is we are doing! Be aware that the world may insist on us doing it, for it may benefit others beyond our own motives and deviate us from the path we are meant to follow. Just because we are good or great at something does not mean we have to become a prisoner of that talent or skill. Learn to know the difference between what will help your purpose and what will not.

So ... what we should do if we are not in the right path? Seek to change it! What you have to do in life is meaningful, supreme, worth living and dying for and you must constantly look for it until you find it (actually, it will find you). How will you know you were found? ... trust me, when it happens, you will know! If what you are doing, if the most important aspects of your life do not seem to resemble such magnificence you must look for your path somewhere else, your life was thought to be blissfully lived, do not waste it!

Arriving at the conclusion that you must seek and initiate change is a paramount moment in the unfolding of your life and one that would mark a before and an after. Take it seriously and give yourself time to think about what you must do. Whatever it is, it will have to be carefully handcrafted, planned with enough details, and thoroughly thought about, especially if you are about to embark into a new phase of your life that may potentially impact other human beings. These are the bold decision making moments, the forks on the road that will make your purpose worth living and dying for, lovingly and gently demanding everything you have to give and more.

You will be asked to stretch yourself beyond reach (not once but multiple times), go to places and experience things you have never gone and experienced before; you will be entering a stage in your life journey when facing the unknown will be the norm and not the exception and you must start to mentally prepare yourself for those encounters.

Prominent life changes may take years to realize requiring a countless number preparation hours and mastership building. When you make a conscious decision to shift the course of your life in a different and meaningful direction, almost nothing will look that different the day after, or the month after, it may take several months or even years for you to realize what the new Life and the new You will look like. It is only after walking the new path for some time that you will be able to see the difference between where you are going now versus where you were going before, the literal fork in the road will not present itself as so life changing in the first few miles of traveling, you have to get further out into the new to see the contrast with the old.

Making changes in your life requires courage, the same courage required not to make a change mandated by the outside world when every cell in your body is telling "stay, hold" and in so doing dare to defy conventional wisdom dictates and expectations. In the midst of confusion, always trust your heart, deep inside you know when to change and when not to, do not disobey the voice within, do not betray who you were meant to be! Knowing what to do or not to do requires no courage other than the one to ask and listen, full of love and duty. The real test to your endurance comes after you have listened, when you have to prove your commitment to your own self by doing what you must do, regardless of anything and everything else. It is in the *doing-according-to-your-beliefs* that you will show the Universe you are serious about becoming yourself. If you are privileged to utterly know what you should do with your life, in a sense visualizing the *who* you must become, do not commit the crime of ignoring, neglecting or defying it. You are among the few and not among the many ... and it is so for a reason.

Such a vast amount of self-awareness is only treasured in the hands and the hearts of those that can handle it, excitingly ready to purposely and consciously pursue worthy and noble ends. The gift of insight has not been given to you by accident, you know because the Universe wants you to know, you have been trusted with the vision of what is expected from you!

There is no need to rush, to take uncalculated risks, or to venture into complex undertakings without enough preparation or practice, take the time you need, get ready, master the requirements to excel and whenever the time to flip the switch comes, do it with confidence, accepting that what happens is exactly what was supposed to happen. You can succeed or not, and if you fall, you will get back up, learn something you did not know and get ready to try again. Don't ask the Universe to push you, ask it to stop you and give you some guidance in the case you may have misunderstood your mission, are going too fast or simply got your priorities mixed up.

Life is not a matter of getting the most you can out of it but rather a long term expedition of doing for others more than you do for. yourself, whatever the purpose you were entrusted with.

If the current stage of your life is one that pushes you more *for taking* than *for giving*, you have a great opportunity to change and start using the gift of choice rightfully and for the reason it was given to you, to be used wisely. One of the best ways to get yourself started in the "*for giving*" side of life is by *for-giving* your self-centeredness and begin to think more about others and what you can do for them. Life is too short and too precious to miss the very reason why we are here.

We were all born ignorant and have to find our way out through the maze of discovering who we are meant to be, nobody was born

*consciously knowing it all, it is fine not to know as long as you start
asking the right questions when the itch of wonder comes to visit you.*

Always remember that the powers we were given (these are the attributes, aspects of your personality, skills, talents, etc where you score above average), were given to us to be used responsibly and altruistically. Nothing in the Universe happens randomly, less so those things we never asked for or went after. When something outstanding comes to you or finds you, it was planned to happen exactly in the way it happened, meaningful encounters are not just random accidents of life, like paths crossing each other out of sheer chance (nothing of magnificence is random but synchronistic). We are all part of a master plan and we are all needed to make it work, like if we were miniature gears of a gigantic mechanical clock, every piece has a reason for existence and is necessary for the whole to operate flawlessly. Do not underestimate your contribution, the Universe needs you!

CHAPTER TWO

Finding True North

CREATING A DIFFERENT FUTURE ...

*The future belongs to those that believe in the
beauty of their dreams – Eleanor Roosevelt*

Being in the second half of my life and in an effort to look in hindsight, all I see is a path full of beautiful circumstances kindly and lovingly escorted by struggle, difficulty and challenging crossroads. Why, What and How questions were my lifelong travel mates gently and caringly forcing me to push the envelope, to raise the standards, to fight the status quo, to test the apparent false assumptions and in a sense go against many of the traditional conventions and the so called realistic expectations of what life can be in the realms of the world-defined *possible.*

*The ultimate measure of a man is not where he stands in
moments of comfort and convenience, but where he stands at
times of challenge and controversy – Martin Luther King, Jr.*

For reasons I cannot easily explain, I was irresistibly attracted to defy the odds of conformity and confront the predictable, daring to imagine what would it be like if what seems to be would just not be, in other words, what if *what it is* would be nothing but one of many possibilities and ultimately nothing but a choice I could pick if I wanted or not pick if I didn't want. Even without consciously noticing it, my curious nature was taking prey of me and sky-rocketing me astray to a world that was not born yet.

I still remember as if it were yesterday, a day in the fall of 1986 when Lili and I went to see a realtor in Argentina looking for our first apartment. We were about to get married and had been saving as much as we could for 7 years, literally penny after penny lovingly treasured in a coffee can. We had close to $14,000 which at the time was not that much of a fund to pay for the apartment we wanted and the possibility of getting a mortgage was not that realistic either (there were no mortgages in Argentina at that time). Anyway, we went to this realtor's office who had a good reputation in the area and we told him what we were looking for. We knew exactly what it was, not only that, we also knew where we wanted it which was not necessarily the most affordable place in town. Our wish list included a brand new one bedroom apartment facing East so we would not have the afternoon sunshine on us (A/C was not common in Argentina those days), not in the last floor to avoid the heat from the building roof, and with opposite windows so we could get a nice breeze circulating during the day. The city we wanted our apartment to be located was called Victoria (which later in life I realized the symbolism of the word, Victoria means Victory in English), a bit upscale town compared to where both of us were born, raised and still lived at the time of getting married.

I still remember the face of the realtor when we listed everything we wanted and then we said "our budget is limited to $14,000." We knew it was not nearly enough the moment we said it, and then came his look, like when your eyes say "you are kidding, right?," but he was professional enough to say "anything else you want?," to which we responded "no, that's all." Long story short, four months later and after multiple visits, negotiations, and apparent mute points, we found it and bought it for $14,500, accepting putting the tile floor ourselves as the building was being finished and the builder would not do this for us at an already bargain price, so we gladly accepted picking, paying for, and installing our tiles, everything else we were looking for was there, every single item on the list.

Carrying high standards require persistence and the ability to renew your energy, your commitment, and your hope, every time you face a dead end, and there will be not one but many! Always remember that there is nothing a brave heart cannot do if it is determined enough to envision and believe on it. All you have to do is keep trying, if nothing else, always one more time.

I can't say that my financial life was a failure but I can't say it was a complete success either. We started planning and saving for our retirement at the age of forty five and to keep up with our plan of record, which had to be very aggressive since we only had nearly half the time that everybody else in our age range had, we would have to live paycheck to paycheck, say *no* to our kids quite a few times and live a life we knew could be a bit better, should no financial concerns about our future were present in our minds. When you compare yourself with those contemporary to you that have made wise financial decisions and realize you are way behind them, you either accept it or do something to change it. We were not the type of humans that would accept things you could change, especially things worth fighting for …

I was never too crazy about material things and accepted this small life crusade as a gift in disguise, another challenge along the road, an endurance test, a sort of conventional impossible that has to be proved wrong. Take with honor and pride whatever life gives you because it is being given to you for a reason, a commendable and meaningful reason, an opportunity to make a difference in the world and do things for others. No matter what it is, you can always think of it as a vehicle to make this world a better place to live, leaving a momentous legacy to the generations to come. In my personal case, I do not want to become financially independent to stop working but to work more, to employ myself on the causes I have been asked to embark on. Financial independence is not for me, it is for them, it is just one of the means to fulfill the purpose I was given by my Creator.

Life's most persistent and urgent question is, 'What are you doing for others?' – Martin Luther King, Jr.

Every man must decide whether he will walk in the light of creative altruism or in the darkness of destructive selfishness. – Martin Luther King, Jr.

If you ask me about the future of those of us embarked in the quest of life meaning, I unreservedly believe it is about to change and direct our lives into a different path, another phase in our journeys where we will be able to help others more and make a greater difference to human kind. I deeply, sincerely believe it. Why I believe it so strongly? ... because this is what we were asked to do. At the end, it is not a plan we created, nothing of our own invention but something that was secretly implanted in our hearts and in our minds, a detour in the road of our lives to head ourselves in a rather different direction, a fork in the road with a strong sign stating *Go Right!* Whatever happened in the first half of our lives was also meant to happen, purposely created to teach us a few lessons, lessons we had to learn to know what we know, and to be who we are.

The future of our lives was designed to be different from the extrapolation of our past and such a fracture in the projection of what we have lived into what we are about to live, where the past-present-future triad is no longer linearly but synchronistically connected to the Universe Master Plan is the key to uncover a future of unseen possibilities, something that was always there just an inch beyond what our limited eyesight could see.

Free yourself from the ties that are chaining you to the "who" you used to be and the "things" you used to do. The future, your future, can be as different as you can imagine it to be, all you have to do is let your heart whisper in your ears to then believe it, with every cell in your body. Nothing is impossible unless you believe it is.

If your vision of the future is conditioned to a simple projection of the past (absent of any positive breakthroughs that would radically change your life and those of others), you are selling yourself short, too short! You are not a caterpillar anymore, you have turned out to be a butterfly (even if you have not noticed it), open your wings and fly, fly as high as your wings will take you, there is nothing to be afraid of, *except refrain from trying!* Paint the most beautiful dreams you can conceive, as dreams are nothing but possible world configurations that will only get materialized if the Universe wants them to occur. You alone may not be able to alter the course of history, but quite certainly fulfill your purpose and play your role on a change reaction that was already conceived but not yet realized. Whatever you can imagine is already contained in the Universe plan, a master piece you are a part of, like being a piece of a giant puzzle that one day will get finalized and will look complete even to the untrained eye.

Refrain from seeking for reassurances it can work, there are no safe bets or ways to ensure your efforts will take you where you plan to go. This is different; you will do what you have to do only because you must do it, out of its inherent rightness and meaningfulness. Whether it works or it doesn't, is not your job to decide, predict or anticipate. Do your part and let the Universe do his. Visions of the future are strong beliefs, not yet knowledge as there is nothing you can scientifically proof about events that are still yet to come (although they have already happened in a different time dimension), but you can feel them with the bravery of a bold heart while sensing with uncanny certainty that such a future world configuration is there, just waiting to be met.

Nobody can predict the future with complete sureness and most predictions are generally built out of projections of the past, a process perfectly crafted to create a gradual evolution of the status quo. If you want to be part of a future different from the past, as different and as beautiful as you can imagine it to be, you have to start with a belief, as strong a belief as you can possibly conceive and hold it true to your heart. It is the belief and what you will do to turn it into a reality what will spark the energy and empower you with the drive to make it happen. A fire, as big and charming as you can envision it to be will never start without a spark … your belief is that spark! If we fail to believe, we will never ignite the fire and it will never get started. Be defiant! If what you see is not the most beautiful dream you can paint, misbelieve it and paint something different, better, more enchanting, more mesmerizing, worth living and dying for.

What is life if not an opportunity to live and die for something noteworthy! If you can't find something worth dying for, then whatever else you found is not worth living for either! We are here to make a difference, don't dare to leave without giving your very best to crystallize it, whatever your life purpose was meant to be!

Some people believe that changing the courses of their lives is difficult, something that can lead to the unknown and carry unnecessary high risks with it. Nothing is difficult or easy, either you learn to do it or you don't, and if you have average abilities for such a field of knowledge then all that is left is your unconditional commitment to get educated and put tons of practice to build the necessary mastery and confidence to do it right.

Creasy: There is no such thing as tough. There is trained and untrained. Now which are you? (from the movie "Man on Fire")

I have seen this pattern enough times to convince myself it is the most common reason why people fail at reaching their goals, those that fail do not fail because what they were trying to do was too difficult or almost impossible but because they did not have the unconditional commitment and the burning desire to make it happen. Somewhere along the road they missed their belief on it and their conviction vanished, as when you stop caring about something you used to care about the most. They never promised themselves to *keep trying until they would either make it or die trying*, they rationalized how much effort they would put into it until they would see some results and if they would not get there when they expected to get there they would quit altogether arguing it can't be done. The truth of the matter is whether you think you can do it or you cannot, you are right! (credits of this concept to Henry ford)

Believing you can change your future and deviate from a life pattern that has been your travel mate for years is crucial and the first step to detour yourself into a different live venue. Without believing, you will not embark in the paramount adventure that changing life lanes may entail.

Changing the course of your life requires that you carry an extraordinary conviction that this is something you must absolutely do, which should emanate from a strong sense of purpose and the vision of a future better than the past, a future in which you are an active participant, a time still yet to come when you will help build something that will blow your most beautiful paradigms away! The strength and compelling nature of your life call will assist you in painting the vision of what it will be like and that supreme depiction will in turn become the drive behind the genuine commitment to live and die for what you came here to do.

The first few years are the hardest, your past memories are so real and the visions of the future so new that the tendency to believe in a future similar rather than different to the past is strong and you will have to fight it! Please do it, fight, with every bit of energy you have! Thank your past for everything it gave you, for you will not be here if the past train would have not given you a ride, a ride you should be grateful for. Now you need to get off the *past* train and stay at the *present* station waiting for the *future* train to arrive. Will it come? Will it be what you thought it to be? Will it take you where you want to go? The answers are only in one place, reach in, seek inside you, what do you hear? Close your eyes, listen to your heart, what does it say? Do you hear "go back, jump on the past train, it is safe, you know it well enough, this is a big mistake" or do you hear "hold, you must do this, have faith, be valiant, venture into the unknown"? I do not know what your heart says but I can tell you what mine *never* said, it never said "go back!" ... and it was not because I was always right and always jumping on a train that will take me straight where I wanted to go, at least half of the things I have done were *apparent* mistakes and things I was meant to learn from, God bless my mistakes, for without them I would have never learned as much as I did.

Jumping off the *past* train will not take you where you need to go *immediately* but *eventually*; this is a key thought to dwell on! Switching trains is not going to be a straight ride into wonderland, rather it will be a challenging road filled with both joy and struggle, a road absolutely worth walking and most importantly the road that was chosen for you, a road you must not refuse to take as it has your name on it … you must go through it. The deeper you get into the new path, the higher the exposure to your desired future … and along the road your past memories will blurry out giving birth to the clarity of that which is about to come.

Your brain needs to be rewired, retrained and it all starts in your heart, if you let your heart lead, your mind will follow. You need to let go off the past to make room for the future, you can't pour milk on a glass full of water and expect the glass to be full of pure milk overnight. You can pour milk and let the overflow eventually replace all the water by milk, making it a bit purer every day or just allow for some water to be taken out and some fresh milk to be poured in instead, your choice. Whatever you do, do not stop pouring milk, one way or the other, you will get there. *If you can't take any water out, just keep pouring milk on top of it, it will take more time and more milk but it will do the job!*

Once you get to what you would consider the middle of your life, you will have your symbolical glasses full of something, your past, especially if it has been consistently following certain patterns, will be imprinted in your mind but not necessarily in your heart. You may believe that you are your past and that your past makes you. *If this is the case, I am sorry to disappoint you, the past depicts who you were, not who you are and quite certainly not who you can be.* You have choice! You can choose to let your past run your life and linearly project itself into your future, repeating the same patterns over and over again for the other half of your existence. This is only one of the many choices you can make and it is paramount that you become consciously aware that it is you and nobody but you who makes that call.

Never refuse to accept what your past was, the glass is filled with something for a reason and be grateful for its content. It is now time to take a look at it and decide whether or not that content belongs to your future life or not, and depending on your assessment of the situation, you must act. It doesn't really matter whether you want to keep it intact, empty it a bit, empty it completely, or just pour something else on top of it letting the old to be gradually replaced by the new, what really counts is that you take the time and make the effort to engage in a deep soul searching exercise to choose, a genuine and laudable resolve about where your life should be led. From there on, it is just a matter of adjusting the sails, cruising the oceans and riding the tides!

WHAT WE WANT VERSUS WHAT WE LIKE ... A MATTER OF CHOICE

I am highly indebted to the great thinkers that in one way or another crossed the path of my life and enticed me into a series of provocative thinking patterns that ultimately helped me get closer and closer to who I was meant to become. One of them, for whom I keep my utmost respect and admiration is Carl Jung, it is as a result of gravitating around his abstract constructs of the unconscious and the fascinating phenomena of synchronicity that I was able to further articulate many of my simple reflections into higher levels of complexity to ultimately reach simplicity at the other side of complexity. Jung's elaborations related to the two most salient phases of life, morning and afternoon, led me to more clearly depict our morning-of-life need to *prove what we can do* and our afternoon-of-life need to *do what we want to and must do* (regardless if we can or we cannot) which facilitated the elaboration of more complex postulates about human behavior and the arrival at a better explanation of why some people do what they do.

It is by further solidifying the foundational premises of the life stages concept that we may also say that we take what we are given in the morning of life and fill our cups with it (we all come with empty glasses at birth and need to fill them with something). The fact that we do not yet know what we truly want (or must do) in the morning of our lives, makes us vulnerable to fill our cups with whatever seems tasteful at the time, not having had the opportunity to really do a good sampling of everything worthy out there and deciding more wisely on the key aspects our life. This is the reason why I believe that the optimal time to start assessing the cup content is at the middle of our life, when the time has come to see the glass filled with something, but not necessarily with that something we consider the best for us and for the purpose we must serve. Once we know, we do not have to prove too many more things, a circumstance that empowers us to better choose what we want to do with the time and the energy we have left. The time to prove what we could do is gone and it is now time to do what we must do, regardless if we prove anything or not (proving our abilities is no longer a need or a drive in the afternoon of life).

The road to a successful life requires us to know what it is that we must do, to know what we are here for, truly and deeply wanting what our purpose requires us to do. Only after learning to love what we came here to do we will be granted with a life of fulfillment and peacefulness for nothing else matters most than to help be what was meant to be.

For those that may wonder what type of freedom is this? What type of choice does it represent to want what our purpose wants? It is a choice like any other, you can choose it or you can choose otherwise, and in so doing ask yourself who has more freedom, the human being that does what he or she likes, or the one that knows what he likes, what he doesn't, and what is expected from him to then decide what he wants to do?

Doing what one likes is not always the ultimate expression of freedom but of blind-sightedness. If all you see is what you like, you are not choosing, you are just picking the only one thing you can see. Choice requires at least two options to pick from. You are as free to choose in direct proportion to the alternatives you think you have and the true knowledge of what you want.

Never let your likes and your self-centered needs drive your most sizeable life choices, we are not here to meet and satisfy our needs but to do good things for other people ... this is not about us it is about them! Let a cause greater than yourself find you and then learn to love it. This is why we are here for, everything else is a filler, a way to spend the rest of the time we are not engaged in what we came here for. Use your time and your energy wisely and focus on your life mission, whatever its form or shape happens to be.

Some doors will close and some windows will open, it is fine, accept it, it is the way your journey is supposed to be traveled. The most beautiful things that will happen to you are those you have never thought about, leave room for the unexpected, be vulnerable and enter the unknown, let yourself be found!

If you give your life to a cause in which you believe, and if it is right and just, and if your life comes to an end as a result of this, then your life could not have been spent in a more redemptive way. I think that is what my husband has done. — Coretta Scott King

A GREAT WINE IS STILL GREAT EVEN IF SERVED IN A PLASTIC CUP ...

For many years I refused to drink water from a plastic cup as I could sense the difference in the flavor, the plastic taste would invade my mouth and cloud my perception of the pure, flavorless water taste. One day, even without noticing it, I realized that a good wine is still a good wine even if poured into a plastic cup. It may not taste the same, but it would be still as good as if it were served in the most expensive crystal glass. The wine does not leave its beauty and greatness behind because the environmental conditions do not favor, overcast or shadow its good taste. Be able to recognize and appreciate *greatness* when the conditions around would fool the untrained eye and cloud the tasting that greatness would offer if external factors would favor it. See the beauty in the imperfect combination of a great wine and a plastic cup as if by means of an imaginary flavor cancelling mechanism, you could suppress the plastic taste of every sip you take.

The brightness of the magnificent cannot be obscured
by the muddiness of the mundane, not if one can see
through the misfortunate and perplexing disguise.

If your essentials are at peak, you are drinking the best wines, don't ruin it by focusing on the cup! The container does not make the contained! You are who you are whether or not the world can see it, taste it, recognize it, honor it, or celebrate it! Your greatness will be many times missed, more so than appreciated. Just accept it as part of the price to be paid to follow your inner path, a path only a few will get to fully know. You need no recognition, praise or approval for what you came here to do, all you need is the opportunity to give your very best to fulfill your purpose!

Be honest to yourself, the wine will not taste the same in a crystal compared to a plastic cup, admit it, it is a fair and responsible action to accept the truth. But the taste does not make the wine, the wine makes the taste, recognize it is a great wine in a plastic cup and imagine, even if only for a split of a second, how great it would taste if poured in a crystal glass instead. Such a hypothetical construct requires creative imagination and the courage to loudly and clearly say, *I do not trust the way this wine tastes, this wine is better, much better than what my mouth tells, I can feel it, I have seen and tasted it before.* Nothing can stop a fearless heart, there are no barriers for those willing and able to break any stretch of imagination. Be daring, be brave!

The passage of time teaches us a few lessons, some to remember, some to forget, but lessons still. I always carried a high set of standards, the highest I could find. I wanted the best not only on the wine but also on the cup side of things. I used to reason that great wines taste best in *glass* cups and if I could not have the best, I would rather not have it at all. My world was a filled with black-and-white choices to make, dilemmas that would not distract those more open and flexible in nature, but big enough of a deal to me. I wanted the best and nothing but the best.

Overtime, you learn to recognize the difference between ideal and real, deep and superfluous, essential and unimportant. I still like (and prefer) great wines in glass cups but I know the wine is as great if all I have to pour it into is a plastic cup, and being that the case, I'll drink it anyway and deliberately ignore the cup, its plastic flavor and with my eyes closed, rescue the greatness of the wine from the ordinariness of the plastic cup. Other times all you can get is just good (not great) wine and you will also take it, plastic or glass cups alike. You always pursue your dreams and go for the best of wines but take what the Universe is giving you at the time. At the end, who are you to say when it is time for great, good, or ordinary wines ... or cups? Accept your place in your Creator's master plan and the role you have been given, become one with the task, learn to love what you have to do until the point when what you do is what you love. It is at that moment when you have become one with yourself, your true self.

Learn to recognize the difference between the bright, the shiny, the precious and the dull, the ordinary, the common. Great things are still great even if surrounded by mediocrity. Don't focus your attention on the minuscule, the optional, the nice to have, concentrate on what matters the most to the reason why you are here! This is the key to your long term success, to living a life full of joy and peace.

Drinking great wines in stylish glasses is neither an everyday occurrence nor something that everyone can aspire to, at least not all the time! If you condition your happiness to those rare gems that appear every so many years, you will miss the many almost-perfect opportunities when you have most everything you need.

The disciple asked the ancient master ... "Master, what is happiness?" The Master looked at him in the eyes and responded with the calmness that a treasured life can give ... "The grandfather dies, the father dies, the son dies." Baffled by the unexpected response, the disciple asked the Master a second question if nothing else to resolve the dilemma posed by the first answer ... "but Master, how can you define happiness in terms of death?" The Master smiled, as if expecting such a reaction out of the awe engendered in his young disciple, and after a brief pause, he looked at the young man in the eyes and with utmost care and love responded ... "my dearest, can you imagine the pain it would cause if the son dies first, then the father and then the grandfather?"

Happiness lies in preserving what is essential to us, the few things without which life would be very difficult if not impossible to bear. Don't complicate something simple in nature, happiness is always at a hand reach, all you must to do is see it, then grab it and finally never forget you already have it!

If your eyes don't let you see well enough, look through your heart! You must find out what your essentials are, what is it you can't live without! Make a promise to yourself to never again worry as long as your essentials are preserved. You have permission to work on your non-essential problems, find what's wrong and try to fix it. Hopefully you will be able to do it, and if you don't, try again, and again, in the meantime you have everything you need to be happy! There is only a handful of things you really need and thousands you don't, why focus your attention on the latter and not on the former? Why reverse the priorities and miss the essential parts of your life by being busy with what matters the least?

I contemplate the number of things I don't need to be happy – Aristotle

Nice-to-have things are only trivially important and even when they may seem to slightly contribute to your happiness, they are sometimes worth pursuing. The key is to always recognize their true nature, they are things you can perfectly live without! As to how hard you will pursue them, it all depends on how related they are to what you believe your mission in life to be. Are they important to someone you love? Do you find them intrinsically right even when they may be non-essential to you and your priorities? Do you feel a burning, inner desire to go after them, to get them accomplished? Do you see your life as more complete if you leave this world having done them? If any of these questions has a true answer or if your heart tells you to go after them, work hard and stay at them, for the rest of your life if necessary! But do not fail to recognize their nature, they belong to the non-essential part of your life.

It took me almost fifty years of living and more than twenty years of soul searching to resolve the dilemma of how to be perfectly happy without some things you regard important (but optional) and at the same time work hard at them, never giving up, never leaving your dreams behind, un-chased, forgotten. During all these years, a part of me connected with the least developed side of the mind, the conscious self, was operating under the belief that *being perfectly happy without some things* and *working hard for them* were mutually exclusive states, as when one has to literally choose between the one or the other. In my former vision of the world, the lack of perfect happiness was the drive to work hard, to get the missing part in order to achieve complete happiness. The passage of time teaches us things that we cannot anticipate by projecting the past into the future, we have to experience life in its different forms to grow into higher levels of complexity, where apparent opposites find a way to meet and reunite. I have learned that unhappiness is neither the beginning nor the end of anything positive, especially when the source of unhappiness is emanating from unimportant sides of your life. Both happiness and unhappiness are not absolutes but relative and temporary states where we find peace and love in the circumstances we happen to live. As far as being perfectly happy, it is no longer one of my desires, there is beauty in imperfection and we are surrounded by it.

In my former and somewhat limited view of the world, perhaps fueled by past experiences, happiness depended on the things you work hard for and their accomplishment was the key to a happy life as they were married assumptions and I could not conceive the one without the other. Evolving into the afternoon of my life facilitated a paradigm shift and I can now conceive a reasonably happy life while I still work hard for things that are optional in nature, missing colors that can complete and embellish the canvas of my quest for meaning without making it less perfect if they don't happen to be. Pursuing dreams is part of the game and a fundamental component of the feelings of happiness. What would life be without breathtaking visions of a future yet to come, without the incessantly chasing of extraordinary causes that may turn into nothing but a fascinating progression of an unfinished business, something that we started for somebody else to continue after our time has passed by. The key to a life lived with honor lies not in the destination but in every stop along the way, when one has the chance to say to oneself ... *well done, I may or may not have accomplished what I was looking for but it was certainly worth the try, and certainly the very best I could have done!*

Once you detach joy and peacefulness from the results of your hard work and accept the eventuality that all the dreams and visions you have treasured over the years may get never fully realized but only get closer and closer to what you envisioned, life becomes incredibly engaging, exciting and fulfilling. Give everything and expect nothing ... this is the principle by which we were created. True love is unconditional.

You will still work as hard, pursue the same dreams and preserve the same visions, but you will no longer condition your fulfillment to it, you know that if you give your very best for something meant to be, chances are it will be, and it is not up to you to decide.

If you are one with the Universe you are not alone, you do your part and the Universe will do his. Free yourself to be happy by only chasing your dreams and giving your very best each and every day of your life without conditioning your peace of mind to what your hard work will bring. At the end, it will bring whatever it is to be brought and at the time it must be brought. Rain does not come when it is expected or most needed but when Nature decides it is time for rainfall. Your dreams may never fully realize, at least in the form you may have visualized them and it is fine, you will still chase them until your very last breath, until there is no time left. If this is the way the Universe wants it, so be it.

Only when you are happy and at peace deep inside, you can bring the very best in you and put it to the service of a cause greater than yourself, a pursuit for the betterment of human kind. Don't sell yourself short! You came here to do great things, to help transform the world, one day at a time, one soul at a time. This impression is counter intuitive and most everything you will hear in the outer world may seem to contradict the premises that each person has a magnificent plan crafted to perfection even before being born. The world will try to treat the masses as nothing but a conglomerate of people running from one thing to another and creating the fabric of everyday life, routines, compliance with accepted societal standards, refusal to defy the status quo ... a symbolical death on two legs. Vehemently refuse to believe in the nonsense of the traditional worry-to-then-be-happy dialog, worrying will make no good to you or your dreams ... choose not to worry but to do what you came here to do. It is by achieving inner peace and giving your very best to the causes you respect that you will climb the mount of your life in a way that you will never regret.

Public opinion will repeat the same message over and over again, until you hear it in you sleep, if something is difficult enough to challenge you in ways of magnificent proportions, it will have the highest chance of getting done only if you regard it as something you can't live without. I have to respectfully disagree. They are not the only ones. It is true that if something you can't live without is missing in your life, say one of your essentials, you will endlessly fight for it, it's a survival reaction. Things you can't live without will almost always get priority attention and get the best of you until they are safeguarded. But this is only the beginning, not the end!

Your dreams, your mission, and your most altruistic inspirations come on top of it, they are above life basic needs, beyond the realm of your essentials. We are entering now into what Abraham Maslow called the world of *Self-Actualization*, when the person can get past the basic need gratification process and climb into higher levels of abstraction, wishes, and aspirations, aimed at being part of *greater-than-the-self* causes, far and away from the narcissistic phases of our earlier life stages.

The self, as we used to know it in our more primitive phases of human life, deeply concerned with survival, affection, and recognition, has evolved into a rather different type of being who is now involved into something higher than fulfilling basic needs.

The quest for a greater contribution to the world has begun. Maslow was not the only scholar that researched into the phenomena gravitating around intrinsically motivated individuals chasing higher order aims and reaching peak performance levels (this is how Maslow referred to those moments when the individual is at his/her best), other renowned researchers like Mihalyi Csiksentmihalyi studied the dynamics of what he coined *flow* states, when the individual was so immersed and engaged with the task that there was a natural meshing of mind-activity to the point of losing track of time and disconnecting from the outer world. Likewise, Deci and Ryan focused on the drivers and characteristics of intrinsic motivation and the environmental factors that make that phenomena possible. Together they have directed their fields of research to the same true north, namely, humans that have found it charming, invigorating, intriguing, or just incredibly tantalizing to engage in non-conventional thinking patterns that propelled them to make gigantic jumps forward in the commitment to the purpose or the task with the subsequent pursuit of goals and contributions to mysteriously satisfy a need far greater than themselves.

It is after you have your priorities in order and your essentials under control that you can lift your-self to the next level in the Maslow pyramid and work on lifelong causes that will complete you and ultimately give true meaning to your life beyond the essentials you treasure the most.

Self-Actualized individuals have their loyalties transferred to *higher-than-themselves* aims where the concern for their personal needs is completely secondary and regarded to something that will have to take care of itself requesting no attention from their part. In a sense, they have evolved from a stage of *self-centeredness* to a stage of *others-centeredness* in which the call towards the doing for others is greater than the call towards the doing for themselves.

The term *others* in this statement represents a metaphorical non-self abstraction and can symbolize many different elaborations for the self-actualized individual. The common denominator to all of them is the focus of their attention and the center of their pursuits, namely their missions, on something greater than themselves. Self-actualized individuals have evolved into beings that can no longer live in a world where basic needs gratification is both the beginning and the end of everything they do. Their questions alone are much more complex and earth shattering than what a simple self-centered answer can provide which enlightens themselves to conform a legion that is working on a paramount and altruistic change to the status quo, on the betterment of the world as they see it and on the transformation of human kind into their maximum conceivable state of being and becoming.

Their imaginations do not have conventional limits, they can go higher and higher, stretching their horizons into unseen levels of contribution and heritage to their future generations. They do not believe in impossibilities, all they know about is difficulty and persistence. Life becomes a metaphorical game where there is no losing, eventually one may need just a little more time to win.

A LIFE ACCORDING TO YOUR PRINCIPLES

Committing to live your life according to your principles is an honorable act and something that will lift your spirit above and beyond the dictates of conventional societal norms, embodying a mysterious transgression into the unknowingness of your existence, the very sacred place you always belonged and were never meant to leave.

Staying true to your principles, regardless of the circumstances (rewards or punishments alike) is an extra-ordinary way of conducting your lifelong affairs. Such a commitment will test every one of your weak spots as such a choice will be neither easy nor the best way to reap the benefits of what the environmental rules of engagement can provide. You simply cannot adore two Gods ... refusal to comply with massive behavioral patterns to ultimately fulfill one's own life call has a price ... and it is worth to be paid! When you commit your life to your principles, your values and your priorities, you are marrying them for life! You are saying *yes* to what matters most to you and *no* to everything else, unless they happen to coincide, to overlap or to align.

This dilemma will hunt you over and over again, pressing on your weak spots, testing your endurance, ensuring you will be loyal to your deepest sense of self and that you will be bold enough to act in a determined manner when and if the world decides to think otherwise.

The outside environment will unquestionably ask you to do what is good for it, for its plans, outcomes and benefits. It is of supreme importance that you recognize that if you are expected, asked or requested to do something, it is not necessarily because such an action is best suited for your purpose over the long run, perhaps not even in the short term, such a petition most always responds to somebody else's need to benefit from you doing what was expected (except those that truly love you, those that always think about you first and about them last).

When the world expects you to act in certain ways is not necessarily coming from a desire to take advantage of you (although some people may try to do it) but for the most part because the world does not know, and sometimes does not care, why you are here for, this is something only you and the Universe know! It is not a matter of if but a matter of when these dynamics will present themselves to you. Be prepared to respond wisely. It is at those times when your determination to honor your decisions and your commitment to what matters most to you has to be shown. Your convictions will be tested not once but multiple times and you must be prepared for when that moment comes!

When you follow your inner voice and act according to your principles you are at risk of disappointing others, a price we must pay and a life contingency that cannot be avoided. You may also get sub-optimal results (as defined by the environment) in response to your apparent rebellious or insubordinate behavior and the world may decide to punish your disobedience, your ignorance, neglect or denial to comply with what you have been asked to do or expected to conform.

You are refusing to follow the crowd and it represents a charge worth being guilty of. Hold! It is always your choice and not theirs, either you stick to your principles and honor your life or take the easy way out, go with the flow, forget who you are, and even worse, become somebody else other than who you were meant to be!

A life based on principles requires strength beyond the conventional, the traditional and the ordinary, it calls for men and women willing to lose it all if required and to never give up or give in. Your moral foundations will have to be as solid as your inner conviction since it is on top of your core that the rest of the Universe will build dreams of magnificent proportions, your dreams! Without a rock solid ethical and moral base, nothing can be sustained, preserved and treasured. The void created by hollow morals will sooner or later lead to weakness, self-righteousness, carelessness and a myriad of soul diseases that will take over the altruistic commands coming from above resulting in a life that, more often than not, will succumb to short-lived dreamful expectations. Your ideals, as you defined them, will become compromised.

Be truthful and loyal to yourself first, then to the world and only as long as you do not violate any of your values, principles, lifelong determinations and priorities. If you don't have them, then find them, they are inside you, maybe deeper than you have ever gone, but there for sure! Nobody comes to the world expected to do great things without the necessary foundations to weather the storms that will come, because they will come. You have been provided with everything you need to fulfill your purpose, either in the form of talents or in the form of potential (which means the ability to acquire the required knowledge and skills). You have what it takes to succeed, to triumph and to honor the Universe with a creation of your own representing your humble contribution to the embellishment of the world. This is the way you will pay tribute to the great men and women of all times, those that gave their lives for the betterment of humanity, for the chasing of their selfless dreams, slaying dragons and venturing into the unknown with the only hope that they will find what they were looking for, regardless of how big of a price they will be asked to pay. You will also honor your ancestors, your loved ones and your future generations, even if they never see or know about you.

Life according to principles is a silent ordeal wittingly accepted, nurtured, cared for and pursued. If you wonder how big of a price will you eventually have to pay, the answer is *big* and *worthy* enough. This is not for the weak and the feeble in character and neither for the light weighted in spirit. This is a lifelong project that will lift your soul to heights you have never thought about, there is no stretch of imagination that can describe the inner peace and fulfillment that living a life according to principles can bring you.

When you do everything your heart tells you to do, sticking to it whether it works or it doesn't, not one day, not one year, not even ten years, but your entire life, you can't find any other reward, any other joy or any other realization that can charm your heart more softly, more tenderly and more lovingly. You will have to be brave since a pursuit like this will test every bone in your skeleton, every cell in your body, every thought in your mind and every feeling in your heart!

You are intentionally choosing to deviate from the conventionality of things, to disjoin the crowd, to run away from the traditional way of doing things to favor your own, whatever form, shape, or color your inner self is dictating. Such a departure from life-as-usual is done with the intent of blending, of meshing and of merging with a Universal Higher Order of things.

You will respect others and their opinions, but only after respecting you and yours, and if in conflict, you will always err to your side. This is not being selfish, self-centered or insensitive to those others around you, to the contrary, in order to help the world, you have to first honor your-self, your values and your mission. Then, and only then, you can take care of the outside world, when everything inside you is in order, at peace and in the dynamic equilibrium that is reached when all the forces of your inner self are in balance.

You cannot listen to the chants of sirens and still head north, your compass must be uncompromised, free from magnetic interferences other than the true north you are after. An oak is an oak from the deepest root to the tallest branch, from the day it is first planted until the day it falls down, and so will you, except that you are expected to be better than the strongest oak, you have been given the ultimate human freedom: *choice.* You were meant to be *somebody*, and unlike the oak what can be nothing but an oak, you will only be the one you *choose to be*, from toes to head, from birth to death ... so choose wisely!

Like the oak that is expected to be an oak and not something else, you are also expected to be somebody and not somebody else!

Some people may wish to be an oak, so they do not have to deal with the burdensome and excruciating task of choosing wisely, carrying the uncanny and unavoidable responsibility of becoming who they were meant to be. Well ... never question Nature. You were given powers because Nature believes you can handle them. You have the ability to make a contribution way *higher* than the one of the oak, and to do that you need *choice*! ... and there lies the challenge, the dilemma and the call to action. We must accept it, we must take what the Universe has given us, because it was given to us for a reason. We could have been born an oak, but we were born a human instead ... why? Do you think the Universe made a mistake? Do you really think that they planted a human seed in your heart expecting you to be nothing but an oak? The Universe makes no mistakes, not of that magnitude. Accept what and who you are and make the best use of it to fulfill your purpose. Everything you have been given was given to you for a reason, no coincidences, no random occurrences but a carefully crafted master plan, a blue print of the future of our kind and you are a part of it, a big part! Choice is the unique attribute that makes human life so different than that of the rest of living organisms. It is the gift of self determination what turns life fascinating, fragile, intriguing and mysterious. Every coin has two sides and the flip side of choice is that humans are the only creatures on Earth that can decide *not* to be what they were meant to be!

Becoming the who you were meant to be is a function of your ability to choose wisely and courageously in the context you happen to be in. Regardless of the outer world wishes and expectations and the many perceived pressures you may feel exposed to, you can always pick your response. Mature self determination requires facing your fears and accepting the consequences of your actions ... for at the end, only wise choices made following the dictates of our heart will stand the test of time ... rightfulness in its purest forms!

Choice is the ultimate human freedom, the ability to choose your response in any set of circumstances – Viktor Frankl

Some people may say … "you don't understand, there is no choice but to do X." I respectfully disagree with that answer, and even if I would admit that in such set of circumstances, self determined action is so limited that you may be led to believe that you have no win scenarios available, being X the less harmful, who stops you from changing the current set of circumstances? Captain Kirk, from the old series of Star Wars used to say that he did not believe in such a thing as a *no-win* scenario, that there was always a way to redefine the problem and come up with at least one alternative that will let you win (perhaps a redefined version of *winning* that is acceptable to you). You can always choose!

> *If the environment is so restraining that you find yourself so limited, so constrained and so unable to steer your boat to the true north of your life, then change it! Change the environment, go somewhere else, find new horizons, start a new life, initiate the change required for choice to be available at its fullest expression, refuse to accept a no-win scenario for the rest of your life! There is always choice … if you want to see the forest, get away from the trees.*

When you start a new phase of your life, whether you initiated it or not (sometimes the Universe will initiate it for us), expect things to eventually get worse before they get better. Life is not always a bed of roses, especially not just because you have been exposed to serious hardship before. The symbolic night of your life can still be darker, colder and longer … but despite the length of the night, always remember that the darker, the colder, and the longer the night, the closer you are to a sunrise!

CHOICE THEORY ... A DILEMMA TO BE RESOLVED

Choice can be seen both as a blessing and as a curse, the two sides of the same coin, a coin expected not to be tossed but wisely used. It can take you to the summit of your life or to the deepest abysses you can ever imagined, it is all in your hands.

Is this a Nature's mistake, a flaw in the design of mankind? Has the Universe placed too much responsibility in our hands? Are we *able* to manage choosing wisely in the fabric of everyday life, both short and long term? Yes we are, the Universe does not make mistakes. Even if for every ten human beings that choose sub-optimally, there is one, only one brave soul that makes wise and selfless decisions, the world will still progress, advance and evolve. It is true that choice is mind boggling for some, especially for those that have some care for doing right and may not know exactly what to do or how to do it best. This is healthy, not knowing what or how to do and being aware of it is the first step towards living an honorable life. The second step is to have a desire, as strong as it can be, of doing the right things. Then you are set off to a good start (and to a better end), you may still don't have crystal clarity of what your next steps will be, but you are aware of it and have the desire to do right. You can't ask for a better context, you do not have to have all the answers before having some of the key questions, problem solving comes after problem definition. If you are there, in that stage of your life ... celebrate!

A problem well stated is a problem half-solved – Charles Kettering

Sometimes I wonder what life would be if humans were given no choice but to be what they were meant to be, like any other form of life. A dog is nothing but a dog, it does not get to choose to be otherwise, so does an oak, or a dolphin. Why? Why were we empowered with the gift of choice?

181

> *Because there are higher expectations placed on us as humans*
> *compared to any other form of life, and self determined action*
> *is one of the vehicles to materialize those expectations. We*
> *were given talents and potential that require the use of choice*
> *wisely and in the service of what we came here for.*

At the end, choice cannot be avoided, we choose even if we don't, not choosing is choosing not to choose, whether we are aware of this dynamic or not. The fact that we were given talents and potential that require choice for those talents to be purposefully used does not imply the existence of the desire to put those talents at the service of the cause they were created for, hence requiring the exercise of self determination. Choice is a double-edged sword in the sense that it was given to us to be used wisely but we can decide not to, and for as bewildering as it may sound, we can choose how to use the gift of choice, either committing to or altogether ignoring the purpose why self determination was given to us in the first place.

Imagine you are joining a construction crew that is building a house. The house is halfway done and you are given a hammer, some two by four pieces of lumber, a box of nails, and a floor plan. You are instructed to continue building the frame of the second floor. You have the tools, the instructions, the skills and the choice. You can do as instructed, better or worse than instructed, or something completely different. You can do nothing, or you can even start using the hammer to destroy what others have done before you. You have the *choice* to: do it right, do it wrong or do nothing. Most people will do what is expected from them, others will do what they believe to be the right thing regardless of what the outside world dictates, and a third group will do what pleases them the most at that very moment. Collectively, human kind has a tendency to handle choice wisely, in other words the number of people with the desire and the determination to do what seems right either outnumbers or outweighs the people with a desire to do what the environment expects them to do or what pleases them the most at the moment. I believe in the power of the Universe to influence the preservation of our species and the betterment of human kind, which is done in no other way than through wise choices aimed at driving rightful deeds.

Quite certainly, the world would not be what it is if humans were to be collectively deprived of the ability to choose. Would it be better? Would it be worse? This is probably a very questionable argument. My personal view, which I recognize is limited to the repertoire of my life experiences, indicates that we, human beings, are better off keeping the gift of self determination than giving it back, in spite of the risks of not using it wisely. But I have not had a loved one killed by a drunk driver, suffered from the atrocities lived in a concentration camp, or been deprived of basic needs by the selfish choices of other people. I have had the fortune of living a life that was not dramatically and negatively impacted by other people's poor choices and I must admit that, because of that reason, my assessment is not completely unbiased. Nevertheless, it is not my opinion what counts but what a statistically sound number of data points would suggest. What do you think would be the most predominant response if we were to ask a rather large and diverse population about the influence of choice in the future of human kind? Would such a poll lean towards keeping it, avoiding it, or some alternative answer not originally thought of? I believe the odds to get a more favorable score towards the retention of self determination would be more probable than not, and I would not discount the likelihood of getting recommendations to educate our future generations on how to choose wisely, including the consequences of poor choices. Ultimately, that should be the center of our attention when it comes to self determined behavioral patterns, how to ensure that choosing wisely will be more the norm than the exception. *At the end, this is what education is all about, to teach how to do right things right.*

Whatever it is, it is, and we are not in a position to change it overnight but over-time, only authority figures can limit, restrain, or remove some degree of freedom from those that have proven unable or unwilling to handle it in a way that is socially responsible and commendable. Law and law enforcement are meant to regulate the exercise of human choice if it happens to invade the right of others (thanks Mom for always teaching me that my rights end when the next person's rights begin).

Unless you are a law professional or a law enforcement agent, what else can you do to help? We can certainly help tilt the odds in the favor of wise choices made not only by us but also by all those we can help, assist, coach, teach, and support.

Below are a few steps, a sort of home-made recipe about how to help tilt the odds of *wise-choice-making* in a favorable direction:

(1) Start by acknowledging there is choice in your life, no matter the circumstances, you can always choose

(2) Choice is both a right and a duty, exercise it when it really matters and recognize that even if you do not choose you are choosing anyway (letting things take its own course without us doing anything is a form of response)

(3) Whatever determinations you make, always take responsibility for your decisions and actions

(4) Remember you were meant to be somebody, special, unique, with qualifications and talents that you, and nobody but you, have

(5) Never forget that power comes with responsibility. You were meant to be somebody for a reason; it was not an accident of life, a mistake in the Universe's master plan, a flaw in the design. Whatever you were given, empowered with, your symbolic personal toolbox is expected to be used for the betterment of the world! Don't let it dust on the side, ignored and unappreciated.

(6) Do your best to uncover and find out *who* you were meant to be. Accept that this task can be such a monumental part of the whole that may take almost a lifetime to get completed. Don't give up!

(7) While you seek to find the *who* you were meant to be, always follow your heart. Your heart is your most accurate compass and will always, without exception, point to the true north in your life. Use your heart as a travel partner, a guiding ally and a counselor

(8) Differentiate *right* from *wrong*, especially in the important aspects of your life, and always choose *right* versus *wrong*. If

you eventually fail to do it, learn from what happened and make a promise to try harder the next time. Sincerely apologize if you hurt somebody else, even if it was unintended.

(9) Do your very best each day, every day, especially in those causes evocative to you, to your mission and what your heart tells you to do

(10) Be patient, be persistent and never give up! Refer to the motto "when it comes to the essential things in my life, I will either make them happen or I will die trying. Either way is fine with me as long as I have given my very best." Make this your *win-scenario*

We also know that the world around us may not know or may not care about the individual purposes we carry with us, our duties and our missions. If indeed cares, it is because it happens to coincide or provide some rewards to the world's interests and not because of an act sympathy, solidarity, or collaboration. The world is a machine that has to produce results, regardless of the individual intents or desires of its components or parts. By the world I mean the external environment we are a part of, belong to or are affiliated with, results oriented organizations that in one way or another expect something in return of what they give to you (workplace, society, government, sport groups, etc). There are some forums that I will knowingly exclude from this logic in the sense that they often share some personal and common visions and not only respect but also honor and feed them encouraging us to pursue our life calls. One example is our immediate family, loved ones and dear friends, whose affection, care and respect for our purpose would be immeasurable. They may want nothing but the best for us and will have few or no other interests of their own in their relationship with us. Their kindness, respect and sympathy are the closest you can find to unconditional love. Family and true friends represent two of the most common nests for us to grow and evolve, but there are other forms of socially responsible and humanitarian organizations that favor the enhancement of our kind, where our efforts and contributions will mutually help the proliferation of principle based conversations and deeds.

Aside from that, you will belong to groups and organizations that will have goals and rules of their own, which in one way or another will be imposed on you, not because they mean to create difficulty in your life but because they have a reason for existence, a mind of their own and it is their intent to manage the dynamics in which they operate according to those rules of engagement. In all cases and without exception, you have the *choice* of accepting or not accepting those impositions (sometimes disguised in the shape of *suggestions*). Remember that you always choose ... even if you fail to do it, you are choosing not to express your desires, your interests, your rights and your duties. Whether actively making a choice or failing to do it, lack of action is a form of response. If inaction is going to be your response, so be it (it was mine several times) but make sure it is a *conscious* and *voluntary* response, not just the unwitting absence of determined decisions on your part, a void of the determined action that would have been taken if you would have seriously reflected on the situation.

> *Every human is born with the unavoidable right to discover who he is and what he wants, which overtime will have to align to who he was meant to be and do, with no compromises of any kind. Such a right cannot be taken away as it has been graciously given to us from above, and if anything, the least we can do is to turn that right into a duty, the most extraordinary and supreme duty of our lives.*

We are social beings and live in social settings, it is true that sometimes we have to be flexible and better adapt to the outside environment, especially those around us that we care about and care for us. I am not suggesting we ignore everything that happens in the world and become blinded by our purpose. We need to be sensitive, kind and compassionate, always respectful of our nature and our reason for existence, the true north of our life, those attributes and considerations should always come first since it is by honoring them that we will help the world the most.

If you have to temporarily deviate from your path for a valid reason, do it, but remember to get back on track as soon as you can. Take your time, do it right, but be back once you have taken care of what needed your attention the most to temporarily detour you from the path you were supposed to follow. Be also able to say *no* when the distraction is not worth it, not related to those you love, or the path of life you have been assigned. Stay focused! It is not possible to please everyone or do what everyone expects you to do. Some people will be disappointed, frustrated and would expect you to do more, less or otherwise. Accept it as the price required to follow your path, to pursue your destiny and to fulfill your mission. It is true that you will have to pay a price, high or small depends on the situation at hand and how important the loss is to you.

Let me offer an example, for some people limiting their career path at work, accepting they will not grow and progress, at least not in the current circumstances or with the speed other people are advancing (sometimes less talented, skillful, or hard-working than they are), is something associated to a high price. For others, it is a relatively small price for keeping themselves honest and truthful to their values. It is all relative to how important the loss is compared to what drives your actions and what produces the loss. Whatever it is that is driving you from within and acting as a foundation of your life must be respected and honored. There are some losses that are not only desirable but something you must initiate. Do not expect the outside world to know what is best for you and your life call, only you know.

Another example of a higher relevance is those you love (family, friends, etc). Many people would not be willing to sacrifice the relationships with those they love to pursue any personal goals, even if the pursuit is related to their missions. They will find ways to go around, above and under to preserve the ties with their loved ones while still working on their life calls, maybe in a different way or at a different pace.

Some things cannot be completely right if their doing is simultaneously creating contingencies that feel wrong, your inner sense of peace and rightfulness must always guide you. There is generally more than just one way to do what you have been entrusted to do and perhaps the perceived conflict of interests is signaling that you have chosen a less than optimal path. At the end, it is you and nobody but you who defines whether the price is high or low and whether you are willing to pay it or not. It is always a matter of choice.

Living a life according to principles will require you to choose your principles and your values over other things and it will require you to sometimes say *no* to the world when saying *yes* will interfere with your essence. You have to be ready to make that call. Mentally prepare yourself in advance and know what the price of your self-determined actions will be, accept it and do not hesitate to act when the moment comes. If you pursue your mission with unconditional commitment, such a juncture will come to you, not once but multiple times, the bigger your life call is, the more buttons you will push, and the more resistance you will get as the status quo of the world will forcefully resist any sort of change. Acting with courage and determination may not be easy for some people, and will certainly benefit from sustained practice. Get yourself started, you can not only learn it, you can master it!

The reason why there are crowds is because humans generally find it easy to do as others have done, to follow already tried patterns of behavior and to go through the most traveled roads. For reasons belonging to Universal wisdom, some people are asked to question crowd behavior and find ways to act according to what their true nature dictates, unflinchingly defying the laws of the masses. They don't have to do it on everything they do, there are aspects of their lives that are just not worth bothering about, they somehow got a sense of which are the areas they will just go with the flow. Wining negligible battles will change nothing of significance. But when it comes to the essentials of their lives, their priorities and their values, they deliberately ignore the voice of the crowd letting it go wherever it wants to go, but without them at its side. They reasonably know where they need to go, and they will go there, with no regard, concern, or preoccupation for what the rest of the world is doing. The world may try to show them in a thousand different ways that what they are doing is wrong, that they must go with the flow and follow the crowd, however they are the ones that get to choose and while they know it is going to be painful at times, that does not change the definition of a wise choice, actually, it reinforces it. Breaking loose and going against the wind has never been easy and you must pick your battles, sometimes accepting temporary compromises to then be able to do what you need to do, to stay in the game and win in the long run. Be wise, be persistent, be patient and see the big picture.

For every ounce of pain I suffered by sticking to my principles and values, I collected pounds of joy, fulfillment and realization. Nothing of significance happens overnight and you must be willing to wait, to keep going in the face of adversity and undesirable circumstances. The pain and the joy sometimes do not come together, you need to be able to trade immediate gratification for future fulfillment, stay put, learn to trust the Universe and do right no matter what. Forget about weighting your effort and your dedication, you do not want to condition your commitment to purpose based on results.

Right things are not done because they work, they are done because they are right. Your mind will think in terms of results, your heart in terms of right/wrong. When it comes to the essential things in your life, listen only to your heart!

Celebrate the small blessings of your life, a child smile after you have made a child-size dream come true will fill your heart with joy and empower you to slay a hundred dragons of compliance and conformity! A tear of joy after contemplating an act of kindness will warm your body to weather two hundred cold and dark nights. Treasure your blessings! The essence of life lies in the simplest things of all, love is always the answer to the most fundamental questions. Learn to save for the winter, sometimes hardship comes in small, frequent doses while joy may only come in a more sporadic manner but in tons and inside huge containers. Learn to treasure your precious moments! Long winters will always come, be ready to weather the storms, have a heart full of joy and hope, a life full of passion and determination and a mind full of beautiful dreams and visions. There is no winter long enough to quench a burning desire and for the same reason to prevent the spring from showing up one more time!

NO MATTER THE REWARD, NEVER VIOLATE YOUR PRINCIPLES

We took a taxi in Rome and not until talking to a tour guide a few hours later we realized that the driver took advantage of us, he used a rate twice as high as the one he should have used and since we knew no better, we paid the price assuming it was a fair cost for the ride. As the tour guide explained it, taxi drivers in Rome had different zones they had to choose from depending on the location where the passenger is being picked. Some drivers, those not guided by principles of respect and honesty, would decide which zone to use only based on their selfish personal interests and profiting from the ignorance of touristic passengers, nothing but a poor choice only aimed at crystallizing a minuscule and unrightfully made personal gain.

No matter how far you can go in life by violating your principles, never do it. There are no rewards that can compensate the offense of betraying your essence and acting differently than what the Universe has thought of you. If you were privileged enough to be given sound values to live by (and every human being was), it is your honor and your duty to follow them in everything you do, you will get only as far as your principles will let you, this is the right way to live your life and the way it was meant to be lived. It does not matter what you see around, what other people do, what the environment tolerates, leaves unpunished or rewards in mistaken ways, you must always do as your inner guidance system tells you to do, you must always follow your heart. Vehemently refuse any benefits emerging from betraying the *who* you are and most importantly, the *who* you were meant to be.

There is only so much time before the two of you will eventually get to know each other, time to be lived according to your principles. Look at the weak spirited with compassion and wish them the

*strength needed to find their way in life for there is nothing more
desperate than a wandering soul that has missed its turns.*

If you choose to ignore, neglect or refuse your nature, life will sooner
or later turn itself into an unbearable burden for you to carry. Live a
simple life and respect your priorities, be always kind to others and do
for others more than you do for yourself. Have your life affairs always in
order, your accounts balanced, your dues paid, be one with nature and
be ready to stay or to leave, bags packed for your next assignment, accept
your humble role as a servant of a benevolent God that has thought of
you highly, loves you unconditionally and has given you a mission to
fulfill, something that you and only you can do magnificently well.

Start each day of your life as it if were your last day on Earth, live
it fully, with dignity, with integrity, with respect for those around
you, with compassion for the weak and the feeble, with passion for
what you have to do, putting your priorities always first and giving
your very best, each day, every day. I like to see each day as a small
(however big it may be) contribution to my most beautiful dreams
and visions. Have enchanting visions of a future yet to come, above
and beyond anything you have always imagined! Commit everything
and compromise nothing. Do all you can possibly do honoring your
priorities and making your future generations proud of what you did,
they need examples to outgrow, somebody honorable from whom to
take the torch and continue the journey! This is just the beginning of
something greater than just you, it is the numinous and mystifying
way in which we complete the will of our Creator, one dream and one
lifetime at a time!

CRYSTAL CLARITY

Springtime was approaching and I was mentally preparing myself for the bloom of the season. Being an engineer I could not resist the temptation of fixing what seemed broken or out of shape and I decided to roll my sleeves and start cleaning the pool. The filter was dirty, full of leaves and debris from the winter closing, the pool walls covered with green algae, dirt on the bottom that came from who knows where ... It was difficult to imagine how it could be worse. It took me over three hours to get the pump back to a clean state where seemingly crystal clear water was flowing through its glass lid, chlorinating the pool and starting to filter the impurities collected through the cold season. That is all I wanted, no matter how big or small the effort, I like when things get done. I had been cleaning the pool and learning something new every year for ten years and it would be fair to say I have done every opening a bit better than the one before, ten times and still learning.

When one embraces too much, one ends up pressing too little ... in Spanish we would say "el que mucho abarca poco aprieta." If you like to get right things done the right way, then pick battles big enough to challenge you to the best of your abilities, but not any bigger. Csikszentmihalyi's *flow theory* postulates that for an individual to be engaged in a task at such a level where the person and the task become one and the same, there has to be a degree of challenge, of defiance, of not being completely certain about how to do it, while at the same time the stretch must be somewhat reachable so frustration will not dominate the overall experience as when one is trying to pursue goals that are way over our head, at least at the stage of maturity we happen to be at the time of engaging with them.

Having access to more of something perceived as good is a temptation we all need to manage and like everything else in life, the secret lies in finding the right balance, the right amount of more, for too much more would not help us get further in our quest for advancement. A little rather than a whole lot more is just about enough and a better dose of unknowingness to dive ourselves into, especially when we are initiating ourselves in a relatively new field of expertise.

There is a delicate balance between what one can do now and what one could potentially do later, if a given amount of stretch is applied, tolerated and exercised. This dynamic calls for a sort of mystical equilibrium between our current and our future capabilities as stretching is not only desirable but also a must-have if the process of human evolution is bound to continue.

Life is a decision making process and one of the keys to live it honorably lies at finding the balance between what we change and what we accept, allowing Nature to do its job. Like in the case of any other major question, always listen to your heart. Stretching for a noble cause represents a wise enterprise but within the confines of what you deem reasonable, you must feel how much you have gone and if you went too far, gently pull yourself back. There is no natural process in the history of mankind that needs no adjustments, corrections and the addition of extra energy to get it back on track. Even airplanes get to the desired destination safely and on schedule after being apart the ideal route 98% of the time, they are normally off-track by just a few degrees, maybe even a fraction of a degree making small adjustments to get back on track so they can reasonably follow the defined route. A plane is constantly adjusting its course to be on top of the imaginary itinerary line as winds, storms, clouds and other environmental circumstances will prompt for a slight change of route that has to be corrected as soon and as safely as possible. Being off-track by just a little, even if it's most of the time, is perfectly fine and one of the best ways to get where you need to get. Those that have helped shape the advances of our civilization always raised the bar a bit higher than where it was, if nothing else to reach it, feel its texture and move it up another notch.

Being on track all the time is like grabbing to the bar and not letting it go, for you to advance in your life call you need to expose yourself to what you have not yet experienced, the new and the novel, that you don't fully understand and comprehend. Confusion creates the lack of clarity, until clarity arrives to displace confusion. The one needs the other as the other needs the one.

It is at that juncture, when you meet the half known that you gently and kindly force yourself to expand your horizons and let alternative views of the world to invade you and come to rescue your old self from the risks of stagnation. You must release the bar you are grabbing and hanging from so you can move it higher, even if not so much higher but enough to keep you thinking: *How am I going to reach it now?* The process of puzzling yourself to do something that does not come naturally and easily will propel you to develop your potential skills and nurture your current talents. *You will never become any better if you do not accept or impose challenges onto yourself. The realm of the comfortable is not expected to last long, it is only a stop on the road to a successful life, most of the time you will be chasing something extraneous to you, like walking through unchartered terrain and feeling deeply inside that if it was meant to be, it will be.*

Although some venues may seem alien to you and create virtual butterflies in your stomach, nothing you decide to embark yourself into is completely unknown and unforeseeable. Your eyes do not see it as it was not supposed to be visible, it was meant to be felt, as if letting yourself go completely and under the command of forces you can't quite describe but trust to be a guiding sort of higher power whispering in your ear "go ... don't be afraid, be strong, be brave." This new path you have chosen lies on a new dimension, a space above and beyond your current level of comprehension, you are not supposed to rationalize it as your conscious awareness is not part of the design.

Piece your journey toward those desired ends in small increments, big enough to keep you engaged but not so huge that would seem insurmountable. A hand reach is too close of a target and a mile is a little too far of a stretch. It has to be just large enough to keep you motivated and feeling confident that you have a shot at it, if enough effort and persistence are applied. Nobody can tell how *big* is *big enough* for you, only you can figure out where that piece of the puzzle goes. It is perfectly fine to think big long term provided you can eventually break a lifelong itinerary into small trips that you can undertake in the short time, as big or as small as your imagination can plan a single trip leg to be.

There will be not one but many pauses before reaching your final destination, this is a multi-point trip that will have many stops, change of aircrafts and even change of travel mates. You will reach upcoming junctures with whoever your travel companions will be and they may not be the same at every stop. Celebrate the small victories, the arrival at the current station and the departure to the next. Every mile travelled is an accomplishment, a conquest, a reached summit, however easy or difficult it happened to be.

No matter how long or short your most recent ride, every new station you arrive at is a major milestone in the journey of your life, a place meant to be reached at the time you got there. Keep yourself moving, resting when it is time to rest and walking when it is time to walk.

You do not want to lose any time, life is so precious and there is so much to do. Use your time and your powers wisely, never neglecting to do what you have to do. Eventually the time to go will come and all accounts will have to be balanced. It is at that time when you want no regrets, no insufficient funds and no debts of yours to be paid by those surviving you. It is at that juncture when you would look back and say … *there are not that many things I would do differently, as I have always done the very best I could.*

DON'T TRY TO BE A HERO, BE THE WHO YOU WERE MEANT TO BE

Let's help populate the world with good women and men ... that's all we have to do. What I am pursuing as an essential part of my purpose on Earth is nothing but leading by example the enduring process of becoming the very best I can be, nothing extraordinary, not a hero of any kind, simply and plainly a good man.

Our Creator has asked us to be somebody, unique and special in our own terms, gifted to perfection for the task we were entrusted with, wise and capable, unconquerable and daring, restless and determined, and most importantly unwilling to settle for anything less than everything we can be and become. That somebody lives inside us in the embryonic forms and shapes of a master piece yet to be crafted.

I saw the angel in the marble and carved until I set him free. — Michelangelo

This morning I was blessed by a comment of my dear friend Alejandro Goyri who was kind enough to share with me a passage from the Bible where God was gracious and kind but loud and clear on what we are supposed to do ...

I've commanded you to be strong and brave. Don't ever be afraid or discouraged! I am the LORD your God, and I will be there to help you wherever you go – Joshua 1:8-10

What a beautiful command and what a great message for those engaged in the process of never giving up doing right and allowing the very best in them to emerge and be offered to the world. The concept of *being strong and brave* is a tremendously powerful motive that requires incredible endurance to be followed. It is easy to be brave when things go according to plan for bravery is not required in the land of the simple, but what happens when adversity shows up, when the odds of success do not seem to be in our favor? How many individuals that have previously committed not to give up will maintain their course of action after their plans, expectations and assumptions have turned upside down? How many of those that had stayed and stumbled would try a second time, a third, a fourth, forever?

> *The test to our endurance is not just an episode but a process and something we need to recommit each and every time we face a moment of weakness or hesitation.*

Have you ever asked yourself how strong your commitment to your purpose truly is? Do you have room for the unexpected? Can anything happen along the way without deflecting your focus and turning your vision away from the ultimate end of your journey? Are there any limits to your capacity to face adverse circumstances? How much is too much? Do you believe in what you do to the point of losing everything you have and start all over again ... not once but multiple times? Are you afraid of cold, dark, long and lonely nights? How long can you wait until the sun rises again? Do you believe it will rise again after a seemingly endless night? Are your worst fears strong enough to make you give up? Can you do as God has asked you to do no matter what? If you have never asked yourself these questions, please start now ... God did not say what He said with conditional statements of any kind or leaving it up to our judgment of how likely, risky or feasible it may seem to be, He commanded us to do it and offered to be at our side wherever we go. His law should be our law and we should follow it, no matter what and until we are asked to stop doing it to do otherwise. We live in a world where things are supposed to work, especially in the *here and now*. That is a totally misleading statement on matters of utmost significance.

> *When it comes to our purpose, whether it works or it doesn't, does not matter at all, we are supposed to follow it, lovingly, unconditionally, dutifully and regardless of the outcomes. If it feels right in our heart,*

> *it should feel right in our hands. Let's do right and give our very
> best each and every day of our life, regardless ... let's be brave!*

Over the last centuries there has been a shift in mankind's preference to gradually move the attention and focus more on what works versus on what is right. It does not take too much reasoning or intelligence to conclude that while they can be one and the same, very often they are not. What is *right*, is so based on its relationship and proximity to universally accepted values and principles. It is rooted on the inherent rightfulness that the deed under question carries within, something that if asked to a large enough number of people, they would agree that it is the right thing to do in such a set of circumstances, something that neighbors the nature of an archetype, a notion ingrained in the minds and the hearts of human kind requiring little or no reason to accept it, it just feels that way and is generally assumed as an inherent aspect of life. Its justification is more unconscious than conscious in the sense that people may find themselves puzzled to explain with words what their hearts have long ago assumed to be truthful and indisputable.

There are however cultural, age, race, sex, and many other demographic connotations that may make something right for one segment of the population and not for another, which represents an acceptable fact of life and the diversity that conforms the variety of the human race. What is right for one person may not be right for another and there are quite certainly some things that are right for both of them. One way to test the universality of right deeds is to have them pass the *harm/help* test. If they harm nobody but help at least someone else other than yourself, you can say it is right (harm and help expressed in utmost positive and altruistic terms).

> *Right by definition has to be something that sooner or later leads to an
> universally accepted principle, value or action that has a benign nature
> or origin. It has to also feel inherently right not only to the beholder
> but also to the recipients in general, all differences considered.*

Conversely, what works is something that leads to a desired result with or without any regard or association to universal laws, principles or archetypes (workability does not require rightness, but can carry it). In its simplest form, anything that leads to its desired result is said to work, with little or no conditions required. It is true that you can enrich this definition by adding an assessment of the means to the ends, which represents a different conversation and a deviation from the pure conceptualization of work. The moment you start analyzing the means to the ends, you are likely making judgments about their rightness what defeats the purity of the *work* attribute of a thought or deed.

Work and right are independent qualifiers with no generalized correlation or causation, although they can be related in certain circumstances. In theory, something can be *right* regardless if it works or not. Similarly, something can *work* regardless if it is considered right or not. One thing does not necessarily lead or exclude the other. For the engineers, the mathematicians and the scientists in you, they are non-correlated and independent characteristics, although in a philosophical form and at a higher level of complexity, one could argue that right things tend to ultimately work in the sense that the two concepts aim at overarching and parallel purposes that connect, blend and mesh into one … eventually. However and when looking at the immediate term, the here and now, work and right may be disjointed and present themselves as non-correlated, ambivalent and independent of each other. It is ultimately up to the individual who has to make a choice between rightness and workability how interconnected the two realms are, a rather metaphysical quandary that calls for a personal determination of which path to follow.

In the same vein and from a higher level of complexity, *workability* and *rightness* can indeed overlap, like parallel lines that eventually meet. Right things work at the end, eventually and if one is patient and persistent enough to stay the course of one's purpose despite the adversity and difficulty that may circumstantially show up. Holding a broad conceptualization of the term *work* can also be a useful tool in our skill inventory as the idea of *work* has to do with actions leading to their expected results, and there is not one but many ways to get something done. In essence, *workability* is defined as the ability of a deed or plan to meet its desired result, whatever that result is at the time of engaging in the task. There can be more than one result and workability can be defined as a continuum, a degree and not necessarily as a black and white attribute.

While the above definition of workability may not directly invoke a connection to universally accepted values and principles, meeting points of work/right dualities are more prevalent over long periods of time, when the engagement on things that are inherently right eventually converge or mature into something that is considered the expected result. On the flip side, it is not so likely that such a duality blending may materialize in short term pursuits started with the workability foot if rightness considerations are not part of the plan. Beginning with an intent to do right can lead to things that work, the opposite is not necessarily true.

Having defined both terms and their respective implications in the fabric of everyday life, there seems to be two different camps of people marking the symbolical ends of a trait with the subsequent bell type distribution of the masses in between the extremes. The two ends of the right/work continuum are:

Those committed to always do what is right
Those committed to always do what works

The postulation that a person can commit to both *right* and *work* would be realistic and acceptable only on a situational basis, when the latitude of both right and work are ample enough to find points of intersection leading to compromises of some sort.

However and when it comes to the essential aspects of our lives, we will come to numerous crossroads calling call for a decision favoring one or the other as a compromise would require a high enough price or sacrifice in one dimension or the other. It is in those intersections that the personal foundation and value system will be manifested and the stronger commitment will prevail.

Dualism in the commitment to work and right would be similar to adoring two Gods, eventually, one of the two will dominate the individual's faith and sooner or later a decision will have to be made. It is wise to keep the concepts of right and work handy choosing one or the other depending on the circumstance, however opportunity-based decisions are not what define your commitment, such a flexible stand would only help you favorably resolve frail life circumstances.

The who you are meant to be is expressed in your response to crucial life aspects, when what you do or what you don't sculpts the masterpiece you carry inside. It is at those moments when you must embody the strength to always do right!

If you are committed to doing what feels right you will have to inevitable accept that some of your actions will not work, at least not all the time and especially based on the world's definition of work. It is like two avenues intersecting and creating a very unstable meeting point, a sort of busy joint calling for a quick decision, standing still is not an option. Think about this dynamic and be able to anticipate your moves.

Know in advance which intersections are those you will choose the work side and which are those you will lean to what feels right. When you get to the stop sign, you will not have a lot of time to think, the decision has to be made before you approach the crossroad. The best way to travel the path of your life is by knowing full well when what is right will supersede what works.

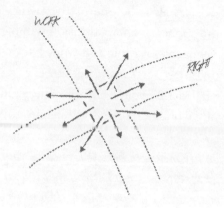

When you elevate your thinking to the overall complexity of human life, it is not just one intersection, but many, like a grid, a city full of stop signs and decision points. It is even multidimensional, not just one layer but many, one for each department of your life, all interconnected, all intertwined, like if you were driving many cars, stopping at crossroads on parallel realities and creating a complex but at the same time simple process of choosing what is right or what works. If you have done your homework, you will know when to go for right and when not to. Deciding is simpler than you may think, it is having the courage to live with the decisions that will test your endurance and your deepest core. Refuse to be afraid, do what you have to do and accept the consequences of your decisions.

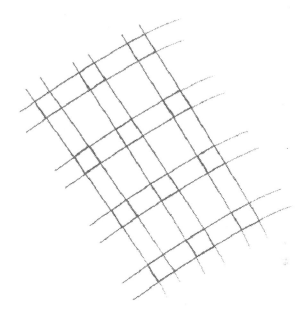

All you need to do in advance is mentally prepare yourself for the possible crossroads and decide whether you will lean to the *right* or the *work* sides based on the anticipated circumstances, knowing that sometimes you will have to wait until you see what the options are (for as much as I love to plan, there are times in life when you can only plan so much in advance but wait until you see more clearly what your choices are). Let's say you want to be a good parent to your child and help him or her get a good college education, so you work hard for the money but it is not coming through, you don't seem to be getting there as you originally planned. The closer your child gets to college age, the more convinced you are that you would not be able to afford a great school for him or her so an intersection is approaching and some decision making will be required. You sit down and analyze the options:

1. Compromise *right* and *work*:
    *   Get a higher pay job that may distort your work-life balance

- Sacrifice part of your retirement funds and eventually create a burden for your child if they have to support you later in life
- Get a loan to pay for the school you or your child always dreamed about, with the implication of getting highly indebted

2. Choose *right* versus *work*:
- Keep working hard for the money doing what you believe to be right and hope things may change for the better in time

3. Expand *rightness* to be more likely to *work*:
- Have a conversation with your child to see if he or she would be willing to get a loan, with your commitment to help pay it off
- See what school he or she would like to go (maybe your dream is not her/his dream)
- Engage your child on looking for scholarships
- Accept that all you will be able to do is to send him/her to a good but not great school and that he/she will have to do his/her part by excelling there and be one of the best (assuming he/she wants to graduate with higher than average grades)

Life is a series of choices and ultimately, those choices are rooted to either a *work* or a *right* standard. You can find compromises where something right also works or something that works is also right, but as any compromise it would neither be the best in the *right* nor in the *work* domains if considered separately. If you can live in the middle and the situation lends itself to a compromised outcome, it may be the best way to go (for instance in the example above if you choose the 3rd group of options and find a new *right* that has a better chance to work).

There are certain aspects of life where you do not want to compromise, you just want the best of one world, not just a fair happy medium. You will know when the time comes. It is in those special circumstances when you do not and cannot adore two Gods. Important and essential life aspects must be dealt with a *right* mentality paying little or no attention to whether the approach works in the short term (remember that right choices tend to work more in the long run than in the immediate present). As far as everything else is concerned, the optional and mundane sides of your existence, you can compromise or simply do what works best.

I would personally never neglect, ignore or refuse to consider the right attributes of choice but I may be willing to compromise, if the relevance in my priority scale is not that high. I know I drive my dear Lili crazy when she asks me "what kind of tea do you want?" only for me to say "anyone, I don't mind." She wants me to decide, as if drinking apple cider tea would make any difference in my life than drinking orange spice tea. They are all teas to me and while I may like one slightly more than the other, I really don't mind it in context of all the other critical decisions I care about. Sometimes I choose one tea versus another only because it would keep me away from arguing over tea choosing affairs ... and that "works" ☺ ... but between you and me, I couldn't care less about which tea she broils as long as she does it with her usual love and charm! I know for a fact it will taste great whichever one she chooses ... anything done out of love does!

You need to have a feel for which decisions are going to be made based on what *works* and which ones based on what is *right*. Have a roadmap! Don't venture yourself into the life driving experience hoping that you will know what to do when you get to the symbolical stop signs, you need to know *before* you get there, think about it in advance. What is it that you want in life? What is it that you came here for? What have you been entrusted to do? How far are you into it? Who is the one you are meant to be? How likely are you to be that one and by when? ... and this is just the beginning.

It is not complicated at all but it will require practice as those questions are far from conventional everyday stuff and can only be answered from the deepest confines of your heart, where your true essence resides. All you need to do is define your priorities, your essentials and to have a *sense* of what you are here for. You don't need to know it for sure (we never do), a guess is good enough as a starting point, overtime you will get to know it better as you become one with it. There will be intersections not worth spending the time to think ahead, trust your heart to identify and ignore them, you will know when you come close their whereabouts. Trifling crossroads may not be the same for every person, we are all unique and special in our own way. We don't have the same purpose and we are not supposed to be the same person at the end of our journeys. Follow your heart, it will lead you where you must go!

A LONG TERM MENTALITY IN A
SHORT TERM MINDED WORLD

The phrase "live one day at a time" comes in to aid humans to cope with the complexity of long term living, in a sense slicing and dicing the overwhelming task of trying to fit a lifetime of potential circumstances inside our minds and figure a way to deal with them effectively. This dynamic, a self-defense mechanism of our psyche, is more prevalent when one is undergoing periods of stress, uncertainty, ambiguity or despair, moments when we seem to find it difficult to anticipate or predict what will happen next and most importantly what our response should be. The pressure to live life on a day-by-day basis is not alien to us humans and represents something that each of us has entertained at one or several points in our journeys. The opposite of day-by-day living is planning for the long run, doing things today keeping the distant future always in mind and using it as our horizon, a final destination for the path called life. Such a careful balance of the present reality and the potential future puzzles the untrained mind and creates a mental challenge not easy to resolve.

First and foremost nobody can tell the future which represents a conglomerate of unknown circumstances still yet to come and even when some of them may be reasonably predictable, everything else remains completely out of mind and out of sight. Being able to cope with the unknown effectively requires the gifts of flexibility and open mindedness so we can adjust and manage the artful talent of navigating through a sea of unexpected circumstances. Unless we possess or develop those skills, we will get frustrated, disappointed and perhaps overwhelmed with the amount of mental reprocessing we will have to deal with each time we face unwelcome, unfavorable or unpredicted settings, nothing more and nothing less than the full encompassing realm of the consciously unknown.

> *The overarching question of how to live with a long term mentality in a short term minded world summarizes the challenge that we, as humans, have to face when the potential stress that comes from managing an increasing amount of stimuli pressing for immediate attention is directed towards us.*

Some may even question … *why must I live with a long term mentality when reacting to the multiple demands of the present seems to fit me just fine?* The answer is simple, you don't have to, living one day at a time is an option. You have the right to live your life in any way you choose, as long as you respect and honor its meaning (life manifests itself both as a right and a duty). Whether you desire to focus on the long term outcome of your existence or opt to live day after day without thinking about what will happen next, is your choice to make. We all came here for a reason and with a purpose unique and special to each of us and seeking to know such a purpose should help us tremendously in the process of fulfilling it.

The world is nothing but what we perceive of it, perception is reality. Things happen inside and around us, some of them initiated by us, others started by the action of an external trigger to then come into our way in an unsolicited, and sometimes undesired manner. Whatever the case, our natural tendency is to respond rather than ignore the stimuli, especially in those cases where a response is expected from us, when the outer world has pushed a button the masses generally react to. Reaction is a more common behavior than inaction or determined ignorance. This inclination to respond to an external trigger is innate and connected to our survival instincts. Whatever the prompt, our brain rapidly processes it, thoughts are born, feelings are nurtured and finally action results from both thoughts and feelings completing a behavioral pattern triad. The typical process is:

Trigger → Thought → Feeling → Action

… and blended into that process are the memories of the past and the visions of the future. In a very simple sense, choice can be described as follows, we tend to avoid what we dislike or are afraid of and go after what we like or want to succeed at. Such a distinction is also manifested in a human trait related to avoidance or action oriented behavior. While in one extreme of the continuum live those that are generally looking for what to avoid, on the other reside those who are constantly looking for what to do. The former are typically focused on what can go wrong and the latter center their attention on what can go right. In a metaphorical way, it is as if each group ignores what the other thinks about by virtue of being so distant of the drivers the other pack mingles with. And the saying goes … "what you focus on, expands," which in turn generates either a vicious or a virtuous cycle preempting a mysterious kind of self-fulfilling prophecy.

The dynamics of the Trigger → Thought → Feeling → Action construct (TTFA) are initially regulated by the most primitive side of the mind, the amygdale, commonly known as the reptilian brain. The amygdale is the fastest part of our brain and it is instinctual in nature, we do not have to consciously decide, not even think, when perceived danger is around it will mobilize us toward action with the ultimate aim of protecting our life. Part of the complexity at managing our life in today's fast paced world is associated to our inability to *quickly* discern between real and perceived risk, when the amygdale senses potential danger, it is not always as dangerous as it is perceived to be and therefore it unnecessary turns on the life protection mechanisms creating a sort of premature overreaction. In actuality, when the reptilian brain steps in, the TTFA cycle is shortcut and it becomes TFA (Trigger → Feeling → Action) as the Think step has been temporarily removed.

More elaborated and superior brain functions can override the amygdale's response and help us manage our otherwise mechanical reaction in order to reach a more mature assessment of the surrounding circumstances. You certainly do not want to interfere with your reptilian brain if life is in danger as you can't be any faster than the amygdale, but when danger is only perceived and not necessary real, you need to allow your superior brain to take over and get in control.

When that superior level of thinking takes place, the TTFA cycle will be reinstated allowing a space between stimuli and response inside of which our self can come up with a more elaborated answer.

The key to being proactive is remembering that between stimulus and response there is a space. That space represents our choice— how we will choose to respond to any given situation, person, thought or event. Imagine a pause button between stimulus and response—a button you can engage to pause and think about what is the principle-based response to your given situation. Listen to what your conscience tells you. Listen for what is wise and the principle-based thing to do, and then act. – Stephen Covey

This extra space created in the *more elaborated* thinking pattern is normally filled with the *think* part of the TTFA process which redirects instinctual responses and turns them into more complex actions or series of actions. Contrariwise, when we allow our reptilian brain to react, we are not choosing a response, our most primitive brain function is. Fear (or anxiety, which is an unidentified type of fear) is by far the most prevalent feeling responsible for the reaction that follows a primitive brain function dominated response. Fear is not to be suppressed but acknowledged, assessed and controlled. There is a reason for fear to exist and we certainly do not want to suppress it, however letting it loose to then become in control of our actions is not recommended either.

Fear will urge us to react, forgetting the long term picture and trying to save the here and now, without which, there is no future. If all responses become a matter of life or death, we will never be able to project ourselves beyond the present set of circumstances and in so doing we would be confining life to become a series of short term settings requiring short term answers.

It is true that the long term vision of a better tomorrow is ultimately constructed by a series of short term actions and the key difference lies in the process of turning those actions more long term framed and focused on the distant future and not necessarily on the preservation of life from a false alarm, a sort of miscalculated threat at the present time. We are not in the business of avoiding risk but in the business of managing it.

Viktor Frankl was absolutely right, the freedom to choose our response in any set of circumstances is the ultimate human freedom, the question in this context is whether or not we are able (and willing) to choose the long versus the short term, the rational response versus the instinctual or emotional reaction. We always get to decide, even if we don't, not choosing is choosing not to choose and whether this is a conscious or an unconscious process, it does not really matter as the choice has been made anyway.

Environmental triggers around you will press your intellect for responses and it is by engaging your more elaborated brain functions and your inner sense of rightness (heart, unconscious, etc) that you will exercise choice wisely. You need time to think and to let your unconscious express its point of view, learning to manage the unnecessary sense of urgency that a fast paced world will try to impose on you. When decisions are mandatory, take your time and avoid being carried away by the rush of apparent urgent matters. What is important, is rarely urgent ... unless you are dealing with a life threatening situation in which case you may want to let your instincts (and not your thoughts) take control.

The reason why I postulate that we have a tendency to see the world as short term minded is because we have an inner urge to resolve the problems that our primitive brain regards as threats as soon as possible and without putting them in the context of the greater picture. Such a framing in a broader vision of life and our role in it, with the subsequent delay or refusal to respond, would be seen as ignoring or minimizing the problem's potential impact. In reality it is a miniaturization of a previously enlarged problem which results in the right-sizing of the troubling incident, a sort of inhibition of the premature engagement of a primitive sensory system that has a tendency to somewhat blindly deal with worst case scenarios in the name of preserving our life from possible uncalculated risks.

> *The same phenomena apply not only to problems but also to opportunities. Letting current opportunities go untouched, or delaying gratification, requires the ability to see beyond the immediate present and realize that the optimal fulfillment of our purpose may not necessarily be in the hands of the here and now but in things that will come to us sometime in the future.*

Things happen for a reason and when something inside tells us to wait, to let this go, to keep preparing ourselves for something even better still yet to come, we must listen to that voice. The key to unlock the best in us lies in our capacity to let some of our today's fortunes and misfortunes to just go by without affecting our posture and our vision of a better and still to come tomorrow. We will not be able to see it with our eyes or touch it with our hands, but if we listen carefully to the whispering of our hearts, it will be impossible to miss! We are all here for a reason, we all carry a unique call that has been assigned to us, whether we know it or not, whether we like it or not. Our purpose was given to us not by mistake but with the expectation that we will feel privileged and honored by having it. The future of the world lies in our hands and only by collectively committing to realize our missions we will be able to turn this place called world into something better equipped to the embellishment of human life. While we work on our life calls every day, they are lifelong calls, long term assignments that we should keep dear and near to our hearts until our very last breath.

We are meant to be someone and to do something and it is our responsibility to be that someone and do that something before we leave. Pursuing our life calls will push us to grow, to become wiser, more loving, more caring and more sensitive human beings. As a result, we will get as much as we give, not because we expect it or because we condition our actions to it but because of the gifts of serendipity and good karma, whatever good and however much love we spread around will come back to us…unexpectedly, unconditionally.

*Those who bring sunshine into the life of others cannot
keep it from themselves – James Matthew Barrie*

When the time to leave would eventually come, our accounts will be balanced, nothing will be owed to us and we will owe nothing to the world. We are in the business of fulfilling our life purpose and spreading love, whether you are a teacher, a parent, a doctor, a musician, a policeman, a gardener, or just a simple human being trying to help another soul in any way you can, makes no difference at all, just focus on the giving part. We all have a purpose to fulfill, nobody is here by accident, there is no such a thing as a purposeless man or woman on Earth.

Finding our purpose and getting to meet and greet it does not always come easy but it is without a question one of the most rewarding experiences you can have in life. The beauty of purpose fulfillment is that you don't necessarily have to realize it or have the opportunity to look at it in the eyes to work on it, there are millions of people that honor their purposes every day without (consciously) knowing what their purposes are or even being aware of what the interpretation of a life purpose is all about. Facing the reason for our existence in a one-to-one manner can be quite intimidating and not everyone is ready for that type of encounter, at least not at every stage of their life. Quite often, the Universe will find ways for you to do what you have to do without necessarily confronting you with the full extent of what you are up against. The Universe knows who can handle purpose awareness, who cannot and when. Knowing our life call can be quite thought provoking and overwhelming for the untrained mind and a medicine that may require a gradually increased dosage before being taken in full strength. In a sense, we always know, although not in a conscious manner, but through a burning sense of rightness.

*If something feels right deep inside and you are mysteriously
attracted to do it over and over again, your purpose is not too
far from it. We are also generally better than average on those
things we are supposed to do, powers come with responsibility*

and when we are asked to do something, we are also generally given the means to do it right, better than most around us.

This is why it is of paramount importance to consult with your heart as it is the gateway to the inner wisdom you carry inside, the pathway to your unconscious and the collective unconscious of the entire human kind. Your ability to see beyond the here-and-now and to override the response of your reptilian brain when it is not needed lies in your capacity to speak the language of your heart. There is no question that the circumstances around you will pull some triggers and you may feel the need to react. Listen to what your brain has to say, primitive and superior, but most importantly always listen to your heart. Weigh the long term impact of your current actions, only rarely we are asked to do something that will not have an either positive or negative impact in the long term view of our lives. Everything we do will be a foundation of what comes next, either a strong or a weak one. Be willing to make sacrifices if necessary, what is life without them? The future rewards of delaying immediate pleasures can be so fulfilling that just the thought of it can be quite comforting and big enough to replace the satisfaction of enjoying that which is postponed.

Reach in for that inner sense of rightness that will be impossible to ignore, it will be your inner compass to get where you need to go. Life is precious and you have been gifted with it. Be strong and be faithful, there will be thorns in the garden ahead but there will be plenty of roses as well!

A NEED TO MOVE FAST

Every night when I go to bed I feel exhausted, really tired, like if every day of my life would have been longer than the day before ... and with almost no single bit of energy left, my body, my mind, and my heart need to let go of the beauty of the day and fall in the charming arms of the night, in a sense allowing myself to be carried away into the silent and mysterious domains of the unknown.

I entrust my body and my soul to the world of dreams, mystical encounters with ancient pasts and distant futures treasuring the hope that they may bring clarity to the still yet to be born new day. I make my moves quickly, I have no time to lose, what I have to do is difficult, will take a lot of time and effort, and most importantly I have to do everything at my reach to maximize the likelihood that it gets done. An overpowering inner sense of direction leads me to believe that the mission I was given is extraordinary, meaningful and a critical part to help change the world for the better. I cannot, under any circumstance, let the Universe down, every second counts.

No wonder I feel so tired, I use every bit of possible stamina in my waking life, my batteries get completely depleted by bedtime and there is nothing else to do other than just lie down and let go. A day is a microscopic version of your life, you live each day with the same passion, hope, dedication, commitment and vision that you will carry out each and every following day, for the rest of your life.

A life, however long or short, is nothing but a series of days, one after the other. You honor life and the purpose you were entrusted only by doing as expected, one day at a time, for what you do in a day counts as much as what you do in a year, eventually a lifetime. You do not spare today only because there will be a tomorrow, you give your very best every day as if it were the last one day left to live ... and when you go to bed at night you hope and pray there will be a tomorrow.

Sometimes I get the feeling that I go too fast, that what some people take months to go through I do it in weeks, that what some people take years to go through I do it in months. It may be true or just a distorted perception of time, a deeply engaged mind playing tricks on me. I am restless and exercise no hesitancy at times of putting effort, real effort into good, noble and sensible causes and I do it without measuring the results, not even expecting anything in return, except feeling grateful and honored for having been given the opportunity to try, to contribute, to help and to be part of something bigger than myself, a sort of mystical ecosystem under the Universe's oversight.

After speeding up for a few years you realize that you can go fast but not any faster, you can't fool Nature, some processes cannot be expedited more than what their essence will dictate. The obstacles you find along the way are meant to be there for two main reasons, first and foremost to teach you a lesson, and second to slow you down if you happen to be going too fast (like symbolic bumps on the road). We will be allowed to run as long as we accept that eventually we will have to slow down, start to walk, come to a stop and perhaps even walk backwards a bit before resuming our next move forward.

Running as well as pausing are temporary states in the doing of whatever we have to do, we are not supposed to just go and never look back, the hindsight contemplation of our accomplishments (or lack thereof) is part of the game and it is there for a reason, a good and noble reason. Learn to respect Universal laws and times, Nature has its own cycles and you can't change that, no matter how hard you try. Nature paces the Universe and it is our job to follow, not lead. Like Albert Einstein said, "everything should be made as simple as possible but not any simpler," you can (and I encourage you to) go through your life fast but not any faster. Perhaps, the central question of this discussion is how fast "fast" is so we go neither any faster nor any slower. The answer is: *only you will know*. At the end, when everything was said and done, you would have gone only as fast as you were meant to and not any faster. If you care for my advice, try to go as fast as you think you should go, chances are you will be slowed down and you will know when it happens. If you are not, then increase your speed a notch … you will get to a point where your speed will be right ... this is a process of trial and error, each of us has an optimal speed of advancement and nobody but us can find it out.

The moment you get over the speed limit that has been set for you at that particular juncture of your life, you will be either slowed down or pulled over to get a ticket, life has their own speed traps, no one is allowed to outrun himself or herself, there is no point to it. The difference with car driving dynamics is that, unlike in a real road or highway, your internal speed limit is unknown until you try to exceed it, and there lies our challenge and our duty. I claim to need no external drive to push me, I hold a burning source of stamina inside, I can feel it, I treasure it, I feed it and I keep the fire always burning. In my partnership with the Universe I ask for two things, if I am headed in the wrong direction, I need help to see where true north is, and if I am going too fast, I need help to be slowed down, eventually stopped. Of course I can be also going the in wrong direction and too fast, a combined disease that has to be prescribed with the same medicines.

In the process of pacing myself there is something I regularly do with the ultimate aim of saving the Universe from having to either correct my course or stop me. From time to time, I just close my eyes and ask my heart two questions. First, "Am I going in the right direction? ... and if the answer is "yes," I then ask "Am I going too fast?." I know for a fact that I am not going too slow as I never had that problem but I did miss my way and/or went too fast quite a few times.

Listen to your heart, it will always answer your pledges, although
it may whisper so softly that you will only hear its voice if
you mean to listen. Don't ask if you don't want to listen, and
when you do, listen with intent and be open to hear whatever
is spoken to you, not just what you would like to be told.

If you are going too fast, slow down, be more patient, more persistent. The sun will rise again tomorrow at about the same time it rose today regardless how fast you go or how early you get up. Nature cares about you but will not allow you to change its cycles to adjust them to your pace, you need to be in synch with the Universe and become one with it.

If you are going too slow, hurry up a bit, you are being patient and persistent enough which is good, just increase your speed a notch. The world is going nowhere, being ahead or behind of yourself will make neither you nor the world any good, the key is to find your right pace. It will not happen overnight, accept the price of getting to know you. Some things just take time and effort. Be willing to put it through ...

LIKE A PIONEER ...

Whether you think of yourself as a winner or as a loser, you are right! You are what you think yourself to be, nothing more, nothing less. The future version of this statement is also true; you will be what you think you will be, nothing more, nothing less.

The world can try anything, make any attempt to tell you who you are but in reality, the world can only talk about what the world sees, and nothing can be more distant from the truth than an external opinion of what you treasure inside. The only person or entity on Earth that can define you, the present and the future you, is you! Regardless of what the world believes, you are special and unique in your own way and this is true whether you know it or not, whether you believe it or not, and whether you want to accept it or not. Knowing who you are and who you are meant to be is not a requirement to becoming it, but it can help.

The Universe has a special trust on those consciously committed to their purposes; awareness is a gift and a privilege that allows you to make conscious decisions to better focus on and align to your life call ... and while your conscious life is only the tip of the iceberg, it feels as if it is all there is! We were all born to be somebody, special in our own terms and whether or not we end up being that person depends on many factors, some within our control, others outside of it. There are many decisions we can't make, but there are many more we can. We cannot decide where we were born or how smart we are, but we can decide where we want to live and how much education we want to get. Things happen for a reason even if you believe there is no reason for what happens. The reason may not be visible to you, may lie in a future or a past time, perhaps a distant future or a distant past, it may reside in a different place, far from where you live, or close enough that you can't see it, a sort of blind spot.

You may have been born in an undeveloped country or in a dysfunctional family only for you to experience life in such a way that would forge the *who* you are, silently and lovingly paving the road to becoming the who you are meant to be. Nothing happens by accident in the Universe Master Plan, sometimes we just can't see it, it may be too big to fit in our minds, too complex for us to reason it or too broad to piece it together with our limited brain power. We will know only as much as we can safely handle, some things are better off left unknown until the time when we can comprehend them, assimilate them, connect the dots of past, present, and future for the related events to make some sense without completely disturbing our peace of mind.

Our conscious minds are limited at best and what the Universe let us know is *all* we *can* know without getting troubled, uneasy or even more confused. Have you ever thought that the adversity in your life could have been pre-planned? That maybe, only maybe it was not just an accident, a random occurrence and a flaw in the Universe Master Plan? What if you had to live through all the despair to experience the change, the growth and the evolution into something greater than what you were? What if you had to turn into a more kindhearted, more considerate and more philanthropic person than the one you once were but needed the exposure to the dark side of life to first hand know how difficult or unfair some life circumstances could be for those in pain, suffering, or simply affected by extreme adversity? What if everything you had to go through was meant to be exactly the way it was? What if you were blessed instead of cursed but you see it precisely the other way around, out of your symbolic shortsightedness? What if you are focusing on the empty rather than on the full half side of the bottle? I am a big believer that we have been placed right in front of the doors to the best and the worst of our lives, it is all about choice and it is up to us to decide.

Kwai Chang Kane once asked his master about evil forces after being frightened by his mirror image. His master, resorting to his usual calmness and wisdom, responded "we all have evil and good inside, it is not a matter of having or not having it but a matter of which one you choose to be." Throughout the course of our lives, we will face the best and the worst of us, not once but multiple times. Acknowledge your dark sides and be compassionate for their existence is part of the Universe master plan. Help your darkness come out and meet the light, we can only be one with ourselves when we have made every effort to reconcile everything we carry inside, bright and dark alike. We are what we choose to be, regardless of what we embody or treasure within.

Expect the unexpected, predictability is an illusion and a need of the weak spirit, be open and grateful to what life will bring to your doorstep. Don't be surprised if some of the best doors of our life will one day close for us to look for windows, go through them realizing they may be suboptimal at first sight to then potentially turn into some of the best things we have experienced! We must have the faith and the courage to go through unknown windows even when all we see is a blurry, yet to be defined forward path. We have to be resilient and endurable accepting the challenge of paving the road to a better future, of going through places we have never been before and in a sense walk the less traveled roads, those ignored, forgotten, or rejected by the masses out of fear or hesitation.

Life is full of mysteries, surprises and treasures waiting to be found, risks and rewards laid alongside the road for those willing to experience their journeys to their fullest extent.

Wondering about the rewards? ... finding the most beautiful sides of your life, fulfilling your purpose and living a life worth every minute of it. As far as the risks are concerned, they comprise everything but your piece of mind, nothing is guaranteed except the feeling that you did exactly as you were expected, rain or shine. We are all asked to wholeheartedly devote ourselves to our life call, our essentials, the things we care about the most, with no promise in return, just our commitment to give our very best without expecting anything in return other than the opportunity to continue doing it, to continue carrying that strong, inner sense of rightness stamped on everything we do.

Each of us has to gauge if this risk/reward proposition is worth pursuing. Nobody except us can answer that question, and if everything

I have witnessed in over 50 years of life spent in two completely different cultures is something to go by, living a selfless life focused on contribution, self-discovery and reinvention is such a mesmerizing proposition to me that I cannot even conceive life without it, all risks and uncertainties considered.

> *I personally need no guarantees, no reassurances of any kind, no insurance policies. I take life for what it is worth and accept the inherent risks of pursuing my ideals. Being allowed to be in the battlefield of a cause I regard as worth living and dying for is enough of a privilege, enough of an honor and enough of a gift that I can't think of asking for anything else. This is it for me, this is all I need and more than I ever imagined I would be blissfully given.*

I was born to be nothing more and nothing less than a good man, a man of honor, a simple and daring human being. I feel like the king of my own little kingdom and when I honor such a vision I feel as being myself in each and every aspect of my life. And the world can think whatever the world wants to think … I have come to terms with anything that may happen out there, with what other people think, want, desire or expect from me. To some of them I will please and to some of them I will disappoint, not because I want to but because what I have to do may not be among their expectations. My silent inner sense of guidance overpowers the eventual loudness of the world's massive yelling at those times when seeing things eye-to-eye may not be the case. Those that I please is only because what I have to do happens to align with what they expected from me, a coincidence if you will, a peculiar and fortunate overlap in the current state of affairs.

Always follow your heart no matter where it takes you! You can't go wrong if you follow your heart. Use yourself as an experimental lab, let yourself explore paths you would have not gone unless directed by a Higher Power, a voice from within, a choice not seeming the best at the time but so burning inside that you can't say no, something that carries an undeniable sense of rightness, an unbearable attraction to comply with your mission, the things you can't leave unfinished by the time you must go.

Life will offer you plenty of choices to pick from, some difficult, others not so, and sometimes you will take the easy way out only to realize you should have chosen differently (there is nothing more provoking than a missed opportunity to choose wisely the next time around).

Other times you will feel confident enough to go in directions you believe on but have no idea where they will take you, it is the faith in what you are doing rather the things your eyes can see what makes you decide which way to go and what things to do. If that is the case, blessed you for accepting to travel the less travelled roads of life, for making paths in the symbolic wilderness of a world still to be born, for leading the way others will follow.

There is a price that has to be paid for paving roads, for having the vision and the faith to walk where nobody else has ever walked before, out of the belief that such a direction is the way we should go, whether there is a path or there isn't. I was once told how to recognize a pioneer ... *they are the ones with the arrows in their backs!*

Vehemently refuse to live in the comfort and the complacency that a routine oriented, overly controlled and extremely predictable life can offer, for that is not living but being lived upon. Honoring life requires venturing yourself into places you have never been before, exploring the unknown, becoming vulnerable to life events, relationships and the mysteries of following nothing but your own heart. Don't go to predictability-land there is nothing there worth living and dying for, sooner or later you will feel you have wasted your time and however big or small your victories were, at the end, they are meaningless in the context of what you came here to do.

We are expected to create variety in our life, to experience new things, to fail and to try again, as many times as necessary if nothing else to finally learn and succeed. We are here to grow into better, wiser, more loving, more caring and more compassionate humans.

The biggest crime a person can commit is to become anything less than what he is capable of becoming, anything less of what he was meant to be. Always remember it! You will not reach the best and the greatest of you by standing on safe grounds, if you don't risk your status quo, if you always go for the easiest and effortless path, you will have wasted a life full of opportunities, hidden treasures and meaningful contributions.

Don't take unnecessary and uncalculated risks, this is not an encouragement to put your life in danger or do things that would not pass your *heart test*, it is though a call to action, to live a life full of adventures, worthy challenges, fascinating exploration and unparalleled choices. Try not to be afraid, and when you are (we all are at times), don't let your fears control you! Be strong and resilient enough to *act* pluckily for what you believe on (even in the face of fear or uncertainty), never failing to do what you deem right and in so doing *not* letting the opportunity train stop at your station only to depart without you!

I can only contribute to this book with more than 50 years of failures, honest and unintended mistakes from which I have learned a great deal, grown tremendously and forged the who I am, if nothing else by being daring to try. Those same failures made me sad, cry and some of them feel I was not going to make it, that it was the end. It is true that when it rains all you can see is water falling but not the sun above the clouds; you have to believe the sun is still there even if your eyes cannot see it. I am who I am because of what I have lived, the choices I have made, the failures I had to go through and the prices I had to pay. There are no regrets, no remorse of any kind, no intent to go back and do otherwise, avoid what happened (even if I could), for everything I have done was done with the utmost positive intentions to do right and expecting nothing in return but to make an astounding contribution to the world, nothing more and nothing less than what I have been asked to do. I humbly confess that I have tried and I have failed, recommitting to never give up each and every time, getting back up always one more time. If we are to succeed in the business of our life it will not be because of the lack of failures but because of them, for it is not the failure itself what matters but what we do with it!

IF I COULD ONLY HELP ...

Some people act as if they would have come to Earth only to give, others only to receive, most everybody else to do a bit of both. For as mysterious as it may sound, those that love giving are as fulfilled by the act of helping that what they get for them is as much, if not more, than what they give. Intriguingly enough, if you wonder whether they do what they do out of personal fulfillment or to help others, the answer is probably "both."

I am here to help, all I ask for is to be given the opportunity to support others in astounding ways, especially those that carry good and noble intentions in their hearts but for strange reasons of fate, life circumstances, adversity or otherwise are struggling to move on, those that truly want but feel restrained by unfair external forces, as if they were expected to do something they seem they can't. I am here to help change the world for the better, to spread love and good deeds everywhere I go, to help others find the reason why they came here and gracefully embrace it. I want nothing for me, the only thought that I am being able to deliver on the mission I was assigned, that I am being able to help the Universe on its monumental task, fills me with joy and peacefulness. I am here to help the needy, the feeble, the kind and brave hearts willing to slay the dragons of complacency, with wooden swords if that's the only armor available ... for at the end, symbolical swords are only as powerful as the hands and the souls that grab them dearly and purposely.

I get fascinated by seeing those that never give up climbing higher in the pursuit of their envisioned summits, no matter how many times they have fallen and regardless how deep their wounds to be. Long days and long nights will befall in their company as they witness their advancement in the everlasting endeavor of doing what they came here to do. They need nothing else but their inner and burning desire to get there. What is waiting for them at the top is believable enough, attractive enough and engaging enough that no other force on earth will keep them from moving higher. They will simply never give up. Some will get there before their lifetime while others will get close and have to pass the torch to future generations. The key lies not on making it but on never stop trying.

When the pursuit is defying, the odds of making it are slim, yet some hearts never stop … why? Because it is not about making or not making it, it is about always keep trying and giving your very best, then and only then you have the highest chance of making it. If the likelihood is low enough that only one out of one hundred trials will ultimately succeed, that one in one hundred possibility is real and someone will make it, assuming there is at least that someone that never quits until that apparent remote possibility is reached. Who says it can't be you? When I was in the early years of college and still in the basic (undefined) side of engineering, I wanted to become an electronic engineer and some of my colleagues tried to help me see a reality that was so obvious to them but apparently not to me. They talked loud and eloquently with the aim of persuading me to change my mind about my engineering major stating that there were going to be more electronic engineers than what the labor market would need, as many as ten to one (computers were blooming and many engineering students wanted to be part of that emerging trend in technology). Their words were indicating that less than 10% of the graduate electronic engineers would get a job; their advice was "pick another engineering major." I looked at them dearly and said "listen folks, thank you for your advice, I know it is well intended, but I guess somebody will have to be in that 10% and I am going to be one of them, I will get a job." I was determined to make it and 10% was an amazingly good probability for something worth doing! What my friends did not know was that at the time, I had been engaged on causes with much lower yields than that, and I did have some wins! Looking in hindsight I can say with confidence that even if the odds would have been one in one hundred I would have still gone after it.

I was never cut to follow the crowd, to go with the flow, act *realistically*, and find refuge under the higher probability or what seemed easier or more likely. If I believe on something, I will go after it, with or without the world behind me. All I need is to believe on what I am about to chase. I define myself as a fighter, a lonely ranger and somebody who needs company or affiliation of no kind to do what I came here to do (although I certainly appreciate heartfelt help and the companionship of kindred spirits!). Fighters are perfectly comfortable with pursuing low probability outcomes and they know from the very beginning that they will either make it or die trying. This is the rule of engagement, there are no guarantees of any kind, all you know is that you will have to keep going until you can go no more. Whether you make it or not, is beside the point. When the vision of a desired future is so prevailing to force you to daydream about it, a one in a thousand, even a one in a million probability is still attractive, very attractive! Somebody will make it and we better die fighting than with the regret and the subsequent intrigue of never having tried to see what would have happened should we have done what we came here to do. At the end it only takes one thousand or one million fearless souls to make it. Either way I am fine, worthy ends are there to test our endurance beyond reason.

Life is precious with meaning, and meaning comes from the doing of what one was asked to do. Life meaningfulness comes from honoring the purpose our Creator has given us, a purpose as noble as our heart and as challenging as our potential. There will be a need for stretch, there will be pain and adversity, but there will be joy and fulfillment as well.

Let's honor our ancestors and our future generations, doing what we have to do without hesitation or remorse. Our existence will be soon forgotten, all that will stay is what we did for others, the love we had spread, the battles we have fought and how honorably and respectfully we lived the life we were blissfully given.

WHAT THE HEART CAN FEEL VERSUS
WHAT THE EYES CAN SEE

We are prisoners of our senses, what we *see* seems to be way more powerful that what we don't, even when something inside us may tell otherwise. We have to resist, push back, reunite with our inner sense of guidance and refuse to blind-trust what our senses dictate. Our senses were created to guide us in the short term aspects of our lives, in the *fight-or-flight* type of circumstances, this is what the reptilian side of our brain does best, quick reactions to preserve our life and keep us out of imminent dangers. The problem with our primary brain is that everything that looks like a threat is thought to be a threat and treated as a threat, even when it may not be something to be threatened by, and if nothing else for the only purpose of not taking potentially fatal chances. Our primitive brain is risk averse and cannot think in higher levels of complexity, actually it does not think, it reacts.

The essence of our existence should not be conditioned to what survival guides of any sort would recommend, a life fully lived rests beyond mere survival. Deep inside we have the wisdom to conduct our lives in a way that we will prioritize the long term aspects and disregard the fears, concerns or fantasies associated to our daily struggle and excitement. In simple terms, we possess the inherent ability to focus and give more weight to the important versus the urgent. Only rarely, the urgent becomes a life or death circumstance, and if it does, we will know.

If we could only connect the dots of the long term events in our lives and see the big picture, we would be much more relaxed, calm, confident and able to make decisions that would favorably impact the overarching embellishment we are after. This, is the main reason why we are here!

In order to do that, to be able to think long term, we must find a way to circumvent the short term mentality, the fears, the over excitement, the need for immediate gratification and the incessant quest for results in everything we do. The recipe is very simple, you only have to do what you believe to be right, regardless of the outcomes ... if it feels right, it will take you where you need to go, just be patient. This process is *incredibly* powerful and works also in the background teaching your brain new patterns, new ways to interact with the reality around you, educating your mind to think long term, to see beyond the obvious, past the basics, to get in the world of the hardly seen, the nuances, the ignored, the underestimated and the conventionally neglected.

We are creature of habits and habits are learned by the gift of repetition and consistent practice (this means even if it does not seem to work), something of paramount value to build second nature foundations.

As you grow wiser, the formula stays the same, you do what feels right, although the definition of right may evolve over time as you widen your spectrum of possibilities, alter the law of probabilities and lift your spirit beyond the world of what can be *seen*. Be open to change, your view of the world will continuously adjust to your new level of maturity and wisdom, fostering the renewal of what you regard as *right* ... and while its core foundations will remain intact, its surface will get polished and eventually refaced. If you follow your inner sense of rightness with a lifelong commitment and the determination of never giving up, you can't fail as you have restated the definition of winning as: "do the right things the very best you can and never give up." Pay little or no attention to what everybody else thinks, says or does, for it is what *you think, say or do* what really matters in your quest. The world will do what the world needs to do, and so will you.

Be patient and persistent, some things will take longer than what you originally imagined. Learn from your missed expectations, improve your ability to imagine alternative outcomes and do better predictions of future circumstances. Mistakes will teach you lessons and after recovering from the frustration that will follow them, you will know better and will be able to visualize circumstances you could not envision before the missed expectations took place, it is all part of the growth journey, it is all part of a master plan, keep going!

The secret to success is not to always win (based on the world's definition of winning) but to never stop trying and to never stop learning.

I will keep trying until I make it and if my last day comes and I still carry some unfinished business, it was because I just needed a bit more time or because the Universe had different plans. However much or little I have accomplished, this is my legacy to the world and it is up to the Universe to decide if somebody else needs to take from here.

Brave hearts with highly altruistic dreams will always leave some degree of unfinished business behind, their visions are just larger than what a lifetime can dearly embrace. They are part of a bigger-than-themselves cause and have unconditionally committed to do as much as can be done in a lifetime, accepting the price of devoting their lives to something still in growth mode. Deep inside they feel that what they do is nothing but to contribute to the Universe Master Plan and that however much or little they will do, has also been already planned for. You just cannot outsmart the Universe!

Travel the roads of your life without worrying about how long it will take as long as you sense progress and you keep learning. The key to mastery in any field is to learn something new every day and never quit. As I once learned from my investment coach … *if I stay in the game, never quit and practice enough, don't I think one day my brain will figure it all out?* He was right, the longer I stay and the more I learn, the closer to mastery I get. At the end, one month, one year, even one lifetime, what difference does it make in the history of human race? We are providing a small but absolutely meaningful contribution to the betterment of mankind, one being at a time, one lifetime at a time. See yourself as part of something greater than just what you embody, a cause so altruistic to live and die for.

If a cause is not noble enough to die for, then it is not noble enough
to live for either! We all came here to make a difference, a BIG
difference. You were created to do something and to be somebody
in life, and even if that something or that somebody remains an
unfinished masterpiece by the time you have to leave, the Universe
will take matters into its own hands and pass the torch to whoever
else needs to take from there. Rest assured that no noble cause
will be left forgotten, not under the Universe command!

Great enterprises almost always take more than a lifetime and require the continuity of heroic spirits tied together by the passage of time and the connectedness of their purposes, synchronicity in its purest forms! Be certain that there will be heroic souls coming after you and picking up from where you left off, you are just one of the many courageous beings that have made a promise to serve a higher order principle and to honor life ... you are not alone! Do your fair share of the work the very best you can, each and every day of your life and let the Universe figure the rest out. This is what the Universe does best!

Perhaps one of the most difficult challenges is to let go and accept that the Universe is on the driver seat, not you. We can and must do our best, and if we have given our unconditional commitment to the fulfillment of our life call, we don't get to decide where to go and whether or not we will get there in time or even get there at all, this is not our decision to make! Our job is to do our best and keep always going regardless of the setbacks, the disappointments or the frustrations we happen to come across. Expect the unexpected and never give up. Doing what your heart regards as right cannot steer you in the wrong direction, not in the long run. It is actually a much better way to conduct your life insofar your heart will weed out all the starts and the stops that may puzzle your daily life and will concentrate on the big rocks (the engineers and scientists in you will call this process *separating signal from noise*) smoothing your path and helping you focus only on what matters most. The type of decisions you will make by following your heart are unquestionably more aligned with your long term life goals and the meaningfulness of your existence. As far as any other decisions are concerned, you make them if you can, nothing astounding is at risk and any missed turns will be simply short lived.

Your brain is very effective at dealing with the here and now, not so with the long term future. When it comes to the distant future, if your heart murmurs "don't worry, keep going" then you don't have to worry and you have to keep going; when your heart softly talks to you, even in an almost inaudible ways, you do *exactly* as you were told, regardless of what your mind yells at you! The statement "don't worry" in reality means "you do not have to do anything else or new, just keep doing what you are doing."

> *Looking into the future and being able to clearly visualize what is waiting for us there requires a completely different mentality and one that can see the present discomfort associated with growth as a point in our development that can and will be evolved, nothing but a stepping stone that will be soon overcome and left behind.*

Linearly projecting the past and the present into the future will only limit our possibilities and create a virtual boundary to what we could potentially do and be. Welcome the unknown and the uncertain for nothing of significance will be found unless we expose ourselves to the new and the novel. Let the future bring its own treasures to you and receive them with both hands, planning to give back everything you get … for at the end, we are here to do for others more than we do for ourselves.

*Throughout our gradual growth and evolution and every certain
number of years have elapsed, we seem to make a major jump to
another layer of complexity, sometimes without perceiving a big
change but catapulting our potential in unforeseen proportions
and expanding our ability to reinvent ourselves to a completely
different dimension, without being fully aware that a realm
of new and unimagined possibilities is about to be born.*

Throughout the course of my life I noticed that most of the astounding events and turning points, those meaningful circumstances that marked a before and an after, an end and at the same time a new beginning, happened approximately seven years apart. It seems as if it has taken Lili and me that much time to develop and nurture what were once the new phases of our lives before being able to take on another incredible jump and literally escalate to a new level of complexity. Not until about seven years after a big change, we became ready and hungry for more, to envision and seek to initiate something new and hopeful, a new break into the unknowingness of life, the reach of a higher complexity realm and something that would allow us to make greater contributions to the world and our future generations.

*I also noticed that nothing dramatically different occurs at the
moment the change takes place which many times presents itself as
something else in the fabric of everyday life, maybe slightly different
from prior enterprises but clearly not as meaningful as time and
effort will prove it to be. Not infrequently such a change is nothing
but a lateral move or even a backwards move to position us on a
new path that while apparently similar to the one we currently are,
carries a potential that is completely unforeseen and unanticipated.*

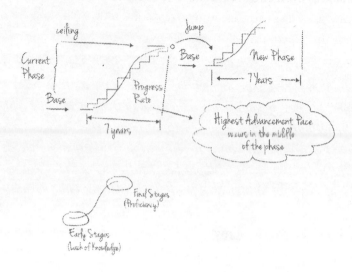

I do not recall being aware of the proximity of a rhetorical maturity ceiling although years later I could see in hindsight that some phases of our lives were almost over; change of a substantial kind was inevitable if we were to continue contributing to the world at a similar rate as we had been contributing up until then. It is captivating to see the enigmatic ways the Universe picks to guide us through the paths we must go, in many instances not asking for our permission or consent (although we have given it up front when we committed to a life of purpose and meaning) and not alerting us when the shift is about to commence.

Some of those germane turning points in our life were *apparently* planned by us (marriage, kids, emigration to another country) although I wonder how many of them were prearranged for us, like when someone else leaves the symbolical front door of life unlocked for us to go through it and face the unknown of the outdoors. There is no question in my mind that the person has to have the desire, the courage and the determination to grab the knob, turn it, open the door and finally venture him or her through it, if nothing else to just see what lays out there. But ... hasn't the Universe also done its part by closing all other windows and letting only that door open, perhaps years before we were able to see it? What else and for how long could a person do in a room that has been explored, known and honored for so long? Life will sometimes asks us in strange and covert ways to look around for doors, test them unlocked and venture ourselves into what lies ahead. Some changes are generally not planned, they just come to us, unrequested, unsolicited, at least at a conscious level of thinking.

When it comes to Lili and me, I have to admit that our personalities are a bit restless, we do not like to live in the status quo of things, to be stagnant, still, not moving. Why deprive the history of mankind to be modestly enlightened by a couple of brave hearts carrying plenty of beautiful dreams and a courage large enough to fight dragons with whatever armor we were given? Whether consciously sought for or not, when we were reaching the boundaries of what at the time were our current life stages, we (either consciously or unconsciously) provoked and finally welcomed the change about to arrive. That evolution, even when far from mind blowing at the time, gradually started to unfold, to grow into full maturity around seven years later. Like getting married, having a child, or moving to another country, eventually the newborn phase in which we once felt confused, uncertain, insecure and inexperienced, came to a point of adulthood and we started to master the once new and novel, feeling more and more comfortable in its company to eventually rank ourselves above average in such a field, something that seven years before was totally unknown and somewhat perplexing.

It is at that time when life will ask us to take on something else, new, different, when our capacity to continue the growth path has almost flattened and we start to entertain an easy ride where the defiance of reinvention has reached a pseudo plateau ... stagnation in its early stages.

Life cycles are different for every person, they are intimately related to the magnitude of your assignments and the velocity by which you can and want to complete them. Speed of action is not necessarily a key factor in the fullness of life, rightful deeds following the guidance of your heart are.

While those changes may not be perceived as the beginning of a new phase in our lives, they most always represent a point of no return, a mystical and meant to be deviation from our old paths, a fork in the symbolical road where we have chosen one way and not another, a direction that secretively suggests the encounter of treasures beyond any stretch of imagination, property of the unknown and intriguing enough not to be ignored or neglected. I can't say with confidence or certainty that the life cycles we went and continue to go through are a pattern-like evolution that most humans will go at one time or another in their life, however I doubt we are the only ones experiencing these phenomena as such a series of events would have been too much of a chance occurrence and a coincidence of no significance (in Jungian terms). I would rather think that it is perhaps not that obvious or easy to identify and visualize the early part of a renewal cycle, the beginning of the new and the ending of the old, in part because they happen simultaneously, overlapping one another, requiring us to look at life as a whole and being able to highlight those significant events that marked the end of a stage and the beginning of another, which at the time are blurry enough to be spotted with crystal clarity. In hindsight, you can pin-point the itinerary you have been following, but it happens so slowly in real time that it is almost impossible to become consciously aware of it. Whatever is being born is happening at clock-hand speed. Can you tell the exact point when the night is starting and the day is ending? I certainly cannot but I can feel a sense of transformation when things have been what they are for quite some time and are beginning to be something else. Not until the day has ended and the night has begun, you will be able to realize what has happened, the emergence of the new happens contemporary with the disappearance of the old, as the moon rises and the sun sets. There is a reason for everything that happens and everything happens for a reason, not all of us are ready to let the old go and the new arrive ... some life events are better left unknown until we are ready to appreciate their magnificent and brilliant nature.

There are reasons behind our conscious ignorance at the time we are going through the transition, reasons beyond our comprehension and our pay grade. Being aware of an upcoming change, particularly if large and unsolicited, can be a great disruption to its natural unfolding and a potential hesitation, refusal or neglect to leave the known and the comfortable behind to embark into the new and the novel, something that in the initial stages will feel as nothing but another rollercoaster ride again. Why we would do it if we are unable to see what lays ahead, that very reason why the change is required to begin with?

The Universe is wise and will share with us only what we can handle without interfering with its plans, whether we like it or not, we will not be asked for permission or consent, what was meant to be, will be.

The visibility of our life cycles requires an atypical abstraction from the present moment and the embarking of oneself in a life-to-date analysis instituting an uncommon habit comprising a rather introspective stretch to seize the sequentiality of our extraordinary life circumstances. This is not an intuitive need the masses find attracted to pursue. Not too many people would find it appealing to engage in a cognitive exercise like this even if they would be able to spot their life cycles after investing reasonable effort, as such a venture requires the *decisive* intent to immerse yourself in the business of lifelong recapping, something abstract enough to suggest sound and tangible returns. For some strange reason that I cannot fully explain, I was entrusted to explore this mental dynamic reeling back years of past life enticingly seeking for patterns of undue relevance that would represent symbolic milestones, mysteriously creating *a before and an after* in the pseudo continuity of life. All I did was to think outside of the here and now looking for clues, signs, apparent nuances that placed in the proper context would reveal the exact location of hidden bread crumbs leading to the assimilation of complex processes disguised in the business of everyday living.

... and so I did, I captured my reflections on a notebook focusing on everything that would appear as out of the ordinary, meaningful in one way or another, and most importantly, intimately related to my priorities and life calls. Gradually and almost unnoticeably, the 7-year pattern started to emerge as if coming from a set of

scattered life circumstances, depicting a revelation as enticing as the magical wonder a child experiences after drawing by numbers!

The more I think about it, the more sense it makes that being creature of habits there has to be some sort of recurrent pattern of self-discovery and reinvention, particularly for those willing to seek the meaning of their lives and in so doing gently and lovingly push themselves in the quest of their highest contributions to the betterment of human kind. If the above reflection created an itch for knowing more about yourself, a sense of wondering about any patterns of your own, the following questions may help you get started:

- Have I taken the time to go back in my life span as far as I can remember and capture those remarkable events that in one way or another marked the end of something and the beginning something else, namely different stages of my journey?
- Which are the utmost positive and valuable events that I happened to go through in life, those milestones that represented indisputable decision points in my quest for meaning?
- Were they something I intentionally created or just a set of an unexpected turn of events in the fabric of everyday life?
- Were those notable events perceived as a blessing ever since the day they arrived or they needed time to mature before their full bloom and glow was evident?
- What was my attitude towards them when their arrival was undeniable and unavoidable?
- How do they fall in the time continuum of my life as a whole?
- Do they seem to occur, coincide or overlap with some recognizable time or repeatable pattern?
- Do they follow some sort of non-chance placement in the span of my life-to-date overall experience?

Extraordinary life circumstances do not happen randomly, even when they may seem they do. The Universe will send new challenges our way when we are ready for them, when we have mastered the one we were given before and we are thirsty of learning and development again. Whether every certain number of years, or following other recognizable patterns does not matter, the key lies in comprehending that your life is somewhat regulated by your readiness to take on something else, new, and more complex, which will rarely happen if you are still struggling with what you were last given. The best way to learn is one prominent challenge at a time so we can focus all our energy, conscious and unconscious on mastering it.

> *Only after reaching a point of proficiency in the current life assignment, we will be kindly asked not to ignore our potential and move up to the next, to our upcoming life phase, one that will better utilize everything we have to give, current or still to be realized, developed and nurtured. Ultimately, our real self is the who we can eventually be, an evolved version of the who we currently are.*

Our passage through Earth is nothing but a pursuit to transform our self into the best human being we can be and become, to reach our maximum potential in the field of our purpose. We are supposed to be the *who* we are meant to be, nothing more, nothing less. The *who* you are meant to be is way different (better, more complex, more loving and more caring) than the *who* you are now, even different to the *who* you *think* you can or will be. The Universe has plans for us that would blow our minds away if prematurely disclosed, *this is the primary reason why you must think very highly of who you must be and what you must do, you can't be told how capable you are, it will just not fit in your mind (… but it will fit in your heart and you can feel it!).*

It is like if the Universe is holding a secret portrait of you in its hands, a forward-looking vision of the future *you* and one that depicts the *who* you are meant to be, carrying beauty beyond reason and sitting far and away from any stretch of imagination. One of the crucial aspects to this rationale is to become conscious that we have choice, that we can either lead our life in a way that we will honor the Universe's master plan and get closer and closer to that human being we came here to become or walk in a completely different direction, in a sense ignoring, neglecting, or refusing to do what we must do. It is completely up to us to decide, choice is a human attribute and we have to inevitably exercise it every day, every month, every year. There will be signals, some of them impossible to miss, and we will have to choose whether we follow them or not, whether we honor life or not.

It is in those meaningful choices where we will express our true life intent, in a sense sticking to or departing from our core set of values and principles, the strongest foundation that holds our sense of love and duty true to the purpose we were blissfully given.

For those of you who may wonder why the Universe does not disclose with us all we can be and become and rather keeps it secret, treasured and sacred, there is a reason, a very important and fundamental reason. Humans can handle only so much change at any given point in their lives and although we get better at it, everything has a limit, a tolerance threshold beyond which we can become mentally overextended, distressed, disturbed and quite certainly distracted from what we need to focus on at the particular stage in our life. The portrait of ourselves will be given to us in bite sizes, small enough not to choke and big enough to comfort our hunger for knowledge. We will be able to see the who we are meant to be in months, perhaps years at a time, as we cannot handle being exposed to the end result of our existence, it will simply defeat its purpose and blow our minds away.

That version of the portrait has to stay in the Universe's custody until we are that close that we may be even able to paint it ourselves. It is at that time when knowing with more certainty what we thought our final destination to be will not hurt but help us get there, when the gap to be bridged is manageable and believable. Be patient, it will come a time when you will be able to see it. Our brain power is limited, especially if we refer to the portion of it that we really use, which is probably less than ten percent of what we have available. That limitation in the way we think is responsible for not being able to transport ourselves into a distant and miraculously different future disregarding the present circumstances. The need to know how we will get there, what will happen when we arrive, what will happen to what we have (not to mention the "why?" questions) would block our ability to effectively function in the here-and-now. Flashes of insight related to the future vision of ourselves will be administered to us in a way we can use them to guide our journey, pointing the next few turns down the road but not the entire itinerary, there is no value in such a vast and detailed vision of the future, we can't do anything with it, it is just too much information.

The unknown embodies one of the greatest human fears and represents a place least desired by the many, yet, it is where the best parts of our life lie, where anything and everything is possible, if we allow it to be.

If the future we are about to live has little or nothing to do with our present, which happened to us in many of our seven-year cycles, we may not be able to switch back and forth, planning for the new while still living in the old. Whether we like it or not, the anxiety to get or not get there will represent a paramount obstacle and inexorably interfere with our ability to give our very best and still be happy with what we have as the perception that the future will be dramatically different alters the way we live the present and could potentially make that future go away or become inexplicably altered … a big enough of a reason why some things are best left unknown.

TIME AND SPACE CONCEPTS REVISITED

While conventional wisdom suggests that the perception of time is sequential, it is not farfetched to conceive an alternative reality containing a different set of the paradigms gravitating around the time continuum and allowing the possibility of the past-present-future triad to be something that does not have to inevitably occur in a sequence. Such a mental construct will remove some of the restrains that tie us to the impossibility of perceiving the passage of time in an alternative way, novel enough that will demand unusual openness to defy the hidden structures of ancient human archetypes.

Past, present, and future are just points in a time tracking mechanism, like the one sixteenth or one eight marks in a ruler, the only difference with a standard twelve inch ruler is that time marks are imprinted in an endless measuring tape called the time continuum. Time has, by definition, no beginning and no end, wherever we are at any given point is called the present, preceded by the past and followed by the future. That time ruler can be navigated left to right and right to left, it is really a two-way street, although we are convinced, with no room for debating, that it can be only navigated in one direction, from past to future. This preconception about time is nothing but a necessary illusion to keep our minds safe, away from the myriad of *impossible-to-answer* questions that would emerge from daring to think otherwise.

For those that can handle venturing into the unknown, I can say with as much confidence as lack of scientific proof, that you can go to the future as easily as you can go to the past, the only difference is that based on conventional wisdom the past looks clear and certain but the future does not. The mere thought of past and future being as certain as uncertain, as reachable as unreachable would puzzle even the brightest minds. You don't need to commit the apparent crime of questioning the unquestionable, why would you do it when you can live peacefully under the protection of the apparently obvious, sacred prototypes that sustained the test of time and perpetuated their far from perfect existence throughout the history of mankind. Why would someone in their right mind defy the odds of living a normal life by not thinking in the same terms everybody else thinks? Only you can guide yourself away from that maze ... and after 50 years of doing it, I can certainly attest that if you are about to defy the laws of conformity, you better be sure of why you are doing it, otherwise you will not have a chance to stand it, sooner or later your initial efforts will become apparently futile, giving up will be unavoidable.

Most human beings spend the majority of their cognitive energy in matters of the present and only occasionally they consciously go to the past for memories and experiences or to the future for visions of what they regard as possible, if nothing else to momentarily escape from the here-and-now in an effort to conceive an alternative form of reality. Conversely, our non-cognitive mind activity, primarily our unconscious, is rarely focused in the present, it travels at light speed from past to future and from future to past, from here to the other side of the world and back and in so doing defies the world of science and accepted knowledge by creating a complex time-space realm where travel with no conceivable human restrictions is simply possible.

The unconscious can literally and temporarily leave the self and expand into the mysterious domains of the Universe, connecting with the collective unconscious, the mystic, the mysterious, the alchemic, the inexplicable, the ancient and the futuristic. It is there, outside of the confines of the known and the predictable where the magic of dreams comes true and the unimaginable can be realized. Let your inner self guide you to ask the questions that need to be asked, whether you are ready for their answers or not. The unknown resides deeper than the whereabouts where your intellect usually wanders and only the unconscious can effectively deal with ambiguous, uncertain, and unpredictable aspects of our existence. You will need to be helped and handheld through the convoluted yet fascinating dimension of the unimaginable. The aim to explore the farthest corners of our self and seek for our true life purpose is a pursuit worth living and dying for, something as exciting as intriguing as life itself. Everything meaningful has a time in our journeys, and finding what we came here to do is not an exception … if you want to do it, you will know when to start!

Challenging the meaning of life is the truest expression of the state of being human. – Viktor Frankl

THE MOST SIGNIFICANT CHANGES IN LIFE

Sometimes you can feel something is changing, something great, paramount or magnificent is being born, however you see nothing drastically different at the present moment, only life as usual. What type of life paradox are your senses introducing you to? What is the meaning of such a feeling, for as feeble or as overpowering as it may be?

You may have just made a decision (or may have been gently pushed into one) that could be striking but since it is so new to you and perhaps one of the many more potentially life changing decisions you went through during the course of your life, you don't have any certainty that this time is different, that this time it will work. While deep inside you know, deep enough to reach the domains of your intuitive self (your unconscious), you are full of doubt and uncertainty on the surface. If the feelings are strong, you must find the courage to operate purely out of faith, conviction and vision. Like when you plant an oak tree seed, it will be weeks before you will even know if the seed will turn into a sprout, strong enough to break out the ground and sneak peek into the outer world in search of the warmth of sunlight and the freshness of a wind blow. You will not only plant that oak seed, you will also plant many other seeds, oak and otherwise, furthermore, you will not only plant, you will also build, repair, take care of, do things for the world, hoping to get nothing but the opportunity to give your very best, to fulfill your life call, to deliver on your commitments, to a be a good man or a good woman, to honor your Creator, your ancestors and your future generations.

The sole meaning of life is to serve humanity – Leo Tolstoy

Planting the oak seed is something you do with all of your love and all of your passion, with all of your hope and all of your dedication, with all your hard work and all of your belief, and most importantly expecting nothing in return, allowing the Universe to work its magic and let be what it was supposed to be. If the seed was meant to be an oak, a one hundred feet tall and five feet wide oak, so it will but not without your care, love and dedication. The Universe alone cannot do it, your help is the spark to light the fire called human life!

> *Somebody must plant the symbolical seed, care for it, nurture it, water it, preserve its sprouts from being eaten by wild life, help it grow straight, protect it from storms, especially when the potentially strong but still feeble baby tree is unable to take care of itself. This is your job, your contribution to the Universe's Master Plan and you must accept it, the Universe needs you!*

After you plant the seed, it will be weeks, eventually months before the sprout comes out and a weak, vulnerable young oak starts to grow taller, wider, stronger. It will be years before the oak reaches heights taller than the average tree and decades before it becomes one of the strongest trees in the forest. Up until that point, your creation will be exposed to the ventures of weather and mother nature, you have to be there watching from a distance and ready to step in if necessary, to protect and prevent, to educate and guide, to preserve, to help the natural progression of the circle of life, to aid the Universe in the turning of events that will ultimately create a better world. From the very first day, you will hope and care for that little, feeble, baby oak tree to one day measure one hundred feet high, and five feet wide!

Even when all that hope, care and vulnerability resides in the future, you can still sense it in the here-and-now, when it is being born, when the seed meshes with the soil to become one with Nature. Something inside you is breaking into the time continuum and messing up with the future, miraculously observing what has already happened at a distant time, like if fast-forwarding a movie that was not yet been filmed in human terms (all movies have been already filmed if you can think of it, and they are all contained in the Universe DVD store, although not available for rent yet!).

*That flash of insight, that moment of truth, that wrinkle of time when
the vision of future greatness is presented to you is like jumping on a
space ship that can time-travel to a future reality where the enormity
of your still unrealized dreams is now a fully functional being, mature,
fully grown and more beautiful than what you have ever imagined.
You must believe in your dreams, for the future that contains them
is nothing but an unrealized present only waiting to be born!*

You have done your job and will now step aside, be available, help
as needed, become a coach, a resource, a supporter. Your craftsmanship
was fully utilized and your creation is complete, carved out to almost
perfection and standing on their feet, strong, independent, with a life
of its own, immutable to the passage of time, growing older and wiser
every day, enlarging its beauty and its taste like an old wine preserved
in an oak barrel.

*Such a vision of a distant future happens in a split of a second, a
glimpse of a blinding form, so vivid and so real that you can't miss it,
ignore it or pretend you did not see it. You did! Most people dream at
night, some dream during the day, it is the latter and not the former
who can change the world! Dare to day-dream! ... and dream BIG!*

THE ILLUSION OF A SEQUENTIAL TIME CONTINUUM

Ever since the dawn of man, visions of a better future have flooded the minds, the hearts and the spirits of those who dearly accepted the noble mission of helping the world become a better place to live, one day at a time, one soul at a time. When those instantaneous flashes of insight, blinding glimpses of a beautiful yet unrealized vision are given to you, you are transported into the future, you can sense it, touch it, feel it, as real and as vividly as if it were in front of you, here and now. You can incontestably say: *it is real, it has just not happened in the present, this is still something that belongs to a future yet to come, a future that has a high probability of becoming present.* Your only doubt, hesitation or uncertainty is whether your vision was meant to be. The feelings are so strong that denying them would just make no sense, like denying what your name is, what you are seeing is as real as the meal you had for lunch, the only difference is it is still yet to arrive (in fact it did, but at a future time that is perceived as having not happened yet).

I am not claiming to have the ability to see the future, nor I am suggesting in any way or shape that anyone can have it. The future, as we know it, is and will always be uncertain. What I am stating is that some individuals have the ability to sense a highly probable future not with their eyes but with their hearts. Such a future state represent a likely outcome they can be a part of, a vehicle to engage themselves in a mystical self-fulfilling prophecy aimed at enlightening the world, aligned with the who they were meant to be and the tasks they were meant to accomplish. Only by believing in your visions of a better future and trusting your heart, you increase the probability of that future state to come true. Some of our higher brain functions (those more intimate with the subconscious activity) are able to ignore the restrictions imposed by conventional notions of time and space continuums, and in so doing dare to defy their nature by thinking in alternative ways, outside of the reach of science and in the whereabouts of an alchemic connection with the yet to be known. Ancient history

248

attributed the ability to engage in this pattern of thought to Gods, saints, wizards, individuals with special abilities and able to see what others cannot, to live in a reality light years ahead of the one the masses are immersed into. It goes without saying that while some of them were respected, honored and remembered, others were condemned, sentenced, ignored or forsaken.

Defying the odds of conformity and the underlying laws that regulate crowd behavior is a path of joy and struggle, as difficult as worth pursuing. Nothing is guaranteed except for the inner feelings of rightness and peacefulness that come out of doing what one was meant to do.

Breaking out of the limits of the time and space continuums and diving into the subconscious realm, whether individual or collective, will allow the visualization of patterns that belong to an uncertain but highly likely future, a place and a time distant to the *here* and the *now*, a symbolic projection of the present circumstances into *what they could possibly be if what it was meant to be becomes what it will be.* You are just for a moment, for a brief glimpse of time, bringing the future into the present, altering the sequentiality of time and alternating the natural past-present-future order of things. You need to be aware that by believing what you *see* you are accepting to disobey the physics of time, at least as our conscious mind thinks of them. Everybody knows that time travel has never been achieved and that any attempt to even think of it as a possibility would code you as insane, ignorant or childish, yet the question is still out there: *is it impossible?*

As far as I am concerned, and at the price of defying the confines of conventional science, something is as impossible as anything that could not be done yet. The history of mankind has witnessed a countless number of stubborn humans believe in their visions of the future so vehemently, so convincingly and so conclusively that for them, the future was set and done and all they were going after was to prove their visions right, if nothing else to just help the Universe at turning the unknown into the known. Can we confidently say that they were able to see (although not with their eyes but with their hearts) that which was invisible to the untrained eye?

> *Visionaries have extra-ordinary powers that paradoxically enable them to see far beyond what the masses can, even if unreasonable stretches of imagination could be reached. The limits are not in how far the farthest confines of massive thinking can go but in how daring one can be when it comes to disobeying conventionalism and being willing to face the unknown, trusting one's instincts beyond reason and regarding the visions of a still-to-be-born future not only as possible but also as truthful enough to be lived and died for!*

If you find yourself embraced by such powerful state of being and can *feel* that the future is so vivid and clear that you can even describe it in full detail, color, shape and form, you are at risk to become labeled and misbelieved, regarded as too creative, naïve, or even mentally impaired. The business of trusting your heart in the process of disputing the laws of empiricism and scientifically sound principles is not for those who depend on social acceptance and popularity, wherever you are trying to go cannot take you farther from those destinations. Believing in what you treasure inside carries guarantees of no kind, reassurances of no sort, expect no sympathy, no appreciation and no praise. At the end, if you believe in what you see, nothing else matters, those visions were given to you for a reason and whatever that reason is, requires the utmost respect and consideration. Don't try to prove anything, neither to others nor to yourself. Visions of indescribable beauty are not meant to be proven, they are meant to be believed. Just believe them to be true!

The time to become one with Nature and let yourself be carried away to where your visions would take you would come in those moments of clairvoyance when strong and irrefutable sensations of something great being born would arrest and invade you, as if coming from nowhere but above. Don't fight them, accept what you are given for it is a gift given to you for a reason, to either guide you in a land of confusion or give you strength and endurance in a land of adversity and disbelief. Visions of a better future that look so real to be ignored are a privilege, an honor and a blessing. Never refuse to believe them, dreams are given to you by the Universe because there is faith in you, there is confidence that you can carry them with all your love and all your care, treasure them, nurture them, embellish them until the point they are irresistible and compel you to act on their inner beauty realizing their splendor and transcendence.

How else would you know, with almost complete certainty, of a beautiful future if not because you have been there and made it back through blinding glimpses of indisputable brilliance residing beyond any extent of conventional imagination? Would you believe something like this to be true if told by someone else, no matter how significant that someone else would be to you? I doubt it ... dreams of blinding nature have to be first hand lived!

> *Visions that carry world-changing powers have to be transferred first hand, from the Universe directly to the beholder, they have to be irresistible, enchanting and mesmerizing enough to create a burning inner sensation, something that cannot be denied but only lovingly accepted and committed to.*

Your unconscious mind knows much more than your conscious mind does and although they regularly and secretly meet, you don't get to remember it, it is not part of the plan. Rest assured they know each other very well, even if they never formally told you about it. There will always be aspects of your life that will remain enigmatic and intriguing, and no matter how hard you may try to solve the puzzle, you will not advance any further if the time when you will be ready to understand is still yet to come. Life can become puzzling and defiant, only to guide us to the exact places we must go, and at the exact times we must get there.

__Matthew Morgan__: Well, you don't love life itself. You love, uh, places, animals, people, memories, food, literature, music. And sometimes you meet someone ... who requires all the love you have to give. And if you lose that someone, you think everything else is gonna stop too. But everything *else just keeps on going. Giraudoux said, you can miss a single being, even though you are surrounded by countless others. Those people are like ... like extras. They cloud your vision, they're a meaningless crowd. They ... They're an unwelcome distraction. So you seek oblivion in solitude. But solitude only makes you wither.*

Pauline Laubie: *So I'm an unwelcome distraction. I'm a cloud?*

Matthew Morgan: *You are the only part of my life I haven't figured out yet.*

From the movie: Last Love

We are getting deeper into the complexity of our-selves and bordering the line with the mystic, the alchemic, the inexplicable phenomena surrounding and sustaining our existence, things that would be impossible to judge in plain, everyday language. I use this type of inner dialog very regularly as it helps me explain some aspects of my life that would be otherwise too simplistic, too mundane, too boring and too immaterial to justify giving the best and the greatest I have to give. There has to be something else to life than just what the untrained eye can see, what the media broadcasts, what public opinion accepts as the ultimate truth and what the masses believe, it can't be just that.

Oliver Wendell Holmes wrote ... "I wouldn't give a fig for simplicity this side of complexity but I'd give my right arm for simplicity the other side of complexity." I could not agree more with such statement. I would even add that it is not uncommon to find people lost in the complexity of simple things, never seeking to find the simplicity of complex and transcendent life matters.

Accept the simplicity of simple things and enjoy them as they are, there is no need to embellish or perfect them as they carry beauty beyond reason. At the same time, never stop trying to find the simple side of complex life circumstances, seeking to understand that which does not seem obvious, what others ignore or don't even think about, know of its existence or simply deny in an effort to avoid complicating their easy lives. It is right there, in the optimal equilibrium of both the simple and the complex where it all starts and it all ends. Once you can better visualize both the simple and the complex sides of your existence, becoming able to tell and accept their differences, everything else resonates in a mystifying unison. It is after recognizing the simplicity of the simple and the complexity of the complex that the stars would align and illuminate the path you were meant to follow.

Past, present, and future are not disjointed, they are not just marks in a sequential time chart where the past comes first, then the present, and finally the future. This is a necessary illusion to keep our mind operating in the confines of its reach and a way to look at the passage of time in such a manner that would not disrupt the use of our limited brain functions. There is however another way, one that would require an extra-ordinary capacity to process information, one that would require the abstraction from currently accepted premises and paradigms, one that would not easily fit in our conventional thinking patterns.

Our unconscious is connected to the Universe through the symbolic pathway that Jung called the collective unconscious, the connectedness of all individual unconscious minds through universal and timeless archetypes, notions, symbols, codes, signals, etc. It is a completely different dimension and one that can be hardly described with words and traditional thinking patterns as it was not crafted to be handled and understood by the conscious mind. The unconscious is more related to the field of feelings, emotions and intuition, what constitutes the non-analytical and non-rational sides of our selves. This is why it is so important to keep reaching out to your heart, it is there where you will find your best partner, your best ally and your best companion to crack and decode the scriptures of the subconscious world, the timeless pieces of your existence, the keys to unlock treasures of the ancient past and the still to be found golden gems of an unforeseeable future.

The answers to life most puzzling questions do not lie inside a tasteful dinner, a comfortable bed, or a luxury car. They are hidden at a completely different level of thinking than the one utilized on the fabric of everyday life, they are treasured far and away from the mundane aspects of our reality, beyond the worries, concerns, wishes and desires that get most of the attention of our minds. To reach the essential aspects of human kind, we have to be both simple and complex in our approach to life, to get past the obvious, the easy, the commonly accepted, the constant blurry of messages that come to us from the outside, unsolicited, useless and only meant to satisfy the basic and primitive intents of those sending them.

Right there, in the meeting point of those apparent opposites, the simple and the complex, lies the key to decode the purpose of our life, the one and only reason why we are here.

If you find the above statement perplexing, it is beating its purpose as it was meant to confuse you, to puzzle you, to challenge your assumptions and to make you think in ways you are not accustomed to think. You must break the thought patterns that have governed your life as you know it, nothing will change unless you start by changing the way you think, which will lead to a change in the way you feel and ultimately a change in the way you act.

We were born to conform and not to, to be part of human kind and not to, to belong and not to. This is not a game of words or a foolish intent to derail you, it is a way to gently guide you to think differently, to be open about the possibility of opposites co-existing at a higher level of complexity, higher than where you are today. Humans were born to be part of a race, we are social beings supposed to live together and share similar patterns of behavior, to have common denominators, to learn from each other and to capitalize our collective advancement, generation after generation. That is the *conform* side of life, the part of our existence regulated by commonalities. There is another side, an opposite side, where we were expected not to conform, not to be equal but different, to be able to think and act independently of each other and according to our very own nature, our very own mission and our very own value system. We will not try to be different than our next door neighbor just for the sake of differentiation but because we were meant to be different, we have to be who we were meant to be and they have to be who they were meant to be, and in the process of becoming ourselves, we will share some traits and not share some others.

You have to raise yourself above the sea level to be able to see the entirety, to climb high enough into the tallest tree to see the wholeness of the forest. We should all eat, but perhaps not eat the same food, or at the same time, or the same quantities. We should all do more for others than we do for ourselves, but perhaps our ways of doing things for others will not be the same. We should all work hard and rest, but maybe our pace, rhythm and tenacity will not be the same, at least not at all times. We should all listen to ourselves more than we listen to others, but perhaps the degree of our inner dialog, boldness to act and acceptance of the consequences of our actions will differ. We are supposed to conform with Universal patterns of thinking and behavior and not to … you decide when, where, how, and why …

Everything can be taken from a man but one thing: the last of human freedoms - to choose one's attitude in any given set of circumstances, to choose one's own way – Viktor E. Frankl

AN ALTERNATIVE THEORY OF THE TIME CONCEPT

Back to the notion of time and the illusion of the sequential continuum, there is a radically different approach to explain the correlation of the past-present-future triad and one that demands a very open mind to question the status quo, the universally accepted notions about the way we think, and in so doing engage ourselves in the process of *meta-thinking* (thinking about the way we think). If you decide to give this reflection some consideration and embark on elaborating more substance around it, you need to realize that you are deviating from the norm and joining a few defiant minds that venture into the exploration of alien mental assemblies that can explain some of the phenomena associated with strong feelings about the future, the persuasive nature of some dreams and the desire to explore aspects of life that many people would not be interested about. Embarking into the discovery of the deepest and most complex sides of the self will bring you no company other than your own, a mystical journey that will remain with you in relative secrecy and shared only with those with a true need to know.

The world refers to anything that falls outside of the norm as peculiar, strange and bizarre, as if those entertaining such a quest would be under the spell of some sort of inexplicable oddity, an apparent impairment that would enigmatically force their minds not to think straight and in compliance with the conventional patterns the masses use, conforming a rare kind of unwarranted rebelliousness to live a "normal" life.

Don't be surprised to find a sizable part of the world's population to be born, live a full life and finally leave without having ever asked themselves once about what they were here for, what was life all about or what was the main purpose of their existence. For many people, life just *is*, and there is no need to dig deeper into the philosophical aspects of it, the true nature of our being here, and the ultimate meaning of our passage through Earth. For them, life is nothing but a sequence of events, some of them randomly connected, aimed at making them do what they are expected to do, what they want to do, or what they have to do enjoying life as they go, to finally leave when their moments would come. It is not uncommon to witness some people walking the final stages of their journeys resisting their departures as if they have not had the opportunity or the time to do everything they *think* they had to do. It is only when you have done what you deemed right that you are equally pleased to either stay or leave, ultimately accepting whatever the Universe decides and the commands of your Creator, a benevolent God that loves you unconditionally.

The questioning, the inquiring and the seeking to understand is only reserved for those who want to know more, the ones in the quest for clues and signals, posing new and difficult-to-resolve dilemmas the moment they know as much as they wanted to know, when the thirst for new insight is starting to invade their symbolical throats. Life is a pursuit to find truth, a hunt for knowledge and contribution, something that never ends but always gets farther, taking each of us ahead in our own calls, generation after generation, regardless of difficulty, complexity or effort.

Past, present, and future are sequential and they are not. We see them as one coming after the other because we cannot imagine it to be otherwise. There are a myriad of aspects in the Universe far beyond any extent of human comprehension, elapsing into dimensions of realism never thought of, bordering the line with the mystical, the irrational and the unreasonable. Something is labeled as non-sense when it cannot be explained by our senses, allowing the possibility that such a phenomenon may carry a complexity beyond comprehension and not necessarily a property of the absurd. When it comes to the general population, especially those conforming with massive thinking patterns, sooner or later mind mechanisms aimed at preserving some sort of stability in the way we think would make us stop diving into extraneous concepts we cannot explain, mental constructs that, if stubbornly explored, would just raise too many difficult to answer and extremely puzzling questions.

There is however a certain number of human beings that dare to defy the odds of conventional thinking, unreasonably stretching their minds to think about what others would consciously or unconsciously refuse to entertain, only because the world they see through the eyes of the masses does not make any sense to them. It is too simplistic and much less elaborated than it could be. These defiant souls live not so much in what is assumed to be but in what could possibly be, and in so doing incessantly chase the demystification of the obvious.

To defy conventional thinking you need to carry a strong belief that we, humans, are unnecessarily complicating the simple sides of life while at the same time oversimplifying or ignoring altogether the complex ones. The essence of becoming one with ourselves resides in finding the optimal equilibrium between the simplicity and the complexity of life, rightfully discerning which is which and investing ourselves with laser focus on that which matters the most.

The natural order of past-present-future triad *can* be altered as *they are actually sequential only in our minds*. Past, present, and future are nothing but points in a continuum, marks in an endless time ruler that can be traveled back and forth, as many times as you want, as far as you want and as fast as you want. I do not believe in coincidences, especially those significant in nature. Carl Jung elaborated this subject in great detail in his book "Synchronicity" where the constructs of meaningfully connected events is developed. Events of substantial relevance and correlation (substantial as defined by you) that do not seem to respond to cause or correlation, are not randomly connected, they are linked and somewhat intertwined by the commonality of their meaning or intent, significant coincidences cannot be explained by chance theory. The phenomena and dynamics that belong to the field of synchronicity are intimately related to the alteration of the time continuum and the notion that the past-present-future triad does not have to necessarily occur in a sequential order. We tend to believe that if two events are connected by causality, meaning that one is the cause and the other the effect, the event that is the cause happened first and at a prior time than the event that represents the effect. This is the only possibility if you assume that past comes first, then present, then future, which will in turn dictate that the causal event must be in a past time compared to the effect (since it created it). I will challenge the paradigm that the past-present-future triad has to occur in that order, in other words that past happens always first, then present, and finally future.

Past, present, and future have already happened and have not. The sequentiality of time is such a powerful illusion that we will not be able to see it from within its confines (for the same reason that the closer you get to the trees the less likely you will be able to see the forest), you have to be able to step out of the linearity of the time continuum, even if only for a moment, to be able to conceive an alternative explanation of it. Only then you may be able to visualize a world configuration outside of the current time paradigms and conceive, even if only for a brief moment, how things could be if what it is, it is not.

Based on the conventional definitions of time, including the order of past-present-future, an event in the future cannot be the cause of an event in the past (defining event as something that either happens in the outside world, a *physical* occurrence, or something that happens in the confines of the mind, a *psychic* occurrence). As a matter of fact, Jung elaborated this unity of a physical and a psychic event and developed the concept of significant coincidences around it. The significant coincidence construct does not have to be limited to any specific type of events, it could be any combination of physical and psychic occurrences as long as you deeply feel they are synchronistically connected, linked only by their meaning and regardless of any causation or randomness in their relationship.

For example, the sense, feeling or thought, that something great is being born, it can be nothing but a *future* physical event creating a thought, feeling or intuition at the present time, a connection between a future, yet to occur physical circumstance and something happening here and now, in your mind, the thought, which conforms a psychic event. In reality, you can think that the future circumstance responsible for your current feelings has already happened at a future time and it is being meaning-fully linked to the mental and emotional activity you are experiencing now. Puzzling? Just accept it for a moment, don't dispute it, assent that there is a small probability it could be true even if you can't explain it.

The outbreaks of current wisdom start to visit us when we allow ourselves to hold notions alien to our current thinking and if even for a moment we become able to accept as possible those things we cannot yet explain or describe. We must respect the fact that deep inside there is something telling us it could be true, when we get the feeling that something we envision is as possible as anything that already happened ... a sort of déjà vu as real as inexplicable.

Allow your mind to lead yourself through unfamiliar terrain, to conceive patterns of change, things that make no sense as long the conventional way of thinking is concerned. To make room for these extra-ordinary realizations, your analytical brain needs to stretch, your conscious mind needs to reach the borders of the unthinkable and befriend the confines of the unknown, the unreasonable and the absurd. *It is at that point when you will dive into the universal pool of knowledge that exists above and beyond what others call reality.* The history of mankind has proven times and again that what was once truthful ceased to be so after somebody proved it wrong, non-conforming, or disturbing the status quo. Everything started with somebody, unafraid enough to defy the crowds, challenging the basic assumptions created by human kind to simplify complexity and make what were the current views of the world to become credible and manageable by the collective (and limited) brain power that existed at the time those beliefs were held true.

But we can and we will evolve, what was once conceived as impossible will stop being so and a black swam will show up again if nothing else to prove the white swam theory insufficient to explain the new set of circumstances. Nothing happens outside of its own time, things follow the order of priority they must carry to allow the history of mankind to seamlessly progress according to our evolution abilities. What we call reality is nothing but a model of what we see, a simplified version of an overwhelming world that if not casted in a mold would simply overflow our capacity to reason and in a sense provoke collective mental insanity. We must limit the possibilities of what we think can happen around us in order to comprehend it and visualize some patterns that would allow us to predict environmental responses in a way that would be accepted by the masses and not only by a few intrepid minds.

All models are nothing but simplifications of a much greater, much complex reality, a dimension so deep and wide that cannot be handled by the world's collective knowledge possessed at the time the model was created. As humanity advances, flaws to the created model are found and a newer version of it is released, one with some upgrades on the areas where the gaps were found. Models of the overarching reality governing the Universe will continue to evolve at human speed, getting more complex in direct proportion of what our collective brain power can handle.

What was once accurate and reasonably explained what was happening in the outer world has now holes, discrepancies and contradictions forcing us to find a more accurate representation that better reflects the new view of the reality that has gained acceptance once the unknown became familiar. Models, no matter how complex or elaborated, have a shelf life, past of which they need to be upgraded or completely replaced (depending on the proportion of the new insight).

This process has been in place since the dawn of times and will continue until the dusk of it. New models would eventually lead humanity to accept that what used to be an indisputable truth is no longer so and that there is a new truth coming to replace it. The truth, as we see it, is nothing but our most honest effort to describe what we see, believe and can explain in regards to what happens in the worlds outside and inside of us. For some, it requires scientific proof, for others it does not, regardless of your natural inclination or preference (knowledge or belief), we call true that what we *know of* or *believe in*, and both our knowledge and our beliefs will evolve as we mature and grow, not only as individuals, but as a kind, as a race and throughout the passage of time.

ELABORATIONS ON THE SIXTH SENSE

Intuition, the human ability to perceive things by non-rational means, has been historically regarded as more prevalent in females where the right side of the brain (responsible for the non-analytic and creative thinking patterns) seems to be more developed than in males. I would not disagree with that statement as I have personally contemplated this postulation supported by enough evidence to believe it to be true. Such a theory is also more prevalent in those cultures where the roles of males and females are in support of this gender differentiation (males more responsible for the analytical societal roles and females more responsible for the emotional ones). Intuition could be defined as having feelings suggesting the possibility of future circumstances to unfold, something that is still unknown for the world but that has presented itself to the person carrying the intuitive feeling in a way inexplicable by conventional logic, let alone proven by traditional science.

How could this happen? Those individuals that are able to experience intuition are synchronistically connected to the future in such a way that something likely to happen will become visible to them in the form of a psychic event (the intuition). One could also hypothesize that the future circumstance already happened although in a different time dimension and is traveling back to the present time to empower the person carrying the vision with the ability to foresee what in conventional terms is likely to happen. Intuition could be also described as the gift to travel the time (and sometimes the space) continuum back and forth, even without knowing one is doing it. It all happens as if one would travel to the distant place/time, see what it holds and in a split of a second come back to the here and now able to describe what one sensed, not clearly knowing how all this happened. At the end, what we call intuition could be nothing but a fancy definition of the old fashioned time/space-travel hypothesis where a person can mysteriously sense what is happening at a place and/or time different from their own and in a way creating a fracture in the time/space continuums. These phenomena are complex in nature and difficult to describe with words. The above definitions are a simplification of all they could really be, modeled in a way that would fit our mind and our capacity to rationalize extra-ordinary psychic activity. Those who have ever experienced episodes of intuition have to be open to non-conventional ways of thinking, feeling and sensing in order to believe the insight they are being provided with, by non-rational means. Trusting intuitive sources of insight requires courage beyond the ordinary and the ability to detach from the fabric of everyday life letting the mind go astray to reach unthought-of levels of consciousness and abstraction. Conventional wisdom (including traditional science) will not accept it as something sound and trustable, regarding it as pure fantasy, an illusion, or episodes of unlimited imagination.

Like intuition, the strength of some dreams (day-dreams and visions of a positive yet to come future), the messages they carry and the enthralling sense of duty derived from their content seem to suggest that circumstances still yet to come have already happened and are reaching out into the present as if begging for somebody to believe in them so feverishly that the future will face a lower risk to be changed.

This theme is related to the existence of parallel realities which helps explain the possibility of something that have already happened to be altered and replaced by something else, a different, alternative, consequential or otherwise synchronistically related event. It all transpires as if the intuitive episode would have mysteriously witnessed a reality that already happened in one of the multiple realms waiting for us at a future parallel time with triggers or causes of unknown origins.

The acceptance of novel and defiant hypothesis like this requires you to stretch your current paradigms and allow for the construction of alternative mindsets that could explain what your current view of the world would not permit. The space and time continuums are unquestionable mental representations leaving you with little or no wiggle room to conceive unconventional world configurations where a different way in which the perception of time should be approached. If you can put what you have learned about space and time to a test and dare to defy conservative thinking patterns, you would embark on a journey that may open the gates of your imagination to venture yourself into *the domains of the unknown and the uncertain* to mystically capture extraneous flavors of an already tasted meal that would completely transform the way you see the world, both the outer and the inner versions of it.

When you get a glimpse of intuition, you are momentary leaving the present, traveling in time to a distant or not so distant future, sensing something and bringing it back with you in the form of hunches, gut feels, perceptions and extra-sensory clues. What you saw there was not seen with your eyes and hence cannot be drawn, perfectly painted or described with incredible clarity. What you saw there was felt with your heart and was presented to you more in the form of a feeling about something believed to have not happened yet, although it has indeed happened, at a future time, and in one of the possible parallel realities yet to arrive.

Have you ever found yourself meeting someone for the first time and having a strong feeling suggesting that this person is a good human being? How do you explain it, especially if years later you find that hunch to be true? You could say it reminds you of somebody else you know, or that you perceived some subtle clues, resemblances, etc. It could also be said that you were able to alter the time continuum and reach out a future and a past you did know about, not consciously. The past of a good person is full of good deeds and the future of your relationship with him or her will be also full of positive experiences. You could have perceived all that in a split of a second. What I am describing is not the world as you know it, it is indeed a different world, as real for some people as your world is for you, and in order to conceive the possibility of such a world to exist, you need to be open to embark in a paradigm shift. You do not have to do it, staying where you are is indeed a possibility and a choice only you can make.

Albert Einstein said *that the solution of a problem cannot be found at the same level of complexity where the problem was created*. If you have a problem with your current view of the world (and I am not meaning you do, but if you do), if you cannot explain why some things are the way they are, you will need to elevate yourself above and beyond your current level of thinking, for the way you think is being part of the problem and to resolve it, you need to start by thinking in different ways. Think about the way you think! This is called meta-thinking.

The possibility of altering the sequentiality of the time continuum and traveling back and forth through it, eventually jumping into past or future times not of our own, either immediate or distant, is intimately related to the fields of mythology, alchemy, spirituality, synchronistic phenomena, and the realms of the unconscious, both individual and collective. Our conscious mind can only deal with the present and the past we remember to then extrapolate them into the future. This is what we do best, it is called linear projection, the human ability to extend present and past circumstances into the future, giving a higher weight to the repetition of what is or once was. It is true that history tends to repeat itself, except when it does not ... fractures inside the history of mankind and inside individual lives do happen! On the other hand, it is our unconscious mind that can more easily depart from the conventional way of thinking and mess around with a whole different dimension of time, space, and meaningfulness. If it is your desire to explore the unknown, you will have to reach inside ... the clues leading you in such a journey can only be found inside the confines of yourself. Reaching in facilitates the conversations of the conscious and unconscious sides of your mind, making it a lot easier for you to engage in the process of finding yourself. The unconscious communicates in symbolic language, for instance the one found in dreams and intuition, this is why it becomes paramount to learn the language of your inner side, the deepest, most intriguing part of your-self, where the gates to Universal wisdom lie and are waiting to be opened.

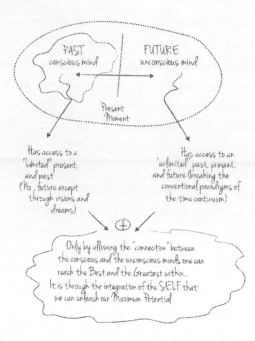

Accepting new and revolutionary hypothesis that may describe what has not been already subject of serious questioning, will call for the *belief* that there are other explanations for what happens around us (a different and future model of the current reality), a sort of unheard theorem not yet conceived by the public and one that, if accepted as *possible (or not impossible)*, would make you look foolish among the many and wise among the few. At the end, why insist on defying conventional wisdom and shake the status quo of what seems to *reasonably* explain what happens, at least on the surface? New models get created by two main drivers: (1) the irrefutable proof that the current representation of reality fails to symbolize that which it was supposed to simplify, (2) the belief that there is a better way to characterize the complexity the current model is trying to reduce. The sequential nature of the time continuum is nothing but a created illusion necessary to comprehend our current reality, a model in its own rights, as precise as our collective conception of the world requires.

New mega models (models adopted by human kind as a whole) only come when indisputable evidence is found, suggesting that the current model is inadequate, inaccurate, or simply mistaken in light of the new knowledge. The world operates under the influence of a strong inertia limiting any proactive and daring drive to look for alternative explanations to accepted and seemingly functional representations of the current and impending reality. Only valiant souls, incessantly battling against all odds, can and will make the paths that would lead the world into the discovery of better ways to explain what would not be otherwise doubted until enough proof of obsolescence would abound.

Without free spirits always looking for the miraculously beautiful, chasing wonders would only be a matter of pure survival.

THE TALLEST MAN ON EARTH

Some people believe that a realist point of view is more effective to cope with life than an optimist perspective suggesting that while an optimist hopes for the wind to blow in the direction he needs, a realist adjust the sails to the direction the wind blows. I always respected this point of view as it contains valid assumptions, especially in the fabric of everyday life, however there was something inside me that suggested that the optimum stand was somewhere in between realism and optimism, something we could call *realistic optimism* which I ended up finding that was a subject studied by some scholars in the field of psychology (Scheider, Hunter, Kilstron, Spiegel, etc).

It is true that realism helps you adjust to the current circumstances in a much better way than pure optimism and pessimism do, however if you are too much of a realist, you are at the verge of becoming imprisoned inside the confines of the reality you are immersed into and forget that there is always a way out, a chance to change things for the better. It is there where the optimism stand comes to help, not by ignoring reality altogether but by adding an optimistic flavor to the mix by empowering you to more creatively and freely find alternative ways to enhance it.

Having a positive, optimistic outlook of life and the future will tilt the probability odds in your favor and in a sense help you create self-fulfilling prophecies of what lies ahead.

Whether you think you can, or you think you can't--you're right –
Henry Ford

I like having one foot on the realistic and another on the optimistic sides of the road … and the question is, would that be possible, can one adopt a realistic view of reality and at the same time become optimistic about what to do with it? Are realism and optimism mutually exclusive?

The short answer is: *they are not.* And here comes the long answer, optimism and pessimism are opposites in the sense that while the former tends to expect somewhat good outcomes out of most contexts, the latter tends to expect the opposite, somewhat negative outcomes from most every set of circumstances. No bias of any kind (neither positive nor negative) is needed to expect good outcomes out of good circumstances or bad outcomes out of negative ones as this is the natural expectancy and the most probable result. To reverse the high probability in either direction, some energy has to be invested in order to redirect the flow of life and in so doing, avoid the natural walk into the path of least resistance, which in one way or another shifts your perspective into the realm of contrarianism.

I have to agree with Martin Seligman on his conceptualizations of learned optimism, like him, I too believe that optimism, realism, and pessimism, can be learned (and unlearned), without attempting to remove the genetic component that can create some unintended bias to a preferred style but educating the mind to counteract it. It would be naïve to ignore the *nature* part of our personalities and believe that everything we would eventually be and become is only regulated by the *nurture* side of life, namely what we can learn and teach ourselves through the *living* experience. There is an undeniable innate tendency built on our DNA, true and irrefutable, we have a genetic code that can't be neglected, but to say that we are predetermined by our genes to carry a life we do not want is a completely different statement and one based on the assumption that we are helpless to offset in any way or shape our natural tendencies, that there is no choice but to be what our genetic code has suggested.

As humans, we always have choice, and it is that self determined action which can at times be directed to counteract our genetic composition as much as possible and to the degree of our ability and our beliefs ... if it fits in your heart it can be done, regardless of how much DNA is against you! It is cornerstone that we first realize that such a choice exists and that the itch of wondering about what we *want* reaches us and starts to gently but persistently pull our triggers waiting for an answer.

We are not what we were born with but what we decide to do with our lives, acknowledging and accepting our initial toolkit, using as many tools as necessary and not using those we do not need while at the same time seeking to get the ones missing to pursue the fulfillment of our missions without conditioning our life to what it would have been should we have decided to follow the path of least resistance, to ignore our calls and let our nature not be nurtured.

I am not what happened to me, I am what I choose to become — C.G. Jung

Unlike optimism and pessimism which stand at the two ends of a personality continuum, optimism and realism are not opposites however they can sometimes be different enough that the mere thought of reconciling their foundations, of being both realist and optimist can be a bit challenging, especially if we fail to see the intersections of apparently diverging traits. To resolve such a dilemma you need to remember that all opposites meet at a higher level of complexity (optimism and realism are not opposites but can seem to oppose or divert from each other at times).

I characterize realism as the ability to accurately expect what may possibly happen with a reasonable degree of objectivity and avoiding the feelings or thoughts of what one may wish, want, or desire to interfere with such expectation. Realism requires a probabilistic mentality, something that generally regulates the dynamics of life as only a few circumstances fall in the camp of the all or nothing, black or white type of odds. Generally speaking there is a variety of possible outcomes to any given situation each of which carries a probability of occurrence based on similar and past settings (history tends to repeat itself, especially the part of history regulated by human behavior, which is habitual in nature). Realists tend to limit their actions to what they believe is reasonably possible given the circumstances and adjust their courses of action to respond to the outside conditions, factors or triggers. In other words, being realist is having your feet on solid ground when it comes to expecting what the future may unfold. The realist's head is a body height above their feet, a body height above ground.

I see optimism as the ability to conceive a future better than the present, an enhanced version of what a linear projection of the past would suggest. Optimism is titling the odds of what can potentially happen to the positive side, *expecting* and *creating* conditions that can change the outcome probability to fall on the wished, wanted or desired side of things instead of where it would fall if no intervention at all would be exercised. Optimism is being able to day-dream and let your mind go astray, in a sense abstracting yourself from the here and now, and from what a realistic or neutral (not optimistic and not pessimistic) expectation of the future may suggest.

Optimists expect and work toward a more promising future than what a realistic view would suggest, as realists tend to accept their views of the future and work around it. In a sense, while realists tend to see reality as something that has to be accepted, optimists refuse to accept anything less than what their visions of a better future would dictate. At the end, it is such acceptance or lack thereof what drives the behavioral patterns aimed at proving ourselves right, optimists or realists alike.

One of the limitations of realism and of realists is their submission to what the higher probability turn of events would suggest, restraining them from defying the odds that the lower probability can indeed happen if sufficient energy and persistent action is applied (actually such a different future does not *just* happen, it is created by forcing the natural course of events to move in a direction different to what reality would suggest, the path of least resistance). Far from explaining the rationale behind the realist mind, it seems as if reality is perceived to be so untouchable, so difficult to change, alter or modify that the only action we can entertain is to accept it and work within their boundaries.

Optimists have their head way up in the air, where their desired future view of the world rests and their feet a body height under it. Optimists, as opposed to realists, tend to ignore the linear projection of the past as a way to predict what the future may bring, defining their own set of desired circumstances instead and somewhat acting in isolation of the status quo, suggesting to act in defiance of its influential power to determine what the future would turn out to be. In so doing, they are consciously or unconsciously ignoring the most reasonable and probable outcome and pursuing low probability occurrences if those circumstances happen to be their desired destinations.

No wonder conventional wisdom perceives realism and optimism as apparent opposites and two stands of difficult reconciliation. Being realist and optimist at the same time would require that you keep your feet to the ground and your head way up in the air, making you the *tallest* man on Earth!

Despite the apparent contradiction and the metaphorical analogy, I hold a strong belief that realism and optimism can indeed be reunited and reconciled although at a higher level of complexity, where the apparent opposing perspectives could intersect. If you intend to find the crossing point where realism and optimism will eventually meet, start by acknowledging that the natural probability of occurrence (the linear projection of what the past suggests the future to be) should be regarded as only one possible outcome, the most probable one if nothing of significance is undertaken to deviate the course of history, in a sense letting the path of least resistance to be followed (history tends to repeat itself). Nothing should be given more power than the one it carries and at the end a higher probability outcome is not a certainty, even events with a one percent odd of occurrence still happen once every one hundred times, statistically speaking.

The following reflections are instrumental to elicit the covert side of the blending points between realism and optimism.

→ *Long term optimist, short term realist.* Hold the highest ideals about what the future may bring without losing touch with reality. There is nothing wrong with shooting for the stars while at the same time realizing the current possibilities one has and what would be required to get there. Assume that if not the stars, you could eventually make it to the moon. Falling short on an aggressive objective will take you farther than falling long on a conservative one.

→ *Commit to either make it or die trying.* There are more people than you would think of that would stop trying only a year, a month, a week or a day before making their dreams come true. *I never lost a game. I just run out of time – Michael Jordan.* Play to win until the very last second of your life, never give up, if anything admit you needed more time to win. *Failure is simply an opportunity to begin again, this time more intelligently — Henry Ford*

→ *If it is in your heart, it was meant to be done.* Nobody is asked to do something completely outside of their capabilities, either current or potential. Maybe you are not able now, or in ten years from now, but to say one would never be able to do something our heart is pledging us to do is a completely different statement. If the voice within says go for it, *you just go,* no questions asked.

→ *If it fits in your mind, it can be done.* This is a derivative of the principle above, whatever you can imagine can be done. Things do not come to you by accident, the Universe does not act randomly, there is a plan for everything under the sun. If you can imagine something it is because it is doable and most likely something you are expected to do before you leave.

→ *Don't be afraid to fail, define your win scenarios. I do not believe in no-win scenarios – Captain Kirk.* Ignore what the world calls failure, define your own *failure* and *success* concepts and live your life ruled by them. Define your *good* deeds as those that meet the definition of *success* and have a life full of them, all you need is to do what you said you will do, and accept the price of your decisions, long term they will lead you to where you need to go, despite the *temporary* and *apparent* failure.

FINDING BALANCE: HOW TO BE CONTEMPT AND DARING

Let's explore the basis of realism (accepting reality) and optimism (trying to change reality) a bit more deeply and from an alternative standpoint. Can someone be contempt with and accept life as it is while at the same time try to change it? Do *accepting* and *trying to change* something represent a dualism of apparently opposed intentions? If such a reconciliation of conflicting stands would be attainable, how contempt with reality and how committed at pursuing their dreams a person can be? Can someone be comfortable with their life experience and at the same time actively pursue their ideals? As if saying …

> *Whenever my time to leave comes, I will be grateful to life for everything I was given and get ready to experience a peaceful departure. Until that happens, there are still a few dreams worth chased and I am all after them.*

Generally speaking those that are contempt with and accept life as is, have stopped trying to change their reality because they have reached what they sought for or they have convinced themselves that they either can't or don't want it anymore. Conversely, those that still try to alter the way things are, have a rather different mindset, one based on a still burning desire to see their dreams come true. They believe they can, have to, and must do more than what they have already done. It could be said that while the first group is in a more passive stage of their lives the second is in a more active one.

It is not that easy to find people that live in such a way that their existence embody both principles, the acceptance and the willingness to do more, it is right there, in that juncture of apparent opposites that the dilemma between acceptance of and determination to change reality resides. What we think and what we feel are intrinsically intertwined with our vision of life and represent the fuel that propels our behavioral engine. If we want to change what we do, we need to first change the way we think which in turn will change the way we feel. This process requires the harmonization of our stands, something that will need us to go deeper, find the way we see life and in a sense revisit some of our most treasured beliefs and mindsets. Soul searching is anything but easy, what we are looking for is not at a hand reach and will stretch every muscle in our body in the quest of hard to find answers.

It is in such a discovery phase when we should relate the reason to be contempt with having the essential parts of life, those key attributes of our existence that make us feel complete, at peace, in love, regardless of anything else under the sun. Happiness has to be associated with our essentials, the few things without which, life would be unbearable and meaningless.

Chasing dreams on the other hand, should be a function of our visions of the future, our purpose and the main reason of our life. If what we see can be pictured in a dream-like manner, full of color, beauty, evocatively, attractively, excitingly, then it should be mobilizing enough for us to regard it as something to live and die for. This is regardless of how much we have reached, tried, succeeded, failed, etc. An enchanting vision of the future should never be traded for whatever treasures we crafted in the past. If it comes to the point of putting everything at risk (except our essentials) so be it. Everything we were given was given to us for a reason, and that reason is to use it for what we came here for. No luggage will be allowed to be taken with us to wherever we go next.

Your dreams were given to you for you to chase them, not to ignore them, neglect them or pretend they are not there. It is imperative that you accept the idea that you don't create or find your dreams, rather your dreams create and find you!

We all come to this world with a purpose of our own, a life call that has been carved out on stone years before we were born, a mold to custom fit everything we can be and become. Such a mission is the origin of our dreams!

While being contempt has to do more with the realist in you, chasing dreams is intimately related with the optimist cells in your body. From a parallel perspective, realism is typically an analytical or logical function (mind) whereas optimism is more of a feeling, an intuition, an extra sensorial perception (heart).

Let's now revisit the original question: *can someone be contempt with and accept life as it is while at the same time try to change it? The answer is Yes.* You can be contempt and grateful with life and at the same time chase your dreams with every bit of energy you have, which is the same of saying you can simultaneously be a realist and an optimist, or what some scholars have coined *realistic optimism.*

One of the central aspects of the dualism between realism and optimism relies at differentiating when to adopt one posture versus the other. Be realistic at appreciating the value of your essentials and be grateful every day for what life has given you! Many people in the world around you don't have their essentials intact. Some have never even asked themselves what their essentials are, awareness is a heavenly gift. Be also realistic at gauging the complexity of everyday endeavors and the amount of effort that takes to live a balanced life. You are here to be great in just a few aspects of life, reasonably good in many others, and to ignore the rest. Such a balancing act requires wisdom and acceptance. Finally, be realistic on what to expect if things do not go as you dreamed, as it is not uncommon for plans to temporarily stall, derail or make an unexpected turn before resuming its rightful course of action. When that happens (it is not a matter of if but of when) slow down, regroup and start again … if nothing else, always one more time.

Be optimistic when you chase your most beautiful visions of a time yet to come, there is no future without dreams and no dreams without dreamers! You must fight the dragons of complacency, be contempt with your essentials and daring to pursue what you believe on with every bit of stamina you can find.

GOAL SETTING, THE ART OF PLACING
THE WHY BEFORE THE WHAT

Those that accomplished meaningful things in their
lives knew exactly what they wanted ... and most
importantly, they knew why they wanted it.

Despite the fact that the *what* seems to be more practically relevant to get things done, it is the *why* what gives you the drive and the motivation to do it. In the purest form of intrinsic motivation, individuals love what they do without too much regard about the reasons why they do it. This is a rather rare psychological phenomenon that happens frequently enough to be referred as the end state in the *task-based* intrinsic motivation continuum. When pure intrinsic motivation is at place, the person is literally *in-love* with the task and in the process of performing it, a mysterious blending takes place where the task and the self become one and the same. The *why* is simply the satisfaction of doing what the person loves doing ...

The most common form of intrinsic motivation takes place when individuals are compelled to engage in an activity based on the *why* (the ultimate reason for doing it) being willing and excited to make a conscious effort to find ways to love, like or perhaps tolerate what they have to do (*the what*) in order to attain the underlying purpose or outcome (*the why*). The ultimate goal or objective the task serves, and not the task itself, takes precedence in the determination and the drive for action. Tasks are nothing but means to an end, steps on a staircase to an enticing vision of a future still to be born, although as real as something that already happened. Unless the individual falls in one of the not so common cases of pure intrinsic motivation, where all that matters is the *what* (the *why* is reduced to just the liking of the task), it is not after you find an outstanding motive (*why*) that you can pull the best in you and direct it towards the chasing of it (*what*). Love to the task is powerful but relatively unstable and inconsistent as it needs to generate positive feelings onto the performer. The task will only be done as long as the person feels like doing it and as long as the task creates the positive psychological states associated with the love to it.

On the other hand, when the person is intrinsically motivated by the *why* of a particular task, there are no requirements imposed on the action itself as long as it continues to be intimately related to the underlying motive it serves. There are no feel-like-doing-it dynamics and the superficially driven emotional states to engage on it, the feelings of contribution to its overarching purpose are very deeply rooted, strong and more than enough of a reason for the individual to get involved on the task. It is in this case where a strong sense of *duty* drives the behavior rather than feelings of *love* to the task. Ultimately, it is a strong sense of love and duty to the *purpose* (and not necessarily the task) what keeps the energy and the passion flowing ... tasks are relatively meaningless and can be replaced as long as one feels that what one does is serving its ultimate intent within the confines of our value system.

When you are motivated by the *why* of a task, something that resonates and vibrates in unison with *who* you are, you need nothing else to stay at it other than the conviction that *it is the right thing to do*. Results do not matter, public opinion does not matter, only your inner reasons for doing what you do are all that count. You need no company, no approval and no appraisal of any kind, a burning *why* is absolutely sufficient to provide the drive you need to go through either easy or difficult paths. Conversely, when the motivation to do is centered on the love to the task, you are vulnerable to the ups and downs of daily living, especially when circumstances are not in your favor, when the winds and waves are not on your side or the overall experience is being perceived as suboptimal. Love to the task requires some level of performance or positive feedback for the drive towards action to continue being refreshed and renewed. Alternatively, when the motivation comes from a strong, absolute and monumental *why*, the individual is led through optimal as well as through sub-optimal junctures, easy as well as difficult crusades, where the occasional complexity and adversity may seem to tilt the probabilities of the average person to leave the behavior behind.

In such a context, those motivated by purpose operate from an inner source energy tied to the ultimate vision, goal, or end with no expected immediate satisfaction or gratification other than the feelings of being engaged with what they have to do. There is indeed a certain level of self-sacrifice in this psychological dynamic, and the person has to be prepared to make such a call, a sort of lower prioritization of a sub-optimal here and now in favor of a beautiful future yet to come.

Adversity will eventually show up at our doorsteps, and when it does, we will feel no less empowered and no less engaged to continue than when everything was almost perfect, our mood will not dramatically change according to the circumstances, no over-excitement or disillusionment will take prey of our feelings and drive our behavior, we will just act according to what we believe on and accepting that whatever needs to happen as a result of our actions will simply happen, in due time. To be able to operate at this level of thinking, we must elevate our logic beyond the here and now, in a sense transporting ourselves to a future point in time where the ultimate reason *why* we do *what* we do is materialized. Such a powerful vision of a future still to come exists only in our hearts and we will be able to depict it as clearly as anything our eyes can see.

The ability to envision a future state where the world and your role in it look different than the present is an attribute of free-willed spirits able to engage in belief-based action as if symbolically numbing themselves to what happens at the present time, including the results of what they are doing to reach that desired future state. There is a kind of blind trust in what their mind's eye can envision (which coincides with what their hearts tell them to do) that completely overrides any current sensory information conveyed by what they see, hear, etc. Their belief system is more powerful and more convincing than every fact laid in front of them by the surrounding environment, any driver of mass behavior, or what the world around them seems to reward and punish. This is so even at the price of becoming an outcast, banned from the flow of life-as-usual as a result of unconditionally believing in a future yet to come, a place in space and time different to the immediate and resounding reality, a realm that only exists in the visions of what can be made possible if one dares to believe in what we came here to do.

Even when we can admit that there is a difference between believing and knowing (the former based on faith, the latter on proof), such a difference is not so marked for these individuals as their beliefs have equal if not greater motivational power than knowledge itself. Actually, they perceive no difference between believing and knowing for they are the two sides of the same coin, a sort of mysterious two-headed coin. Belief is a form of knowledge, a rare kind that is acquired through extra-sensory means, something in the form of a feeling, more intuitive than logical, more unconscious than conscious, outside of the field of science and not subject to proof of any conventional kind. Belief holders are not in the business of proving what they believe on, their love and faith are just enough of a reason to follow their inner compasses wherever they point true north to be. They feel privileged and grateful to the Universe for having been given all they have, truly and deeply knowing that powers and blessings come with responsibility, wise choices, faith and courage will be required … and they are willing to give it all!

Those focused on a noble and altruistic purpose reach a state of being where whatever they are after is much greater than themselves and the price of living a life that may seem a bit (or a lot) more complex and difficult than those of the masses is a perfectly reasonable offer for the outcome being pursued. Their minds and hearts do not neighbor with the known and the familiar, actually they have been catapulted astray to a distant place and to a future time where they can more philanthropically contribute to the fabric of a different world configuration, a vision that has gapped away from the reality around them and enticingly migrated to a dimension where the custom becomes standard and the standard becomes custom, a kind of upside down domain, an opposite day resulting from a series of fortunate and synchronistic events assumed to be nearly impossible, as far as conventional wisdom would suggest.

These individuals live in low probability worlds perfectly suited to meet and even exceed the inherent beauty of their inner visions, dreams and the artifacts of their creative imaginary. They will never rest on their laurels as their targets are constantly moving as if they were seeking no victory other than the continuous improvement of the conditions they are after. The moment their dreams are realized, new dreams start being crafted ... for they were born out of a need to keep a continuous reason to give everything they possibly can.

Events will happen throughout your life, there will be starts and stops, ups and downs, things will change, fluctuate, some things will end and others will begin. When it comes the time for the Universe to test your endurance and how lovingly you want what you are after, the inner, rock solid *why's* will come to rescue you. Stick to them, they are your life savers, you will not only survive but reach the shores of a new world. Being endurance tested is inevitable if you want to grow, mature and evolve, eventually being promoted to the next level of life complexity where the answers to your current questions most likely lie, along with new wonderings you had never thought about (at least consciously).

The Universe will not give you a higher complexity assignment before making sure you can handle what you currently have in your hands. If you want to get more and do more, you have to prove you can manage what you have. This is what an endurance test is all about, namely proving that you both *want* and *can* handle what you are after, that you are capable enough to weather the storms, showing undue resilience to keep going even when the conditions around you are far from optimal and when all you have left is nothing but a loving vision of a future yet to come ... like a Phoenix bird emerging from its ashes.

Anyone can stand their ground on good weather, under the sun, covered and protected by a blue sky. But who are those that can stand still when the night gets dark, cold and long enough for the weak and the non-believer to lose the hope that another day will eventually come? You are as strong as your weakest belief.

Those of you that are invested in lifelong journeys know that some things will take time and that the paths you have to follow will not always lead to a true north, eventually you will come to a pause, maybe a temporary stop, a bump on the road, a retracement maybe. When that happens, be ready to say:

> *I am fine with the current state of affairs, I expected joy and struggle to eventually come and I am here to stay, rain or shine alike, and if I fall, I will get back up, always one more time*

Whichever the stage of life you are in, your mission is not over yet and you need to be open to any possibilities your most beautiful dreams can suggest while being grateful for everything that life has given you. Eventually the time to go home will come and you will have to pack and leave, we all will but not any earlier than our time, when the Universe has determined that our job has been done and there is nothing else we need to do. You are not supposed to outsmart the Universe, accept its superiority and subdue your will to its command.

> *Fear no death, for death is only an interim stage in a higher order journey, a step up to a superior dimension, a jump into the unknown that only exists beyond our most evolved level of comprehension, a new and still mysterious beginning to the afterlife side of our existence rather than the end to all known and experienced.*

Find your burning *why's*, this is one of the most important and life changing tasks you have to do, and the earliest you do it the better. You may need to ask, times and again, and keep asking until you find them. Some will wonder … *how will I know that I truly found them?* Trust me, when you find them you will know you did. If you are in doubt, you have not found them yet. You *why's* represent your life call, your mission, your mental and spiritual representation of the work ahead and even when truthful enough to be trusted, they can still be diffuse and blurry but sufficiently clear for you to know they are a strong part of the answers you have been seeking to find.

It took me almost fifty years to find my way and I can certainly tell that I know that I know. The beauty of soul searching is that you can sense you are getting closer, you can smell the flowers when you approach the garden! If your life has been somewhat erratic, with no clear sense of purpose or meaning, you must embark in the search of your *why's*, we all have ours, they are there, like golden gems in a treasure chest waiting to be found (or better said, waiting to find you!). You cannot delegate this task, you and nobody but you can only do it. Expect no bed of roses, no free lunches, this is not going to be easy in any way or shape, but knowing what you have to do in life and why you have to do it will quite certainly become so fulfilling, so rewarding and so life transforming that any effort, even way beyond any stretches of imagination will be absolutely worth it!

Your *why's* and your *what's* will point you exactly to the ultimate reason you were sent down to Earth. Deep inside an impossible-to-miss sense of rightness will invade you and make every cell in your body to vibrate in unison only by the sheer thought of doing what you came here to do to the best of your abilities. If your heart is full of love, and we are all capable of such a blessing, you can't escape from fulfilling your mission, it is wired to your DNA, it is part of who you are and an unavoidable step in the mystic and mysterious process of creating the *who* you will one day be.

> *You have been given the power of transforming the who you are and turn it into the who you are meant to be. It cannot get any simpler than this. This is it, this is why we are all here, we share a common purpose with a unique and personalized call to action, tailored to our stature, not our current but our potential stature!*

You can't fool Nature, it is not worth it and you won't be allowed to do it without paying an incredibly high price, a price that has been set that high for a reason, for almost nobody to be willing to pay it. Why take shortcuts, why would you deprive yourself from the most rewarding and most exhilarating experience you can possibly live? ... only because it is going to be eventually hard or difficult? ... is that it? ... is that the greatest fear holding you back? *If you think and feel that following your inner path is going to be difficult, try following somebody else's and live somebody else's life … then you will really know how hard life can be!*

We are here to do and not to avoid doing. By choosing what to focus on you will naturally leave some things behind, you will prioritize, you will pick your battles, you will decide what to do and what not to do (which is not the same as avoiding in the sense that deciding what *not* to do is action rather than avoidance), that is the way it is supposed to work. Whatever selection strategy you use, never pick by the *easiness* of the task or the pursuit, choose by the relevance and the significance of it in regards to what you feel your mission in life is. This is the way you honor your life, if it feels true in your heart, you must find ways to ignore how hard it can possibly be … the journey of your life is something you must embark yourself on.

When we go to bed at night we should be as exhausted as fulfilled. Fulfillment will come out of doing what we had to do and exhaustion out of having done it the very best we could, using up until our last bit of stamina. There is no tiredness that a good night sleep cannot remedy and good hearts always find a way to a peaceful rest. Live by example and teach your children about these principles, the world would be a much better place to live if more people would seek for their *why's* instead of just going with the flow, joining the crowds, or choosing what gives them the most immediate amount of gratification. Refuse to live a self-centered life, a life where you don't do for others more than what you do for yourself, think big and step out of what your eyes can see!

You have not been sent down to Earth just to have a full belly and to rest well, there is more to life than just the immediate gratification of our basic needs. Defy the status quo that the masses live by, look at things from a non-conventional and non-traditional perspective. Find the meaning, the reason for your existence, that one thing you can absolutely not leave without giving your very best to it. There is always one and even if you can't see it quite yet, it is there waiting to be uncovered, undusted, polished! Things happen for a reason, even those things we don't want to happen which carry the burden of at least teaching us something we did not know or have forgotten about. We all have a purpose to fulfill, an unavoidable accomplishment to realize and it is our honor and our duty to find what that purpose is and then realize it to the best of our abilities.

We were given talents to be further developed and used wisely, opportunities will arise to sharpen our skills and to use them for a noble cause, be on the watch, you are not here by accident! The master planning is on the Universe hands but the hard work, the preparation and the doing is in ours. Pick your battles!

There will be a thousand things in your everyday life that if not done or done differently will not make the slightest difference. Conversely, there will be a handful of things that must be done and must be done to the very best of your capabilities. These are your right things and where you should focus your attention, everything else is more or less avoidable and has to be regarded as a far second priority. Learn to know the difference and do what you must do!

WHOEVER YOU WERE MEANT TO BE YOU WILL BE!

If you listen to your heart and are committed to give your best, you will eventually get there, to the place you were meant to be and at the time you were expected to arrive.

You can speed up or delay your pace, you can take shortcuts to get there faster or ignore the roadmaps altogether by using your inner navigation system. All you will be able to do is either accelerate or delay your arrival and in so doing comply with Nature's master plan. Loving hearts follow their predestined paths, making choices all along and in response to their sense of rightness … what was meant to be will simply be.

We live in a world of fantasies and we believe we are in control of our lives, our destiny, what happens to us and what we do. In a sense, in a very narrow and limited sense, we are. If all we have to drink is water, we have the choice of drinking it cold, at room temperature or warm, we can also choose to drink it now or drink it later, drink it slow or drink it fast, drink it all or only part of it, and that is it so far our alternatives are concerned. The illusion that water is *all-there-is* makes it easy for our conscious mind to believe we are in control of anything possible, that our ability to choose is as ample as it can be. The truth of the matter is, Nature will build a *virtual* reality for us to best fit what we have to do, to guide us in the journey of becoming the *who* we must be and become.

If you carry a loving heart urging you to do for others more than you do for yourself, there is no way to escape your destiny, whatever you were meant to be, you will be!

There will be some room to maneuver within the road you are supposed to follow, your pre-destined itinerary, left or right, faster or slower, it does not really matter, the destination stays the same. We were given choice within a limited realm, a free-will fantasy framed in a somewhat confined space where our decisions will have to be made. The fact that we ignore this dynamic makes it easy for us to accept it without feeling the need to defy Nature in an effort to prove our imperfect depiction of the Universe to be right. Some things are best left unknown!

If you are privileged enough to visualize your mission, to get a sense of what the direction of your life is, you have been trusted by Nature to be the recipient of sensitive information, something that only a few humans can handle. If you are among them, you certainly know the many things you can but are not supposed to do, some of them attractive enough for the crowds, especially when they can be good or even great at them. It is your duty to honor Nature's confidence on you, ancient secrets only shared with the few and not the many have been disclosed to you and it is your responsibility to live your life in a way that maximizes your contribution to your purpose. You will be allowed to choose from as wide a range of options as you can handle and the wiser you become the higher the number of choices you will be given!

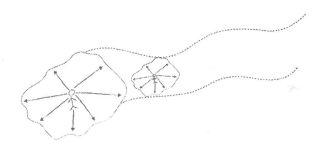

For as contradictory as it may sound, your acceptance, submission and commitment to your life purpose will determine how much say you will have in the shaping of your life. Some people are just told *what* to do and *when* to do it, others have more room for decision making. It all comes down to how much self-discipline and control you can exercise when it comes to choosing wisely among the many alternatives you have at your disposal. You don't ask a child to do grown-up work for the same reason you don't give more control to every person than what every person can handle.

If we don't know how or don't want to control ourselves beyond the pleasure principle, ignoring or refusing to selflessly drive our actions to maximize our contribution to the collective good, it makes no point to ask for greater authority and more control of our lives, we would simply steer our ships to ports not meant to arrive at.

It is only when we can choose as Nature would that we would be given the ability to see beyond the here and now, to know that there is more than just water to drink, that no-drinking *is* indeed an option and that there is also more to just drinking in our lives. Knowledge is power and power comes with responsibility.

We must feel morally obliged to fulfill our purpose, to know we can choose otherwise and yet refuse to do it in a profound and heartfelt manner enticing ourselves to do what we have been entrusted to do. Choice is a gift given to all human beings, however and based on how such degree of self determination is exercised, not all humans will get the same latitude or decision making power.

The amplitude and the variety of choices has been expanded for those able to choose wisely, the Universe wants you to have all you need to do your job, and do it right. Conversely, if you can't make sound decisions, the options will be narrowed and you will be presented with less of a spectrum, a reduced set of alternatives, a controlled environment where your suboptimal choices can do little harm to the collective good of the world. There is nothing wrong with admitting our ignorance in any field of life, if we are uncertain about how to choose wisely, it is sometimes better not to choose at all (unless you are in a learning stage where trial and error are part of the process of mastering your field).

Fooling Nature should not be considered an option and you should never try to do it ... even if you could (free will is only an option for those without limits), it is inherently wrong and a self-destructive behavior that threatens human kind preservation. Nature is the maximum authority in the business of dictating what to do, how to do it and when to do it. It is also the simplest way to discern between right and wrong, to easily know the way things were meant to be. Become one with Nature, one with the Universe, walk with it, blend with it, merge with it, mesh with it, like flesh and bones, mind and heart, body and soul. Like the bone that cannot disjoin the flesh without hurting us beyond reason, you should never deviate from Nature, from your very own Nature.

Seek to follow your heart for it is the closest to Nature you can get. Your mind can at times play tricks on you, give you the illusions that you are in complete control of a situation and that you can do as you please without any further consequences. Your mind's job is self-preservation, survival, workability, it is not meant to find the optimal ways to prioritize the long term future of the human race. Your brain is highly regulated by short term processes that tend to linearly project current circumstances into the near and distant futures, whether good or bad. Use your brain functions for logical, extremely analytical processes requiring decisions that must be calculated enough to not miss a desired outcome, especially when failing could be too risky, too painful or too dangerous. Your brain is your rational part and your best ally to make logical, non-emotional, non-intuitive decisions. Do not use your brain to debate with your heart on lifelong calls, purpose related concerns or philosophical right-or-wrong, good-or-evil dilemmas. For those matters surrender to the command of your heart as it will guide you well, taking you kindly to the places you must go, places you may not choose to go if not because directed by your heart. Always listen to your heart and never contradict it, do otherwise, or ignore what you hear. If what you were told is not what you wanted to hear or what you thought about doing, always follow your heart's lead and accept the possibility that you may not be seeing clearly, holistically enough, that some things may be there although hidden or camouflaged to your untrained eyes. Your heart should always takes precedence over your brain on legitimate life matters, especially those that will determine where to go or what to do when the end is in mind.

Self awareness is a gift that will enlighten your path in ways you may have never imagined. It is as if you were able to take your tinted sunglasses off and look at them, not through them. It is through exercising the gift of self-awareness that you will discover parts of the self hidden to most humans, in a sense becoming able to get inside of your brain and think about the way you think, the way you do what you do, and why you do things you were not consciously aware you do. Sometimes it is not enough to ask what you do or why do it, it is also important to understand why you think the way you think and how you do the things you do.

JUST DARE TO TRY!

What do you see when you are in the middle of uncertainty? When your glass is both half full *and* half empty? You can go either way, but what is your tendency, your first inclination, your most common reaction to the unknown in the face of possible fortune or misfortune? Do you have any kind of bias towards one side or the other? Do you generally see the positives out of any circumstance? … or the negatives? … Are you a more neutral type of person remaining skeptical until you see to then know? … or you can believe before you see?

I was, still am, and perhaps will always be fascinated to imagine the positive side of life, what can go well, especially when I can influence it, when I can do something to tilt the probability odds in the Universe's favor! It can always be done, the likelihood of something good occurring can always be improved, if nothing else by a quarter of a percent, and the fact that sometimes it may just take more time and more effort than others should not shy you away or give you the impression that it is not possible.

Nothing in this world can take the place of persistence. Talent will not: nothing is more common than unsuccessful men with talent. Genius will not: unrewarded genius is almost a proverb. Education will not: the world is full of educated derelicts. Persistence and determination alone are omnipotent. – Calvin Coolidge

Can you see the can-do mentality, the spirit of never giving up until the last second? We were expected to do meaningful things, things that will stretch every muscle of our body, and if we are going to, it will not be because things will come easy, but because we will never stop trying and learning. When it comes to the earth-shattering aspects of our life, the battles worth fought, either we make it or we die trying, and one outcome is as noble and altruistic as the other. As my investment coach would say … *if you stay long enough at it and try hard, one day your brain will figure it all out.*

Your brain and your heart will piece it together, will crack the code, decipher the riddle, find the way out, and the way in. It is not farfetched to conceive that a vision, for as high up in the air as it may be, can become real, especially if you believe that the biggest limits of human kind creations were always contained within the confines of our minds, deep down where all the fears rest, irrational qualms to be all we can be and become.

No matter how highly you can think of yourself, you are always an inch or a mile under the best of you. What you came here to do and the *who* you were meant to be have to remain mysterious and unknown so you can always get a foot deeper into the forest of your life seeking to reinvent your most beautiful self. Everything magnificent starts with a thought, a vision, a *what-if* type of wondering. Always remember that the most splendid man accomplishments started at some point in time with a dream, an idea, as remote and as distant a future world configuration can be, maybe close to what the masses regarded as an impossible picture of what the future may look like, a defiance to the status quo preserved generation after generation, until somebody had the bravery to challenge it and dare to try!

The whisper of epic hearts ignoring the everyday messages of the masses, the high probability occurrences and the common denominators of human behavior, while rare, are powerful enough to set an example that the so called impossible is not so if unreasonable amounts of belief propel an uncanny and exhilarating vision of a future yet to come, regardless of how low its probability of occurrence maybe in the collective mind of the crowds.

Some people, even when few in number, are heroic enough to defy the odds of the extremely difficult and venture to think in ways that would frighten the non-believer, the fearful, and the hesitant. This is by all means a high risk bet, there is certainly too much to gain and too much to lose, and we must take it. *But ... why?* Why should we embark in such a risky proposition? What type of reward would be waiting for us at the other side of the bridge? Making our dreams come true, becoming the one we were meant to be, leaving the world and our future generations a legacy, a token, a symbol of our existence, a vivid proof of our passage through Earth and what we did for others. As far as the risks are concerned, they are nothing but one, the biggest risks of all, our failure to give our very best in the pursuit of that we came here for!

The biggest crime a human being can commit is to stop trying, to deprive the world of what could have been his best contribution, to give his very best in the quest of his ideals, failing to be all he could have been and become, failing to be the one he was meant to be!

Can you see it? The reward and the risk are nothing but the same, just expressed in opposite ways, the abundance and lack thereof. The risk is nothing but not reaching the reward! … and there is no way to lose! … if you always give your very best, you will always win, hit or miss! Don't try to avoid failure by playing safe in the game of life, leave that for the masses, they are great at it; take risks, get exposed, give everything you have, be courageous, be brave, be bold! You came here to make a difference, not to cruise, not to have an easy life, and not to stay out of the possible trouble that may come out of pursuing your most beautiful dreams!

Almafuerte, a great Argentinean poet, once wrote "no te des por vencido ni aun vencido" which means don't consider yourself defeated even if defeated. To reach this type of mentality you don't have to think in terms of *reasonable* returns for your effort investments. When you embark yourself in a *make-it-or-die-trying* journey, you are making a promise to keep going no matter what, and most importantly whether things work as you expected or not.

Being in the game and playing to win, giving your very best at every moment is enough of a reason to do it, it does not get any better, no circumstance is more fulfilling than the inner feelings that you never gave up, you never stopped trying, you never kept the very best to yourself but brought it all out.

This is the true gain, the only win scenario you can control and the framework you need to live by every day. It is the love for the game what should keep you motivated and needing nothing else but the chance to give everything you have for a cause worth it! Love of the game, the ability to imagine a future better than the present is an extremely powerful drive to give the very best of you in a way that feels effortless even when your body may insist in telling you otherwise. You can get tired physically but your mind will be so fresh that can go on and on for hours without feeling any signs of stress or tiredness. Sometimes your body will say ... *stop and get some rest, so you can go back to it with a full blown of stamina in the morning.* Accept the proposition, take your time, especially after a long day.

You will get up in the morning only wishing you can spend most of your day at it, advancing one day at a time, consistently, with no major interruptions. The possibility of getting closer to your vision is so much of a drive that you can't even resist it, let alone do something else. It does not matter how far or how short you fall, at the end of the day and as long as you have given your very best, there is nothing else or more you could have done, and that is enough, just keep doing it. Doing your very best will always revolve around the same basic principles, you have to be open, flexible, learn from your mistakes, and adjust your definition of *very best* according to the circumstances. This is the essence of learning and growing! Think about children learning to walk, don't you think they are adjusting their attempts every time they fall down, in a sense, getting a bit more proficient with each try? They do not do the same things, repeatedly without any changes whatsoever. They repeat the task but gradually and slowly they perfect their styles, they get more in balance, they step a bit more firmly, they move more in synchrony with the needs of the next step, they practice, and they reap the benefits of continuous repetition. You do things over and over again, changing them a bit every time, turning the knob just a little bit more to the right or to the left each time, listening to the tunes of your effort and hearing what happens. What now? ... left or right? ... a tiny bit or a little more? ... again, and again, and again. As long as you never quit, one day your brain will figure it all out. It will be that day when self-confidence will pay you a visit, and stay with you for life, and it is that day when you will be able to lift yourself above the one you used to be and say ... *I know that I know.*

294

Intrinsically motivated people have a tendency to set the bar high (higher than those motivated from the outside), they do not want an easy life, actually they want to be as far as possible from *easy* as it will convey a sense of waste, of underutilization, of not trying hard enough, of having missed an opportunity to contribute, an opportunity to do something else, something more for the causes they are committed to. They know that everyone has unique powers above and beyond the masses and feel compelled to do something about it, something with them, something worth being done. As Peter Parker said in Spiderman ... *with great powers come great responsibility.*

We can all make a difference or live an ordinary life, it is our choice. We are all unique in certain ways, we all have great talents of some sort, finding them (or letting them find us) is the key to maximizing our contribution and live a life worth lived! Refuse to live an easy life! We were all meant to be somebody and to do something, somebody and something the Universe needs and the world will remember.

The heavenly command of giving our very best was not created just for the few but for the many, and it is not fair for the few to bear a load heavy enough to be carried by the many, help them, the Universe needs you!

Intrinsically motivated people feel compelled to do more, they have higher than normal expectations and this is in part due to the self-awareness that they are above average in what they do, that they can do more, better, work harder than the crowd. They also know that the masses will ignore the call, that the world's future lies in the hands of those intrepid souls who will always strive to make a difference, to give their very best for the missions they have been entrusted. This feeling, this call to do more also comes from the realization that what you have to do is astonishing, out of the ordinary, something that can really aid in the betterment of the world, even if only one soul at a time. There is no better and no humbler way to transform the world than helping one human being at a time, focusing on the person next to us that needs our help the very most. In time, and only if it was meant to, you will go to the next, a heart in need of comfort that may require your undivided attention and everything you have to give. Always remember it, if all you do in your life is to make just a few souls happier, lighten their burden, illuminate their paths, fill their hearts with love, or simply be there to help alleviate their pain, then you have done enough. But don't stop there, keep going …

People with a strong sense of purpose may not be intrinsically motivated by the very task they do but by the realization that the task is a means to a greater end. Whatever they are after, the ultimate result of their work is so indisputable that they get fixated on it and find ways to love what they do. They tie and mesh the task with the ultimate result (not the immediate outcome, which may be something totally different) to the point that they can't tell the difference between the one and the other. Their creativity spurs actions above and beyond the stretch of conventional wisdom and reaches the field of dreams, ancient knowledge, alchemy, universal unconscious and archetypes. Deep inside they can sense there is a way to do it, even when the outside world may be shouting … *it can't be done, it is impossible.* A whisper of their inner voice will sound louder than the outer world's scream, they know that the answers to their most fundamental questions lie nowhere but within themselves and it is there where they will seek for guidance. They can sense the Universe to be on their side, the night can be long, dark, cold, and lonely; it just does not matter enough. The longer, colder, and darker the night, the closer dawn is! They must stay at it, they must learn, they must grow stronger, wiser, become more loving and more compassionate.

Those fighting for noble causes, pushing hard for their assigned enterprises, have the Universe behind them and they can feel it! The history of mankind has plenty of examples proving that what the masses believe, for as respectable and credible it may be, means nothing for a soul daring to do what it was meant to be done. Nothing can be labeled impossible as long as there is a heart, a brave and fearless heart believing it is not!

Just dare to try! … and keep always trying!

All the best in your Journey!

SUGGESTED READING

Bach, Richard. Jonathan Livingston Seagull. A story. Avon Books, 1973

Beattie, Melody. Journey to the Heart. Daily meditations on the path to freeing your soul. HarperSanFrancisco, 1996

Belitz, Charlene & Lundstrom, Meg. The power of flow. Practical ways to transform your life with meaningful coincidence. Three Rivers Press, 1998

Buscaglia, Leo. Living, Loving, & Learning. Fawcett Columbine, 1982

Covey, Stephen R. First things first. Simon & Schuster, 1998

Covey, Stephen R. The 7 habits of highly effective people. Powerful lessons in personal change. Simon & Shuster, 1989

Covey, Stephen R. Principle centred leadership. Simon and Schuster, 1992

Csikszentmihalyi, Mihaly & Csikszentmihalyi, Isabella Selega. Optimal experience. Psychological studies of flow in consciousness. Cambridge University Press, 1988

Csikszentmihalyi, Mihaly. Creativity. Flow and the psychology of discovery and invention. Harper Perennial, 1996

Csikszentmihalyi, Mihaly. Finding flow. The psycholofy of engagement with everyday life. Basic Books, 1997

Csikszentmihalyi, Mihaly. Flow. The psychology of optimal experience. Harper Perennial, 1990

Csikszentmihalyi, Mihaly. The evolving self. A psychology for the third millennium. Harper Perennial, 1993

Damasio, Antonio. The feeling of what happens. Body and emotion in the making of consciousness. Harcourt Brace & Company, 1999

Daniels, Aubrey C. Bringing out the best in people. How to apply the astonishing power of positive reinforcement. McGraw-Hill, 1999

Day, Laura. Practical Intuition. How to harness the power of your instinct and make it work for you. Villard, 1996

De Saint-Exupery, Antoine. The little prince. Harcourt, Inc., 1943

Deci, Edward L. Why we do what we do. Understanding self motivation. Penguin Books, 1995

Deci, Edward L. & Ryan, Richard M. Intrinsic motivation and self-determination in human behavior. Plenum Press, 1985

Dyer, Wayne W. Your erroneous zones. Funk & Wagnalis, 1976

Feldman, Henry David & Csikszentmihalyi & Gardner, Howard. Changing the world. A framework for the study of creativity. Praeger Publishers, 1994

Fisher, Robert & Kelly, Beth. The owl who didn't give a hoot. Lectorum, 2002

Frankl, Viktor E. Man's search for meaning. Washington Square Press, 1959

Frankl, Viktor E. The will to meaning. Foundations and applications of logotherapy. Penguin Books, 1969

Fromm, Erich. Escape from freedom. Henry Holt and Company, 1941

Fromm, Erich. The forgotten language. Grove Press, 1951

Gardner, Howard. Frames of mind. The theory of multiple intelligences. BasicBooks, 1993

Glasser, William. Choice theory. A new psychology of personal freedom. Harper Perennial, 1993

Goleman, Daniel. Emotional Intelligence. Why can it matter more than IQ. Bantam Books, 1995

Harrison, Allen F. & Bramson, Robert M. The art of thinking. Strategies and techniques you can use everyday to achieve more personal growth, wealth and happiness. Berkley Books 1982

Herzberg, Frederick & Mausner, Bernard, & Snyderman, Barbara Bloch. The motivation to work. Transaction Publishers, 1993

Jung, Carl G. Man and his symbols. Laurel Book, 1964

Jung, Carl G. Memories, Dreams, Reflections. Pantheon Books, 1963

Jung, Carl G. Modern man in search of a soul. Harcourt Brace & Company, 1933

Jung, Carl G. Psychological reflections. Princeton University Press, 1973

Jung, Carl G. Synchronicity. An acausal connecting principle. Princeton University Press, 1960

Jung, Carl G. The undiscovered self. Back Bay Books, 1957

Jung, Carl G. The development of personality. Princeton University Press, 1954

Kabat-Zinn, Jon. Wherever you go there you are. Mindfulness meditation in everyday life. Hyperion, 1994

Keen, Sam. To love and be loved. Bantam Books, 1997

Kleiber, Douglas A. & Maehr, Martin L. Advances in Motivation and Achievement, Volume 4. Jai Press, 1985

Maehr, Martin L. & Ames, Carol. Advances in Motivation and Achievement, Volume 6. Jai Press, 1989

Maslow, Abraham H. Maslow on management. John Wiley & Sons, Inc., 1998

Maslow, Abraham H. The farther reaches of human nature. Viking Press, 1971

Maslow, Abraham H. Toward a psychology of being (2nd Edition). Van Nostrand Reinhold, 1968

Maslow, Abraham H. Motivation and Personality (3rd Edition). Addison Wesley Longman, 1987

May, Rollo. Man's search for himself. Delta Books, 1953

McGregor, Douglas. The human side of enterprise. McGraw-Hill, 1960

Neill, Humphrey B. The art of contrary thinking. Caxton Printers, 1992

Peck, Scott M. Further along. The road less travelled. The unending journey toward spiritual growth. Touchstone, 1993

Peck, Scott M. The road less travelled & beyond. Spiritual growth in an age of anxiety. Simon & Schuster, 1997

Rogers, Carl R. On becoming a person. A therapist's view of psychotherapy. Houghton Mifflin Company, 1961

Sansone, Carol & Harackiewicz, Judith M. Intrinsic and Extrinsic Motivation. The search for optimal motivation and performance. Academic Press, 2000

Seligman, Martin E.P. Learned optimism. How to change your mind and your life. Pocket Books, 1990

Smith, Ann W. Overcoming perfectionism. The key to a balanced recovery. Health Communication, 1990

Sternberg, Robert J. & Barnes, Michael L. The psychology of love. Yale University Press, 1988

Urdan, Timothy C. Advances in Motivation and Achievement, Volume 11. Jai Press, 1999

Wallace, Doris B. & Gruber, Howard E. Creative people at work. Oxford University Press, 1989

Walsh, Neale Donald. Conversations with God. An uncommon dialogue. Books 1-3. Hampton roads, 1995-1998

Wheelis, Allen. How people change. Perennial Library, 1969

Williamson, Marianne. A return to love. Reflections on the principles of a course in miracles. Harper Perennial, 1993

Printed in the United States
By Bookmasters